CATHOLICISM

AN
HISTORICAL
SURVEY

by John P. Dolan

PROFESSOR OF HISTORY
UNIVERSITY OF SOUTH CAROLINA
COLUMBIA, SOUTH CAROLINA

1368

Barron's Educational Series, Inc.

WOODBURY, NEW YORK

Preface

THE MANY DIMENSIONS of Catholicism are perhaps the greatest obstacle to presenting a clear picture of what is often termed its intangible comprehensiveness. It would be a simple task to sketch an external picture of it, to explain its organization, to outline its doctrine, discipline, and ritual, to accumulate statistics. Yet when the reader had absorbed this mass of information, he would still stand at a great distance from a comprehension of its true nature because the soul or spirit of Catholicism might well escape him. On the other hand, to reduce it to a philosophy of life or a code of ethics would also betray its claim to being a living organism.

Therefore, rather than attempt to present a static outline, we have endeavored to explain its origin and transformation in space and time, its complex relationships to various civilizations, and its richness and diversity in terms of its historical development. We cannot understand Catholicism at the present time unless we have first understood the whole of the Christian past. To limit this study to what is at present alive in Catholicism, or to what appears to be alive, would run the risk of writing an apology, shunning the human elements in the Church—power, sin, and failure.

This approach is based on the belief that Catholicism is the continuing work of Christ in the world, the constant development of His Mystical Body which is led by the Holy Spirit toward the totality of truth. It is wholly the work of God but at the same time entirely man's endeavor as well. The historical character of Catholicism is founded ultimately on the Incarnation of Christ, the entrance of the Logos into the ever changing stream of history. It rests on the fact that Christ willed His Church to

iii

be a society of human beings, "the people of God" under the leadership of human beings, and thus subject to human actions and human weakness. Hence, in addition to its official teachings, creeds, and decrees set within a chronological framework, we have also included the literary expressions of those who shared in and contributed to its development. Without an Origen, an Augustine, an Aquinas, or a Lacordaire, neither the basic continuity nor the changing expressions of Catholicism would be intelligible.

University of South Carolina   John P. Dolan

Table of Contents

CHAPTER 1

Catholicism in the Hellenistic World

The Jewish Background

ALTHOUGH CATHOLICISM has for many centuries been identified with the spirit of anti-Semitism, it is one of the paradoxes of history that in its doctrines, its cult, and above all its very origin in Christ it can be understood only in terms of the Jewish religion, a fact that impelled Pope Pius XI to proclaim that spiritually all Catholics are Semites. Hence any understanding of the Catholic religion must begin with an appreciation of the Jewish background of its founder, Jesus Christ.

The evangelist Mark tells us that Jesus came into this world "when the fullness of time was come"—a definite reference to the Messianic hopes of the Jewish people. Their basic belief, which they defended at times fanatically in the midst of completely different types of religious convictions and forms of worship, was that they were being led by one God, Jahweh. This one true God had manifested Himself either directly or through His prophets throughout their long history. Every pious Jew directed his daily life on a basis of God's faithful and merciful guidance. As a chosen people, they awaited the appearance of a Saviour sprung from among themselves who would establish in Israel the kingdom of God and raise Israel above all the kingdoms of the earth.

During the half-century before the birth of Christ, the Messianic hopes of the Jewish people had taken on a political coloring. The Idumaean Herod the Great had obtained from the Roman Senate the title of King of the Jews. In 37 B.C. he had captured the city of Jerusalem and cruelly murdered the Hasmonaean descendants of the Maccabees, who a century before had defended religious liberties against the Syrians. His efforts to gain popular support by rebuilding the temple and improving the economic and social condition of the kingdom came to nought. He divided the country among his three sons. Judea, Samaria, and Idumaea went to Archelaus, who was also to inherit the royal title. Philip received Trachonitis and Auranitis, while Herod Antipas succeeded to the provinces of Batanaea. Because of the incompetence of Archelaus, the Romans deposed him in 6 B.C., and a procurator residing in Caesarea and sharing responsibilities with the governor of Syria was placed in charge of the military and economic affairs of the area. Although the Sanhedrin, under the presidency of a high priest, governed purely religious affairs, the stationing of Roman troops in Jerusalem and the Roman tax policies continued to antagonize the Jewish population. Their hopes increased for a Messiah who would liberate them from the Roman yoke.

Within the Jewish community itself there were a number of varying interpretations of the Law, although all were in fundamental agreement. The Chasidim, or Assidaeans, felt that the Law was so sublime that they desired to observe it with unconditional obedience. Theirs was the fanaticism associated with the Maccabees. On the other hand, the Sadducees, for the most part members of the upper classes, and influenced by Hellenism, held to a sort of rationalism which rejected belief in angels and belittled the idea of the resurrection of the dead. The Torah—the five books of Moses—formed the basis of their more tolerant religious beliefs. Far more influential than either of these were the Pharisees, "the separated ones." Like the Assidaeans, they emphasized the importance of the Law, but they endeavored to apply it unswervingly to every possible situation in daily life. Traditional interpretation of the Law embodied in the Mishna and the Talmud and a subsequent casuistical attitude fostered a number of various schools known by the names of their leading scholars, such as the school of Shammai or the school of Hillel. Far more warlike in their opposition to pagan domination were the Zealots, who refused to pay tribute to Caesar and advocated a holy war against Roman domination.

Although voluntarily withdrawn from public life, the Essenes, another group of Jewish religionists, must be mentioned to complete the spiritual background of Palestine at the time of Jesus. The recent discoveries at Qumran, west of the Dead Sea, have shed much light on this previously enigmatic people. Their beginnings can be traced back to the time of the Maccabees, and they flourished about a century before the coming of Christ. It was their belief that Belial, or Satan, had spread three nets over Israel: unchastity, stolen wealth, and the defilement of the temple. They separated themselves from the "men of corruption," the Pharisees, and under the leadership of "The Teacher of Righteousness" proclaimed an unconditional commitment to the Law. A new interpretation of the Old Testament prophecies was announced. In the last age, the final struggle, two Messiahs were to play an important role: The high priest of the last age, the "Anointed of Aaron," and the "Anointed of Israel," the prince of the final age. There was an element of predestination in the ultimate selection of the saved. Some were given the spirit of truth and light, while others received the spirit of darkness and wickedness. Salvation was an unmerited grace. Among the Qumran group a monastic religious community was established. The members were obliged to swear an oath to observe the rules of the order, all property was held in common, and celibacy was enforced. A rigid order of precedence, with the priests forming the head of a caste system, also prevailed. There was a great interest in the events that were to take place at the imminent end of the world, the final judgment, and the everlasting glory of salvation. The monastic center at Qumran was destroyed by the Romans in 68 A.D., and it is quite probable that the sect was involved in the conflict against the Romans in the rebellion of 66-70, as they would have interpreted this as the final struggle between the sons of light and the sons of darkness.

Christ and His Work

It was into this diversified religious milieu that the Messiah was born. The sources of our knowledge of the life of Christ are the writings of the New Testament, especially the first three or synoptic gospels and the Acts of the Apostles. Actually none of these are or were intended to be historical biographies of Christ, but rather supports to the claim of the first preachers of the Gospel that Jesus of Nazareth was the Saviour whom they proclaimed as the source of salvation for all men.

Soon after his birth, some four or five years before the beginning of our era (in terms of our present calendar), Jesus was born in Bethlehem of the Virgin Mary. According to Jewish custom, He was circumcised and presented in the temple. Forced to flee Palestine, He was taken by his parents to Egypt until the death of Herod. At the age of about thirty He left His parental home and, after being baptized by John the Baptist, began to proclaim the advent of the Kingdom of God. All peoples, not merely the Israelites, were called to salvation. The supreme law of the religion He taught was the love of God and for His sake the love of one's neighbor. In opposition to the Pharisees, with their external observances of the Law, He proclaimed that sincerity of intention was the basis of moral action. In this way He gave the individual conscience the principal role in formulation of religious piety. By curing the lame and the blind and by casting out evil spirits, He proclaimed His divine origin. Like some of the Jewish sects, He preached a complete and total commitment to God, but what distinguished His doctrine from all others was the fact that no man could come to God the Father except through Christ.

Although He attracted great crowds by His preaching and His miracles, actually a small minority of the people joined the specifically religious community which He was preparing. From among this small group He selected twelve men whom He particularly instructed concerning the nature of the new society He was founding. He called them Apostles, or those who are sent, and commissioned them to preach the doctrines He taught throughout the entire world, giving them special priestly powers. Among them, Peter was selected to hold a position of leadership. He was the rock on which the Church was founded, and he was to feed the sheep of the flock. Although an external framework had been worked out which gave the group the marks of a visible society, it was the death of Christ that infused the community with its inner mysterious life. For the message that Christ preached was not a new code of ethics nor an new intellectual system; it was above all life and the communication of divine life that gave the movement its real significance. The death of Christ, occurring on the fourteenth or fifteenth day of Nisan between the years 30 and 33 of the Christian era, completed the work of redemption, and His resurrection confirmed it.

For a picture of the primitive Christian community, we must turn to the first seven chapters of the Acts of the Apostles, which cover a period of some fifteen years. The story begins with the election of Matthias to succeed the traitor Judas. It describes the descent of the Holy Spirit upon the Apostolic group and their enthusiastic preaching of Christ's Messiahship. The resultant conversions disturbed the Jewish authorities, and the Apostles were arrested and forbidden by the Sanhedrin to preach. We get a glimpse of the early organization of the Christian community in the appointment of seven men to engage in charitable activities while the Apostles carried out their preaching mission. These men were appointed rather than elected, and some of them—for example, Stephen, a Hellenistic Jew—engaged in theological disputations while Philip was active in missionary work. Some trace the office of the deaconate described in the Pauline epistles to this group. A third group within the early community were called the elders or presbyters, a title taken over from the Jewish heads of patrician families. The existence of these three groups, apostles, elders, and seven, indicates an early hierarchical structure which, although dividing the faithful, did not create a gulf between the clergy and the laity.

The early Christian continued to attend services in the temple. The Jewish hours of prayer as well as the ceremonies and gestures were retained, particularly the recitation of the psalms. Prayer was still addressed to the God of Abraham, Isaac, and Jacob. Although there was no break with the liturgical practices of Palestinian Jewry, one detects certain new forms of piety and ritual. Baptism was the basis for membership in the new community. Christ as a person was the center of this liturgical act, and it was from Him that it achieved its supernatural results, the forgiveness of sins and entrance into the community of the faithful. Unlike the Jews, the new community assembled on Sundays for its own form of worship. Their fast days also differed from the traditional Jewish Mondays and Thursdays. Friday was selected because it was on this day that Christ had been crucified, Wednesday because it marked the beginning of His Passion.

In doctrinal matters, the early community emphasized the resurrection of Christ. It was this belief (that the risen Christ was none other than Jesus of Nazareth) that above all separated the new Christians from their Jewish brethren. The resurrection was also the most compelling proof that He was the Messiah. More and more He was called Christ and "The Lord." He was the Judge who would come at the end of time to judge the living and the dead. He was the Holy One and the Just, the bringer and the Origin of Life. Finally He was the Saviour without whom man could not attain salvation. "Neither is there salvation in any other. For there is no other name under heaven given to men, whereby we must be saved" (Acts, 4:12). The message of salvation was called "Evangelium" or the "Good News." It is referred to as the "Word of the Lord," "the Promise," or "Peace through Jesus Christ." Circumcision could not save, but only the grace of the Lord.

After the notion of the resurrection, the sect of the Nazarenes, as their Jewish adversaries called them, stressed the idea of the kingdom of God and eternal life. They were filled with the hope that Christ would soon reappear and bring about the "restitution of all things" and the "times of refreshment."

The spread of the Christian faith outside of Jerusalem was a slow process, partly because of the continuing sense of being a chosen people. Peter and John had journeyed to lay hands on the new converts in Samaria, and there were Jewish Christian communities in Joppa and Lydda. Yet it was not until the destruction of Jerusalem, after which the Christian community moved to the land east of the Jordan, some settling in Pella, that a move toward the Christianizing of non-Jews is evident. The first pagan to be baptized was the chamberlain of Ethiopian Queen Candace, and the reception of the pagan Captain Cornelius of Caesarea and his family gave an impulse to the growing conviction that the new faith was for all men. The real thrust, however, toward missionary activity among the Gentiles began with the sending of the former Levite Barnabas, a member of the Jewish Diaspora in Cyprus, to Antioch. Here, with the aid of Paul of Tarsus, the formation of a large Gentile community was begun, and here the term *Christians* was first used, whether for political or derisive reasons is not clear.

Paul, considered by some historians as the real founder of Catholicism, was born in Cilicia, in the city of Tarsus. Although of strict Pharisaical Jewish parentage, he was exposed to the Hellenistic culture of this imperial city, a fact that was to be of vital importance in his later missionary journeys throughout the Mediterranean Basin. He went to Jerusalem to be trained as a teacher of the law in the Pharisaical school of Gamaliel and, as he admits, one of the early persecutors of the nascent Church. His change from a violent persecutor to an ardent disciple was the result of a direct apparition from Christ. After baptism and a brief retreat in the Arabian desert he preached the gospel in Damascus and Jerusalem, but, meeting with little success, he retired to his native Tarsus. It was in Antioch, at the urging of Barnabas, that he began the conversion of the Hellenistic world. The synagogues of the cities of the Mediterranean provinces of the Roman Empire were the starting points of his Apostolate.

Here many former pagans had joined the Jewish communities as "God-fearing ones," and here Paul found a ripe harvest for his dramatic preaching of Christ crucified. His message was addressed to Diaspora Jews and former pagans, although it is quite evident that the majority of the latter repulsed him. A central point of his preaching was the emancipation of Gentile converts from the observance of Jewish law—a point that alienated him from the extreme wing of the Palestinian Jewish Christians. He strongly castigated Peter, who had feared to offend "the circumcised" in Antioch by dining with Gentile converts, and he proclaimed that "man is not justified by the works of the Law, but by faith in Jesus Christ" (Gal., 2:16).

After many missionary journeys, Paul was executed in Rome during the reign of Nero. His epistles to various Christian congregations throughout the Hellenistic world present a picture of the early Church and its organizational life. As a divinely appointed Apostle to the Gentiles, Paul was keenly aware of his office and full authority. For those to whom he addressed his letters, he was not only the highest teaching authority but judge and lawgiver as well. He made decisions binding upon them and laid down regulations governing worship and moral behavior. Whenever he preached he established a local hierarchy of presbyters or overseers, "episkopoi," who were to remain with their particular congregations. Perhaps the most important feature of the external structure of the Pauline congregation was its sense of belonging to a larger community of the faithful. Christians of all congregations, whether Jewish or pagan, served one God; were members of one body. It was this awareness of unity that kept the primitive church from splitting into two different denominations, one of Jewish, the other of pagan, origin.

The center of religious life for the Pauline congregation was belief in the risen Saviour who as the Son of God was Himself "the power and the wisdom of God" (I Cor., 1:24). Baptism was to be understood in terms of its relationship to Christ's death and resurrection. The Christian dies to himself and is given new life in and through Christ. The focal point of divine service was the Lord's Supper. The Eucharistic celebration was the confirmation of internal unity, since all shared in the same bread, which was the body of Christ. It was also this awareness that gave Christianity its early Catholic dimension. By the time of his death, Paul had planted the seeds of a religion that, at least in terms of the Hellenistic world, was universal.

The Struggle with Paganism

Unlike the first generation of Christians, who were more concerned with the conflict with Judaism, the second and third generations turned their attention more to adapting themselves to the philosophy of Hellenism and the religious situation in the urban centers of the Roman Empire.

Although the entire Mediterranean Basin had been united politically by Rome, and the Hellenistic culture with its common language had penetrated the urban centers from the Rhine to the Indus, there had been nothing resembling religious unity in the empire. In Greece the ancient polytheism had succumbed to the rationalistic criticism of the Stoics and the the Epicureans. The rule of the Diadochi had witnessed the breakup of the old city-states, with their shrines and religious cults. In Rome the ancient religion had been Hellenized in spite of Augustus' attempt to revive an interest in the gods and the colleges of priests. Although in 12 B.C. he assumed the title Pontifex Maximus, his efforts came to nought. Yet in adopting the eastern ruler cults, Augustus was to pave the way for one of the chief hurdles to the spread of early Christianity. Later emperors, who less modestly deified themselves while still alive, came into open conflict with Christians, who opposed any form of divine honor paid to humans. This led to the conflict between Christianity and the Roman state.

Not only had the ancient Greek and Roman religions greatly declined, but the spread of the mystery cults had changed the religious complexion of the Hellenistic world. Stemming from Egypt, Asia Minor, and Syria, after the Alexandrian conquests they gradually moved into the West. From Egypt came the cult of Isis and Osiris, the former the goddess of morality and civilization, the latter, her husband, the god of vegetation, whose dying was mourned by his followers and whose resurrection was celebrated with great joy. Later the veneration of Osiris was eclipsed somewhat by the Ptolemaic Serapis, god of life and death, the helper of the oppressed and the lord of fate, who led the soul unharmed into the next world. In Syria the mistress of nature, Atargatis, was worshiped, while from Asia Minor the cult of the Great Mother, Cybele and Attis, spread throughout the empire. The latter cult was served by a special college of priests, who were often led in their ecstaticism to flagellation and self-castration. All three cults were concerned with the idea of death and resurrection. The eschatological element and their strange and exotic initiation ceremonies made them popular with the middle classes, who had not as yet succumbed to the gross materialism of Hellenism. Mention must also be made of the cult of Mithras, which was widely practiced in the West, especially among the military. It was Persian in origin, and its disciples were initiated with the sprinkling of the blood of a bull after a long initiation of endurance trials and ablutions. The members looked for a final and glorious resurrection and participated in communal meals which prefigured the happy life to come.

Due to their esoteric and sophisticated nature, the mystery cults did not appeal to the lower classes as much as did a belief in astrology and magic. Very widespread throughout the Hellenistic world was belief in the miraculous, particularly as it affected the recovery of health. Aesculapius was the helper of mankind in distress, the "savior of all." His shrines were places of pilgrimage to which flocked the lame, the blind, and the afflicted. Where cures occurred, thanks were expressed in the donation of costly gifts. It was this god that Julian the Apostate later attempted to reinstate in opposition to the God of the Christians.

The Persecutions

It was in this atmosphere of diversified but enthusiastic religious interests that Christianity made its first confrontation with the Roman world. The established state cult of the emperor could hardly be expected to favor a religion founded by an executed criminal. The mystery cults with their extreme licentiousness were quite alien to the laws of chastity and mortification that formed the moral teachings of the Christians. The real cause, however, for a growing animosity on the part of the pagan population toward the Christian community was the latter's claim to absolute exclusiveness in the matter of religious truth. In a culture and civilization toward which they had contributed nothing, the Christians, by rejecting the religious pluralism of the Roman state, made themselves public enemies. It was not so much their objection to emperor worship, which at least during the first century had not been fully integrated into the state religion, as it was their constant bickering with other groups and consequent disturbance of the peace that provoked official repressive measures. The chief cause of the persecutions was the exclusive and absolute claim of the Christians to possess the true religion, and this did not seriously threaten the imperial government until the third century.

As to the early persecutions under Nero and Domitian in the first century, there is no evidence that they were directed on the basis of a legal proscription against Christians. The infamous human torches in the garden of Nero in the year 64 were a guise to cover up the emperor's arson. The persecutions of Christians, at least until the middle of the second century, were of a local nature with a relatively small number of victims.

It is important to note that all accounts of the persecutions were written by Christians, and the image of the emperors as the cruel oppressors of the righteous—an image created by writers like Lactantius and Eusebius—is much in need of re-examination. There has been a great deal of exaggeration and a failure to recognize that the Roman state did not persecute citizens solely because of their religious beliefs. The tenfold enumeration of the persecutions is nonhistorical and is based on the Old Testament prefiguration of the ten plagues.

Although there were a few Christian voices raised against the Roman state in the pre-Constantine period—Hippolytus of Rome, for example, identified the Roman state with the first beast of the Apocalypse—many Christian leaders, especially in the East, recognized the authority of the state. Clement of Alexandria praised Roman law and urged the payment of taxes and military service. Origen found in the unity of the Roman state and the Pax Romana a special and providential condition for the spread of Christianity. The Christian community in Antioch appealing to the emperor in a case involving a lawsuit against the heretic Paul of Samosata, and the rescript of Emperor Gallienus restoring confiscated properties to Christians, are indicative of a slowly developing attitude of mutual forbearance on the part of the Church and the state in the century before Constantine.

Early Heresies

Far more disruptive than the persecutions to the early Catholic community, as it was termed already in the writings of Ignatius of Antioch, were the heretical and schismatic groups that grew apace with the spread of the new religion. The Ebionites, a term probably derived from the Jewish 'ebjon (poor), are a good example of this divisiveness. They held to a dualistic view of creation, the principles of good and evil. Christ was but a human prophet of the same rank as Adam and Moses; His preaching rather than His redemptive death was the means of salvation. Many of the early heresies were directly related to heterodox Jewish groups who mixed Christian elements with a dualistic view of creation, with the principles of good and evil. In addition to the Ebionites, the Elchasiates and the Manicheaéns are representative of the strange mixture of Christianity, Judaism, and Eastern mystery cults.

Perhaps the gravest threat to early Christianity was the Gnostic movement. The remarkable discoveries at Nag Hammadi in Upper Egypt in 1945-1946 have thrown a great deal of light on this movement, which had such a strong attraction for the Hellenistic man. Like Christianity, it sought to answer the basic question of man's purpose in life, his birth and rebirth. For the Gnostic man, banished into an imperfect world by a lesser god, longs for a reunion with the true, perfect, but unknown God. He can free himself from the lesser deity only if he realizes that he is separated from the perfect god; this knowledge alone will enable him to return to the upper world of light where the true god dwells. This message was proclaimed by the heads of respected schools of philosophy in a literary style that soon gave indication of undermining Catholicism. Equipped with an attractive liturgy and possessed of a closely knit organizational life, it attempted to destroy the Church from within by utilizing the terminology and parables of the New Testament and focusing its piety on Christ, "The Living One."

The appearance in Rome about the year 140 of the Christian Gnostic Marcion forced the Church to revise her entire attitude toward Scripture and faith and to reorganize her external structure. The local bishops became more fully aware of their duties as guardians of orthodoxy, and their office became more monarchical in nature. A whole school of anti-Gnostic Catholic writers developed, among whom Irenaeus, bishop of Lyons, and Tertullian, of Carthage, were the most effective. Since the Gnostics claimed to have sole possession of Christ's revelation, the Catholic defenders were forced to reaffirm what they meant by Apostolic tradition and the cannon or authentic body of the Scriptures. The four gospels were gradually united with the Pauline epistles. The books of the New Testament were placed on the same level as those of the Old Testament. In determining the authenticity of sacred writings, the principles of ecclesiastical tradition and Apostolic succession were invoked. This development guaranteed the place of tradition as an essential part of Catholic faith and theology. The war against Gnosticism also stimulated the formulation of what Irenaeus called the "Rule of Truth," a summary of basic truths required of those to be baptized. Baptism now demanded a profession of faith that rejected the nonhistorical or spiritualistic doctrine of the docetistic elements of Gnosticism. The human birth, passion, and death of Christ were reaffirmed. Also in opposition to the Gnostic doctrine of self-redemption, the gratuity of grace was emphasized as well as the relationship between faith and knowledge.

Whereas Gnosticism in its various forms is considered one of the greatest threats to the early Church, the sect of the Manichees must also be mentioned as an organized religious movement that threatened the early Catholic community. Although until recently Manichaeanism was known only from the writings of its adversaries, the discovery of certain Manichaean writings in Turkestan at the turn of the century and the more recent uncovering of a Manichaean Coptic library in upper Egypt (Medinet Madi) have given modern scholars a more complete picture of its doctrines. Born in the capital of Parthia in 216, of a strict Mandaean family, Mani formulated his universal religion in a number of writings entitled *The Great Gospel from Alpha to Tau, Treasure of Life,* and *The Book of Mysteries.*

The religion is characterized by a radical dualism; the forces of light and darkness are the two highest principles of being. They are equal and unbegotten. Man is created by the father of light to combat the demons of darkness, but as he fails in this combat, he is given the living spirit who also emanates from the father and who will gradually save him through self-knowledge. To aid in mankind's salvation, God has sent a number of prophets or messengers; Buddha, Zoroaster, Jesus, and finally Mani, who differs from the latter three in that he is not restricted to any region and has put his teachings into writing. Mani is the last messenger of light and the apostle of the ultimate generation. His message is the final appeal to salvation. The perfect follower of Mani renounces the material things of this world and subdues his appetites, renouncing impure words, menial work, and marriage. The head of the church resided in Babylon and was the direct successor of Mani, from whom he derived his authority. Lower ecclesiastical orders were the 12 apostles, the 72 disciples, and the 360 priests. All others were designated deacons. Since Christ held a special position in the religion, He was "a part of the Father having the same nature as He." Mani calls himself a disciple of Jesus Christ. It is Mani upon whom the paraclete has descended.

It was perhaps this close similarity to Christianity that made it so dangerous. The religion spread rapidly through Mesopotamia into Syria, Arabia, and Egypt, whence it extended throughout the entire Mediterranean Basin. St. Augustine was captivated by Manicheaism for more than ten years, and his Christian writings give evidence of its influence. It flourished in Italy, Spain, and the Balkans, continuing to manifest itself in the latter area well into the Middle Ages. It was condemned by Emperor Diocletian, and the Christian Emperors Theodosius II and Justinian continued to harass it with penalties of confiscation and death. The Albigenses, or Cathari, and the Bogomils of the twelfth century show a definite similarity to this dualistic heresy.

All in all, the defense of the Catholic faith gave the Church, at the end of the second century, a deepening awarness of herself as the guardian of orthodoxy and the living word of God. By then Catholicism was established not only in Asia Minor but in North Africa, Gaul, Germany, and Spain. The rapid spread of the faith was due to the enthusiasm of the individual believers. There is no evidence of any central control and direction of missionary work.

In spite of a number of severe persecutions, especially under Emperors Decius and Diocletian, Catholicism continued along a path of coexistence with the pagan Roman state. In 250 Decius undertook a policy of extermination that far surpassed the sporadic attempts of his predecessors to eradicate the Christian community throughout the empire. The testimony of contemporaries, especially Cyrian of Carthage and Dionysius of Alexandria, show that many, including the higher clergy, were prepared to offer a token acceptance of paganism rather than endure martyrdom. Yet the great majority of those who had lapsed quickly returned, once the persecution ceased with the death of the emperor. Under Emperor Gallienus (260-268) there began a period of toleration lasting forty years, which witnessed a great flowering of Catholicism.

Missionary activities penetrated the entire empire, and from centers in Antioch, Alexandria, Carthage, and Rome a strong doctrinal, liturgical, and organizational current of development was in evidence. As more and more of the educated classes became attracted to the new faith, a correspondingly more intellectual presentation of its doctrine emerged. Schools of theology developed at Alexandria and Antioch, where, in contrast to Rome, there was a tradition of interest among the upper classes in religious and philosophical questions. The Ptolomies, by establishing the great libraries of the Sarapeion and the Museion, had laid the foundations for what was to become the greatest center of Hellenistic learning and neo-Platonic philosophy in the East.

Unquestionably the greatest luminary of the Alexandrian school and the most important theologian of Greek Christianity was Origen (d.254). The victim of episcopal suspicion during his life, he was forced to leave Alexandria in 230; as late as 553 he was posthumously condemned by the Second Council of Constantinople. Hence, very few of his original writings are extant. In spite of this, his influence on the subsequent development of Catholic thought is inestimable. The real basis of his theological contribution is the Scripture, critical commentaries on which form the greater part of his writings. The allegorical method of interpretation which he developed led to the clearest understanding of Christ. The daily reading of the Scripture, which was for him the chief source of his life of and his striving after perfection, had a tremendous influence on monasticism both in the East and in the West. He is the first representative of a deep devotion to Jesus and the founder of that mysticism and Christocentric spirituality which found its medieval representatives in the Victorines and Bernard of Clairvaux. In a way he set the course of theological speculation for centuries to come in composing the first manual of dogmatics, *Concerning Principles,* which dealt with the central problems concerning God, creation, sin, freedom of the will, and Scripture as a source of faith.

A contemporary critic has rightly declared that not only Christian antiquity but the entire Middle Ages lived on the treasures accumulated by Origen in his commentaries on the Old and New Testaments. In systematizing the allegorical interpretation of the sacred writings, he developed the great love theme of the New Testament, the identification of the Logos with charity, and the marriage of the Logos and the soul within the union of Christ and the Church. In this way he prepared that Catholic mysticism which revolves about the notion of the spiritual marriage between Christ and the soul. He constantly reiterates the fact, often lost sight of in later centuries, that there is a compenetration of the life of the Church and the life of the soul, the mystery of the Church and the life of grace. The following selection from his commentary on the Song of Songs especially demonstrates the interdependence of the Old and New Testaments:

We should remember what we brought out in the introduction—namely, that this book which has the appearance of a marriage song is written in dramatic form. We defined a drama as something which has characters coming, going, and speaking their parts, thus creating an interchange between themselves. This book will be like that throughout and from reading in this way we will receive a simple record of events. As we already indicated there must be a spiritual interpretation. The terms *Bride* and *Bridegroom* designate either the Church in her relation to Christ or the soul in her union with the Word of God.

In reading this simple story, we see a bride who has received for her engagement a dowry with gifts from a very noble bridegroom. But when the bridegroom delays in coming, she waits at home and grieves, doing all she can to bring herself to see her spouse and to enjoy his kisses. We see that the bride, who can neither give up nor gain her love, prays and petitions God, who is her bridegroom's Father. Let us consider her, "lifting up holy hands without anger or contention, . . . in decent apparel with modesty and sobriety," dressed in the worthiest ornaments befitting a bride, longing for her spouse, troubled by her inward love, pouring out her prayer to God and saying of her Spouse, "Let Him kiss me with the kisses of His mouth."

This, then, is the main substance of the story, presented in dramatic form. But let us see if the inner meaning can be supplied along these lines. Let it be understood as the Church longing for union with Christ. By the Church we mean the assembly of all the saints. So it is the Church, as a corporate personality, who says: "I am filled with the gifts which I received as betrothal presents or as dowry before my marriage. For of old, while I was being prepared for my wedding with the King's Son and the Firstborn of all creation, His holy angels put themselves at my service and ministered to me, bringing me the Law as a betrothal gift; for the Law, it is said, was ordained by angels in the hand of a mediator. The prophets also ministered to me. For they it was who uttered all the things that were to tell me and to show me concerning the Son of God, to whom they desired to betroth me, when all these so-called betrothal gifts and dowry presents should have been taken away. Moreover, in order to inkindle in me a love and longing for Him, they with prophetic voice proclaimed for me His coming; filled with the Holy Spirit, they foretold His countless acts of power and His mighty works. They described His beauty also His charm, and gentleness, that I might be inflamed beyond all capacity with the love of Him by all these things. But, since the age is almost ended and His own presence is not granted me, and I see only His ministers ascending and descending upon me, because of this I pour out my petition to Thee, the Father of my Spouse, beseeching Thee to have compassion at last upon my love, and to send Him, that He may now no longer speak to me only by His servants, the angels and the prophets, but may come Himself, directly, and kiss me with the kisses of His mouth—that is to say, may pour the words of His mouth into mine, that I may hear Him speak Himself and see his teaching. The Kisses are Christ's which He bestowed on His Church when at His coming, being present in the flesh, He in His own person spoke to her the words of faith and love and peace, according to the promise of Issaias who, when sent beforehand to the Bride, had said: Not a messenger, nor an angel, but the Lord Himself shall save us.

Let us bring in as our third point the soul whose only desire is to be united to the Word of God and in fellowship with Him and to join in the mysteries of His wisdom and knowledge as did the Bride enter into the chambers of her heavenly Bridegroom. For, just as the Church's dowry was the books of the Law and the Prophets, so also is natural law, reason, and free will the soul's dowry. Let the teaching which comes to her from her masters and teachers be her earliest instruction. But since her full desire and love does not find perfect satisfaction in these, allow her to pray that her pure and virgin mind will be enlightened by the illumination and visitation of the Word of God Himself. When she is not empowered with the services of human or angelic agents but none the less is filled with divine perception and understanding then and only then can she be assured that she has received the kisses of the Word of God Himself.

For this reason and for the sake of these kisses, let the soul say in her prayer to God: "Let Him kiss me with the kisses of His mouth." Of necessity she receives "kisses," or interpretations from the mouth of teachers, as long as she is unable to receive the solid and unadulterated doctrine of the Word of God Himself. She will receive the kisses of the Spouse Himself, that is, the Word of God when she begins to distinguish what was obscure, entangled, involved and is able to interpret parables and riddles and the sayings of the wise along the lines of her own expert thinking.

Furthermore, the plural, "kisses," is used so we may comprehend that a kiss of the Word of God bestowed on the perfected soul is the cause of the illumination of every obscure meaning. And it was perhaps with reference to this that the prophetic and perfected soul declared: "I opened my mouth and drew breath."

And let it be known that by the "mouth" of the Bridegroom is meant that the power by which He enlightens the mind. By some word of love spoken to her He also makes clear all that is unknown and dark to her. And this is the truer, closer, holier kiss, which is said to be granted by the Bridegroom–Word of God to the Bride—that is to say, to the pure and perfect soul: It is of this that the kiss, which we give one to another in church at the holy mysteries, is a figure.

We may believe that kisses have been given to us by the Bridegroom–Word of God when we find some problem that pertains to the divine teachings and meanings revealed to us without an instructor's help. But when we seek and cannot find the meaning of something of this sort we should make this prayer our own and ask God to grant us the visitation of His Word, saying: "Let Him kiss me with the kisses of His mouth." For the Father knows each soul's capacity and at what time it should receive the kisses of the Word.[1]

Antioch also produced an important theological school which, in contrast to the allegorical, interpretive methods of Alexandria, clung more to a literal and rationalistic understanding of the Scripture. Among its noteworthy exegetes were Lucian and Malchion. Alexandria and Antioch prepared the way for the Christological and Trinitarian controversies of the fourth and fifth centuries and the subsequent clarification of many points of Catholic doctrine.

Along with the doctrinal development of the third century, the community also underwent a constitutional formation that gave the Church a more complex character. The bishop was recognized as the undisputed leader of the Christian community. His authority was founded on the words of Christ conferring the power of the keys. His election was the responsibility of the entire community, who were to see to it that he was a man of proper moral and intellectual disposition. In the East, it was recommended that a bishop should have attained the age of fifty years, that he be not married more than once, and that his wife and children lead lives in harmony with his high office.

Although the office of the priest or presbyter gained in importance (he was permitted to celebrate the Eucharist and in times of special peril to hear confessions), his role in the daily life of the community was overshadowed by that of the deacon, who continued to be the "ear and mouth, heart and soul" of the bishop. The third century also saw the appearance of the lesser ministries of subdeacons, acolytes, exorcists, lectors, and door-keepers. The lector, who read aloud during services, was held in special regard. Appointment to all lesser offices belonged to the bishop, who consulted his congregation on the suitability of candidates. As the Catholic population increased, the bishops' authority extended over larger areas, and gradually ecclesiastical provinces were formed. In the West these provinces did not at first correspond to the existing imperial dioceses, but often included all the episcopal sees in a larger territory. Carthage, for example, summoned synods for all of North Africa, while Rome was the center for meetings of the bishops of southern Italy.

In the realm of the liturgy, the feast of Easter held the central position, since it commemorated the death and resurrection of Christ. The exact date of the celebration was for many centuries a cause of dispute. In the West the Sunday that fell on or followed the fourteenth Nisan was widely accepted as the day of the resurrection, whereas in proconsular Asia the fourteenth Nisan, regardless of the day of the week, was observed. In both East and West the day was preceded by several days of fasting. The center of the rite was the nocturnal vigil, for which the entire Christian community assembled. The vigil consisted of prayers and readings from the Psalms, the prophets, and the gospels. The central feature of the service was the solemn baptism of converts. There was little uniformity in the length of Eastertide; some communities kept it for forty days, while others extended it to fifty. The third century also gives evidence of a calendar of feasts commemorating the deaths of martyrs.

In the sacramental sphere an elaborate system of instructions for converts arose. The catechumen underwent a prolonged series of tests and instructions aimed especially at proving his moral qualities. Witnesses were called upon to testify with regard to his qualification, and a rigid code was applied that excluded certain classes of society. Prostitutes, charioteers, temple workers, and for a time soldiers were excluded from the catechumenate. The period of probation lasted over three years and culminated in a series of inquiries and penitential practices. Baptism itself was administered by immersion. For the third-century Christian, Baptism was believed to bring complete forgiveness of sin and to liberate the soul from the power of the evil spirit. On the positive side, it was a rebirth, the beginning of a new life in the kingdom of the Father. With the infusion of the Holy Spirit, one received the gnosis, or true knowledge of God. Spiritual writers, especially Origen, refer to the life that flows from baptismal grace as an imitation of Christ with whom the baptized person is united. He speaks of the Old Testament prefigurations of Baptism, as seen in the exodus from Egypt, the crossing of the Red Sea, and after wandering in the desert, the entrance into the Promised Land. Just as Israel was freed from the Pharaoh, so the baptized person is freed from Satan. In Baptism,

Christ becomes the bridegroom and spouse of the soul. Yet fidelity and the spouse can be kept only through constant vigilance and combat against the powers of darkness. This constant struggle leads to all the virtues, especially a love of one's neighbor and an enthusiasm for martyrdom. Gradually the desire for martyrdom was channeled into other forms of self-immolation, such as virginity and retirement from the world. Many Christians embraced celibacy, and we read of women who have become the "Brides of Christ." Yet even at this early date excesses were in evidence. The practice of ascetics living together in chaste marriage as brother and sister gave rise to definite abuses.

The *Life of Saint Anthony* by Athanasius demonstrates how baptismal spirituality had laid the fundamental ideals of monasticism by the end of the third century. The vows taken by the monks were considered equal in value with the promises of baptism. The Encratites of Mesopotamia are an example of extremism in early Christian asceticism. They admitted no one to baptism who did not renounce marriage and promise to observe absolute continence. Origen himself, in his ascetical enthusiasm, had undergone self-castration.

It is difficult to ascertain the exact nature of the marriage ceremony during the period before the Church emerged victorious over paganism. Ignatius of Antioch had recommended that it take place before a bishop, although it cannot be concluded that this was a requisite. Marriages with Jews or pagans were forbidden, and parents who consented to such a marriage incurred ecclesiastical punishment. Second marriages, although disfavored, were not condemned. Abortion was considered as murder, an indication of disagreement with the legal attitude of Rome, which regarded only the born child as a human being.

The question of reconciliation in the case of sins committed after baptism was a stormy one for the early Church. The belief that the death of Christ is not efficacious a second time in the case of a lapsed sinner was widespread, especially among the Montanists. Tertullian, for example, denies the Church the right to forgive grave sins since God Himself would not forgive them. Yet it is from his polemic against Catholic penitential practices that we gain an early view of the process. In what he terms exomologesis, or "Confession," the sinner must openly admit his need for forgiveness. The sinner was excluded from the prayer and Eucharistic service of the community. He was to don sackcloth and ashes and kneel before the door of the Church, supplicating passers-by for readmittance. Finally, the bishop received him back into the Church with the imposition of hands and the petitioning prayers of the congregation. In the writings of Origen it is clear that confession was to be made to the bishop. In the case of priests, their power of granting remission is bound up with their own personal perfection. It is interesting to note that this power is also attributed to ordinary Christians who have attained a high degree of personal holiness.

The Eucharist, of course, continued to maintain its important position in the liturgical life of the faithful. One of the earliest descriptions of the rite is found in the writings of Justin Martyr dating from the year 150. The ceremony, described in connection with baptism, consists of the reading of the memoirs of the Apostles and the prophets, prayers in common, and finally the consecration of the elements of bread and wine, their reception by the faithful, and a communal prayer of thanksgiving. The entire function is one of thanksgiving for the gifts received. Praise and honor are given to the Father of all things in the Son and the Holy Spirit. During the third century there is little evidence of any uniformity in the prayers used at the Mass. Yet in both the East and the West the basic formula was the same. The faithful received communion under both species. The consecrated bread was placed in the hands of the recipient, and he drank of the same chalice. Originally the Eucharistic celebration was preceded by an "agape" or love feast, a meal intended to foster fraternal charity, especially aid to the poor and indigent. Because of abuses the practice was discontinued in the fourth century. Although the Eucharist was celebrated on Sundays, there is early evidence of its taking place during the week, especially in connection with burial services.

As far as places of worship are concerned, the earliest services were held in the private homes of the faithful. Tertullian could speak of the "House of Our Lord" in Carthage and in Rome; Hippolytus refers to pagans breaking into the "House of God." The first written evidence of Christian churches is found in reference to a flood in Edessa about the year 205. Excavations in the Roman frontier garrison at Dura-Europos on the Euphrates in 1931-1932 disclosed a Christian church built about 232. On the walls are frescoes of the Good Shepherd among tombs, the healing of the man born lame, and Christ walking on the water. The burial places of the early Christians in Rome, called after the ninth century "Catacombs," are also a source of the liturgical art used by the early Christians. Here themes such as Daniel in the lions' den, Noah in the Ark, and the resurrection of Lazarus give evidence of the anxieties and hopes of the Christians during the first centuries.

In spite of our sporadic knowledge of the Catholicism of this early period, it can be rightfully asserted that in organization, dogma, and liturgy the basic elements of this religion are already in evidence during the second and third centuries.

Catholicism the State Religion

The final attempt on the part of the Roman state to eradicate the new religion occurred during the rule of Diocletian. Here again, as was the case with his predecessors, Diocletian felt that Christianity was an obstacle to the wide-reaching political and economic reforms with which he had hoped to forestall the collapse of the Empire. He had already secured the frontiers and reorganized the fiscal policies of the government but was convinced that the widespread sectarianism so evident in the religious field was inimical to the preservation of peace. The persecutions began with a purge of the military forces, as their support was essential to carrying out his policy of return to the ancient religion of the Roman state. The persecution finally attacked the ministers of the Church, and after 304 an edict was promulgated against all Christians who failed to sacrifice to the gods. The persecution lasted until 311, when an edict of Galerius, applied to the entire empire, called a halt to the attacks. For the first time in two centuries the Roman state finally recognized Catholicism and put it on an equal footing with other cults. Populationwise, the Christian community by the beginning of the fourth century probably numbered seven million out of a total population in the empire of fifty million. It was this fact that no doubt convinced the emperors that persecution was no longer an effectual means of suppressing the new religion.

It is evident that the Edict of Toleration of Galerius was but a final step in the gradual process that was to culminate in the establishment of Catholicism as the official religion of the Roman Empire. In the eastern part of the empire, the process suffered a temporary setback when Maximin Daia again expelled Christians from the cities. The persecution struck especially in Antioch and Damascus. The desperation of the pagans to discredit the Christians is evidenced in their calling on prostitutes to bear witness to their alleged debaucheries. In some places documents were forged attributing to Pilate a whole series of blasphemies against Christ. This final persecution, however, terminated as a result of a strange development in the West which must be listed as one of the great turning points in the history of the world.

In October, 312, Constantine, son of Constantius and the former innkeeper Helen, who had been Augustus of the West since 306, defeated the usurper Maxentius in the celebrated battle of Milvian bridge outside the city of Rome. The victory, which was in no way a contest between the foes and friends of Christianity, was nevertheless the occasion for Constantine to declare himself in favor of the God of the Christians. This declaration is evident in a number of monuments: the triumphal arch erected by the Roman Senate and ascribing the victory to an "inspiration of the divinity," the statue of the emperor in the Forum bearing a standard described as the "sign of suffering that brought salvation," and finally the appearance of the Christian monogram on coins as well as the imperial helmet.

Following the victory, Constantine called a halt to persecution of Christians in the East. He manifested his turn to Christianity in other ways as well. He communicated with the Catholic bishop of Carthage, granted him a considerable sum of money for the clergy "of the lawful and most holy Catholic religion," and freed the clergy of that city from obligation to public service. Confiscated property in North Africa was restored. In February, 313, at the Convention of Milan, in agreement with the Eastern ruler Licinius, he furthered the cause of Christian recognition. Although it is not correct to speak of an Edict of Milan, the far-reaching decisions drawn up there and later published in Nicomedia gave an indication of the radical changes inaugurated by Constantine regarding the official attitude toward the Church and affecting future Church-state relationships. Everyone, including Christians, was given full freedom in pursuit of his personal religion; all confiscated property, whether in private or public possession, was to be returned; and finally it was expressed that this amicable treatment of Christianity was to be a token of imperial gratitude for favors granted. Certainly a long step from the hesitant tolerance of previous edicts!

A further indication of Constantine's growing interference in ecclesiastical affairs was his involvement in the Donatist schism in North Africa. This disturbance was occasioned by the question of the validity of sacraments administered by traditores, those who had turned over the Scriptures to pagan authorities during the persecution by Diocletian. According to the Donatists, so-called after Donatus (d.355), bishop of Carthage, the spiritual disposition of the minister of the sacrament was a factor in its efficacy. The appointment of Caecilian to the see of Carthage sparked the controversy when it was noted that he had been consecrated bishop by a traditor, Felix of Aptungi. The followers of Donatus regarded the appointment as invalid and refused to recognize it. Informed of the disturbance, Constantine turned the matter over to Miltiades, bishop of Rome, where the case was heard by bishops of Arles, Autun, and Cologne. Donatus was deposed. When the Donatists contested the decision the emperor took matters in his own hands, claiming it was his task to eliminate error, maintain order, and protect divine worship.

This action was a preview of the pattern of Church-state relations that were to continue until modern times. Gradually a number of laws were enacted which gave a unique Christian imprint to what was definitely in the process of becoming an exclusively Christian state. In 321 Constantine passed a law ordering cessation from work in courts and manual labor on Sunday. Bishops were given permission to set up courts of arbitration even in civil matters. A special edict was passed allowing legacies to be bequeathed to the Catholic Church. Penalties were imposed on those who attempted to force Catholics to attend pagan services. After 324, when Constantine became sole ruler of the empire, his open sympathy for Christianity became even more pronounced, and he could speak of the complete establishment of the Catholic Church as the state religion.

There is a conflict of opinion on the beneficial effects of the complete change that was to make Catholicism the official religion of the Roman state. For some it marked the beginning of a sort of Caesaro-papism, making the Church dependent on the state and thus limiting her missionary efforts and secularizing her hitherto religious interests. For others the conversion of Constantine presented the Church with tremendous opportunities for proselytizing and consolidating its doctrinal and liturgical functions. Above all, it offered Catholicism an opportunity for closer adaption to the pagan culture against which its lack of recognition had forced a defensive position. The new situation naturally brought about a lowering of the high standards that the persecutions had forced upon her, and it exposed her to a dilemma that was never to be resolved successfully: the question of rendering to Caesar what was Caesar's and to God what was God's. By the end of the fourth century, the policies inaugurated by Constantine culminated in the creation of a Catholic state under Emperors Gratian and Theodosius and sealed the union between the Church and the state.

Although state intervention in the case of the Donatists gave a clear indication of the independent policy taken by Constantine in religious affairs, the advent of a new dispute on the nature of Christ proved even more that a Christian-state religion was a mixed blessing.

The Question of Christ's Nature

The century that witnessed the completion of the political adjustment of Catholicism to the Roman state was strangely enough also a period of one of the Church's greatest internal crises. It involved an attempt to explain in terms of Greek metaphysics the exact nature of the God–man, Jesus Christ. Since the identification of the Logos in the prologue to the Gospel of St. John with the second person of the Trinity, the question of Christ's divine nature had been the cause of varied and often conflicting explanations of His relation to the Father. In the prologue of St. John's Gospel it was proclaimed that Christ as the Logos and a divine being had existed from all eternity and had come from a previous existence into the world. The Logos or Word was well known in Greek philosophy. It was the highest of a whole scale of intermediary beings between the Godhead and mankind, between the creator and the creature. As Christianity became more intellectualized, the reconciliation of belief in three persons with the strictly monotheistic belief, inherited from Judaism, became articulate. Origen, for example, had spoken of the second person as a second God, although stressing His eternity and divine nature. Other theologians began to speak of the three persons in the Trinity as being nothing more than manifestations of the one God.

The notion that the Son was inferior to the Father was elaborated by Lucian, a priest of Antioch, in his efforts to emphasize the eternity of the Godhead. Many now believed that the Logos was a creature of the Father—that there had been a time when he was not. The stage was now set for the emperor to intervene in a matter of great dogmatic importance.

Arius, a deposed priest of the Church in Alexandria, became the acknowleged leader of a group who refined the doctrine of Lucian and made the Logos a creature of the Father whose existence was not from eternity. As in the case of the Donatists, Constantine intervened not because of any theological appreciation of the dispute but rather to maintain peace in the empire. To quell the threatening storm, a great synod was convened in Nicaea in 325 at the imperial summer residence. Here, under Constantine's direction, a formula of belief or creed was drawn up and promulgated as the law of the empire. The formula excluded equivocally any subordination of the Son to the Father and spoke of the Son as being "of the substance of the Father, God of God, light of light, true God and true man."

There is no official record of the proceedings of this first ecumenical council, but a few facts concerning the membership are of interest. Over 250 bishops attended, most of them from the East. Representation from the West was negligible. There were but five priests from this area. The bishop of Rome was not present, nor did he send special legates. In addition to the formulation of a creed, the council also busied itself with a number of disciplinary problems, important because until this time the Church had no uniform disciplinary code. The date of Easter was to be henceforth the Sunday after the first full moon following the spring equinox. It was decreed that bishops be consecrated by at least three other bishops. The practice of usury was prohibited. Although an attempt was made to enforce celibacy upon priests and bishops, it was unsuccessful.

The council concluded with the Fathers participating in a great banquet provided by Constantine, who was celebrating the twentieth anniversary of his rise to power. Yet the peace proclaimed by the council proved a failure. The Arian groups which had been condemned reasserted themselves in the East and were able to convince the emperor of the dangers of referring to Christ as consubstantial with the Father. The leader of the consubstantialists, Athanasius, bishop of Alexandria, was banished to Trier. His presence in that German city has been hailed by certain historians as an important step in the introduction of monastic ideals in the West.

The spread of various versions of Arianism, often receiving imperial support, continued until Emperor Theodosius in 381 convened an ecumenical council at Constantinople which reaffirmed the Nicene creed, condemning all forms of Arianism as well as those who denied the divinity of the Holy Spirit—"the pneumatomachi." Often ascribed to this second ecumenical council is the creed formula which is used even to this day in the Roman liturgy of the Catholic Church. Actually, it was a profession of faith that originated in Jerusalem sometime earlier. As accepted in the West, this creed included a clause that was to be the occasion of a seemingly interminable disagreement between the Latin and the Greek Church: the "filioque." In the Latin version the expression implied that the Holy Spirit proceeded from the Father and the Son, whereas for the Greeks the third person of the Trinity proceeded from the Father through the Son. The Greeks considered this formula a falsification of the text, and it remains to this day a cause of contention between Catholic and Orthodox. The Nicene-Constantinopolitan creed is as follows:

We believe in one God the Father almighty, creator of heaven and earth, and of all things visible and invisible. And in one Lord Jesus Christ, only begotten son of God, born of the Father before all time; light from light, true God from true God; begotten not created, consubstantial with the Father; through him all things were made. For the sake of us men and for our salvation he came down from heaven, was made flesh by the Holy Spirit from the Virgin Mary, and became man; he was crucified for our sake under Pontius Pilate, suffered and was buried. And on the third day arose according to the scriptures; he ascended into heaven, sits at the right hand of the Father, and is going to come again in glory to judge the living and the dead. His reign will have no end. We believe in the Holy Spirit, the Lord, giver of life; he proceeds from the Father and is adored and honored together with the Father and the Son, he spoke through the prophets. We believe in one holy Catholic, and apostolic Church. We profess one Baptism for the forgiveness of sins. We expect the resurrection of the dead and the life of the world to come. Amen.[2]

The strong position that was finally assumed by the emperor against Arianism and its various manifestations was also reflected in the declaration of Catholicism as the official religion of the state. In February, 380, he issued a decree (*De Fide Catholica*) which called upon all subjects of the empire to accept the Nicene creed as a rule of life. Three years later he passed definite legislation against heresies. In the West, largely due to the influence of Ambrose, bishop of Milan, severe measures were taken against paganism. The Altar of Victory was removed from the Roman Senate, and the colleges of pagan priests and vestal virgins were deprived of subsidies and immunities. Finally, in 392 paganism in all its forms and manifestations was proscribed throughout the empire. From what had been a position of tolerance toward the ancient religion, there now developed a policy of suppression. Nor were pagans the sole victims of this reversal of policy whereby the persecuted became the persecutors. Already in 388 Christians had stoned a Jewish synagogue in Callinicun, and the command of Theodosius that local bishops make restitution was rejected by Church authorities. In Alexandria an infuriated Christian mob burned the famous temple of Serapeum. The cruel murder of the neo-Platonist Hypatia in the same city in 415 is indicative of the triumph of intolerance. Freedom of worship no longer existed; Catholicism had become the sole state religion.

At the same time many of the privileges hitherto enjoyed by the pagan priesthood were transferred to the Catholic clergy. They were exempt from taxes and in certain cases were not to be tried before civil courts. The pagan practice of "sanctuary," whereby certain offenders could take refuge in ecclesiastical property, was transferred to Catholic Churches. Laws against heretical groups multiplied until it was the established practice to consider nonorthodoxy tantamount to crime. Heretics were no longer suppressed by the state simply because they disrupted public order but because they were considered as criminals in the same category as adulterers and murderers.

The Christological Controversy

The establishment of a definite Trinitarian creed for the Christian empire at Nicaea and Constantinople did not terminate the controversies that continued to revolve around the exact nature of Christ. Known as the Christological heresies, they are traced (as were the questions relating to the Trinity) to the continuing conflicts between the schools of Antioch and Alexandria, which were, of course, accentuated by political as well as ecclesiastical considerations. The Antioch school was represented in the recently founded capital of Constantinople, which now overshadowed the patriarchate of Alexandria in learning and importance. Nestorius, patriarch of the new capital, following a more Aristotelian and rationalistic interpretation of the nature of Christ, had taught a doctrine that seemed to some to attribute two persons to Christ. The Logos dwelt in the person of Christ as an idol does in a temple. This indwelling of the Logos, which allowed one to speak of two Sons of God, one by nature and one by grace, had been developed by Diodorus of Tarsus and Theodore of Mopsuestia. They argued that the Son of God was not born, but rather Christ was born a man, in whom God dwelt. In the case of Nestorius, this was given a new dimension by his denouncing the use of the title *Mother of God* and insisting that Mary's title was *Mother of Christ*. The Alexandrians under Cyril brought the quarrel to a head, and a general council was called at Ephesus in 431 by Emperor Theodosius II. After much disagreement between the Alexandrians and the Antiochians, Nestorius was finally excommunicated and forced into exile. His followers, however, continued to flourish, and during the following centuries they spread throughout the East into India and Asia. Before World War I there were as many as 100,000 Nestorians still living in Kurdistan. In recent times groups of Nestorian or Chaldean Christians have entered the Catholic Church. Historians are in disagreement as to whether Nestorius was actually a heretic or not. Some feel that he was the victim of political intrigue, as was his teacher, Theodore of Mopsuestia.

The controversy over the nature of Christ was not, however, terminated with the condemnation of Nestorius and the declaration of the real unity of the two natures in the Son of God. Here again the difference between the Alexandrians and the Antiochians came to the fore. For the latter, influenced by a historical association with Judaism, the question of the person of Christ was moral rather than philosophical. Like the Jews, they were more concerned with the problem of a divine unity than that of a divine Trinity. By overemphasizing the real union of the two natures, they concluded that the bond was so strong as to constitute one nature; hence the expression "monophysite."

The Alexandrians, influenced by Aristotelian philosophy, were more concerned with the problems of free will and self-determination. For them, man's salvation depended on a return to obedience to the will of God through the divine Logos in whom Man and God are united. Due to their insistence on God's manhood, they attribute to Him two natures. The discord that had prevailed in the East after the condemnation of Nestorius was also aggravated by the attempt of the Alexandrian school to reassert itself as the principal center of orthodoxy in the East. Against this background Emperor Marcian convened a council at Chalcedon in 451, which was by far the greatest of Christian antiquity. Some estimate that six hundred bishops attended, although historians now agree to a smaller number.

In a sense, the doctrinal decisions of this council settled for all time the perplexing questions as to the nature of Christ. The council followed a middle path, rejecting the extreme claim of Nestorius, who considered Christ as two persons and attributed to Him two natures. It also rejected the view of the extreme anti-Nestorians as represented by the monk Eutyches, who maintained that Christ's human nature had merged with the divine and upheld the humanity of Christ as necessary in the economy of salvation. The formula of faith drawn up excluded those who would make Christ two distinct persons as well as those who overemphasized His divinity to the exclusion of His humanity. It expressed belief in "one and the same Christ, Son, Lord, Only-begotten, made known in two natures, existing without confusion, without change, without separation; the difference of the natures having been in no way eliminated by reason of the union, but rather the properties of each being preserved and concurring in one person and one hypostasis." The answer to the question "What think ye of Christ?" was now set upon a sound theological basis that would protect His uniqueness as both God and Man.

As was the case with other heresies, Monophysitism continued to flourish for centuries after its condemnation. Yet the Council of Chalcedon must be listed as a landmark in the development of Catholic doctrine on the mystery of the Incarnation.

The controversies concerning the nature of Christ also had an influence on the liturgical life of the Christian communities. The old doxologies which terminated prayers with expressions like "Glory to God through the Son" or "Through the Son in the Holy Spirit" were modified to read "Glory to the Father and to the Son and to the Holy Spirit" or "Glory be to the Father with Christ together with the Holy Spirit." In the East, prayers were terminated with the expression "For thou art a good and benevolent God and to thee we send up the glorification, to the Father and to the Son and to the Holy Spirit, now and always in all eternity." Also noticeable as a result of the Christological controversies was a shift in attitude from what unites man to God, Christ as his Brother, the sharer of his human frailties, to what separates him from God, His infinite majesty. The great gulf between the human and the divine was henceforth emphasized. The two great feasts that evolved at this time, Christmas in the West and the Epiphany in the East, are also indicative of a trend to emphasize the Incarnation of Christ, the coming of the Logos into the world. The date of the celebration on December 25 has, of course, been a source of debate among historians. The strongest evidence points to the replacement of a pagan feast of the Unconquerable Sun, kept on this day, as the source of the date. Mention is made of celebrating Christ's birth on this day in Rome in the middle of the fourth century. The emphasis on the divinity of Christ also had its effect on attitudes toward the Eucharist evidenced in a considerable dropping off of the reception of Holy Communion. Christ was to be received with fear and trembling, and the Mass was celebrated on the "terrible and awful table." The Council of Ephesus, in proclaiming the notion of Mary as the Mother of God, had already stimulated a greater interest in the Virgin. The consecration of a Church dedicated to the Mother of God at Gethsemane on August 15 marked the beginning of the feast of the Assumption. Another Church dedicated to Mary on September 8 occasioned the feast of the Nativity of Mary. The Annunciation and the Purification, since they were related to the manifestation of the Logos in human flesh, are also traceable to this period. The former was celebrated on March 25, nine months before Christmas, and the latter forty days after this feast.

The condemnation of the Monophysites was responsible in the East for the adoption of national Coptic and Syrian languages rather than the official Greek, and hence the diversity of liturgies in the East evident to this day.

While the eastern part of the empire continued to exhaust itself in seemingly interminable quarrels over the nature of Christ, the West, less sophisticated and more inclined to the practical than the speculative, focused its attention on problems of discipline rather than of philosophy and metaphysics. In contrast to the East, the attitude was more pragmatic, direct, and in a sense authoritarian. Two heretical movements bear out this difference—Donatism and Pelagianism. The former, already referred to with reference to Constantine, had taught a doctrine of holiness that excluded from the Church all who were contaminated with sin. It was held that the valid administration of the sacraments depended on the minister's being in the state of grace. Although Augustine refuted these doctrines in a series of treatises proving the objective efficacy of the sacraments, they continued to flourish until the Moslem conquest of North Africa. Pelagianism, a doctrine attributed to the fourth-century British monk Pelagius, held that man was capable of avoiding sin and meriting heaven by his own powers. In refuting this doctrine, Augustine gained the title of Doctor Gratiae, the Doctor of Grace. He pointed out that according to the Scriptures all men, with the exception of Christ, are sinners, since no one observes the commandments perfectly in spite of grace and free will. In his work entitled *De Spiritu et Lettera*, written in 412, he also demonstrated that grace consists not only in the external fulfillment of the law but in an internal sanctification of the will. Grace itself is a gift of God and therefore unmerited. The question of the relationship between grace and free will continues to haunt Catholic theologians down to the present day. The accusation of Pelagianism became the rallying cry against those who overemphasized the role of the will in working out salvation in the late Middle Ages and during the post-Reformation period.

It would be incorrect to assume that the West was lacking in great theologians. Hilary of Poitiers; Ambrose, bishop of Milan and great antagonist of Arianism; Jerome, translator of the Scripture into the Latin Vulgate; and above all Augustine of Hippo were outstanding representatives of Latin Christianity.

Yet, just as Christianity itself had arisen in the East, it was that area which continued to produce its most articulate theologians. This was particularly true in the case of the Cappadocians St. Basil (d.379) and his brother Gregory of Nyssa (d.394) and Gregory of Nazianzus (d.390), son of the bishop of that city.

Basil's great contribution to the development of Catholicism was his influence in changing the direction of monasticism. The social and economic difficulties of the late Roman Empire as well as the constant doctrinal conflicts had led many Christians to escape the world by taking refuge in the desert. The monks, or cenobites, as they were called, are, of course, to be distinguished from the numerous hermits and anchorites who lived either alone or in more loosely knit organizations. It was the great service of Basil that he projected the monastic ideal of seeking perfection by following the evangelical counsels of poverty, chastity, and obedience into a more social or community arena. He advocated sharing with others the spiritual riches acquired from meditation and contemplation and in so doing he integrated monasticism, hitherto a divisive and often misguided asceticism, into the life of the Church. Monastic institutions were henceforth engaged not only in social-charitable work; they were also to aid in the organized Church by supplying recruits for the ministry. What had been an institution aimed at freeing the individual from responsibilities now became an organized effort that engendered collective responsibilities. In short, Basil gave earlier monasticism a stability and a place in society. It is this ideal that was taken over by the Latins and was to form the perfective ideal of Catholicism in the West for centuries to come. Both Augustine and Jerome were strong advocates of the superiority of monastic life over life in the world. It was Augustine who perhaps more than any other in the West gave monasticism its clerical or sacerdotal character. Monasticism in the East had not been a priestly vocation, but was restricted for the most part to men not in holy orders. Thanks to Augustine, the monk of the Middle Ages was generally a man in priestly orders, and the vows of chastity, poverty, and obedience were adapted to the sacramental life of the Church in terms of his role as a priest with pastoral concerns.

There were, of course, other elements at work in the ferment that was to develop into the monasticism of the early Middle Ages. Cassian, laboring in Provence in the early fifth century, helped to preserve the Eastern tradition that the real fruit of self-denial is in the attainment of charity: chastity, poverty, and obedience did not constitute a supernature, but were merely means of attaining the charity. His *Institutes* gave the Latin imprint of orderliness and subordination to the movement. Benedict of Nursia is generally recognized as the patriarch of Western monasticism. Yet the rule attributed to him did not bear fruit until the Carolingian Renaissance of the ninth century. The chaos that followed the collapse of the empire, the Germanic invasions, and the rise of Islam gave Augustine and Benedict an almost unwarranted influence in the life of Catholicism during the Middle Ages; the former in the formation of the pervading piety which was monastic, the latter in shaping the *Weltanschauung* of the Latin West by imbuing it with a deeply subjective otherworldliness influenced by his long association with Manichaeism. Their writings, in spite of bridging the gulf that was to separate the West from the more primitive Christianity of the East, tended to obstruct much of the more positive message of that earlier and more productive period when the spirit of Christ conquered rather than retreated from the world of men.

Unfortunately, the growing political division between the East and the West and the gradual eclipse of literacy in the West, especially the loss of Greek, curtailed the influence of the great Fathers of the East until the time of the Renaissance. Taken up by the reformers of the sixteenth century, the points at issue formed the arsenal from which charges and countercharges of deviation from the early Church were drawn by Catholic and Protestant alike.

Early Religious Practices and Beliefs

A look at religious practices and beliefs among Catholics before the collapse of the empire, which they had succeeded in Christianizing, is illuminating because it reveals much that was to dominate Western thought in the Middle Ages.

Infant baptism did not come into practice until well into the fifth century, probably as a reaction against Pelagianism. Even when both parents were Christians, many did not receive baptism until adulthood. Hence the catechumenate, the long period of instruction and scrutiny, was still an important feature in the preparation of those who had decided to be baptized. It consisted of exorcisms, the confession of sins, fasting, and memorizing various creeds and prayers which were recited before the assembled community. It is significant that many of the Fathers of the Church were not baptized until reaching adulthood. Although a catechumen since childhood, Augustine (d.430) was not baptized until the age of thirty-three. Ambrose (d.397) was not yet baptized when he was elected bishop at the age of thirty-four. John Chrysostom, patriarch of Constantinople toward the end of the fourth century, was not baptized until the age of twenty-five. The earlier Fathers, Origen, Tertullian, and Cyprian, advocated the reception of Baptism only after the recipient had reached a certain maturity. Perhaps one reason for opposition to infant baptism was the emphasis placed on the complete forgiveness of sin attributed to this sacrament. There is no doubt that Augustine's teaching on the nature of original sin brought about a change in this attitude. It is interesting to note that many of those who wrote of the nature of Baptism were themselves men who had experienced the deeper significance of the sacrament by having received it later in life.

Also closely associated with the baptismal rite were the various creeds or symbols that expressed belief in the Trinity and the divinity of Christ. All of them demonstrate a belief in the Holy Spirit as the principle of the new life conferred by Christ. The Holy Spirit dwells in the Church; hence the immediate reference in the creed to belief in the Holy Spirit and the Holy Church. The "communion of saints" mentioned in the creed refers to the community of men here on earth made holy by Baptism. The "remission of sins" is also associated with the effects of Baptism, and here again it is the Holy Spirit who is the effective agent of forgiveness. There is little reference to the notion of "grace" as it was later developed in the Middle Ages, and the "I believe in God" expressed in the creed was not the object of the speculative analysis it was later to become. Once attributed to the Twelve Apostles, the Apostles' Creed is now known to have been a distillation of various formulas used not only at baptism and in the Eucharistic celebration but along with the *Our Father* as a daily prayer of the Christian. St. Augustine introduces the creed to the neophyte in this sense in the following words:

Accept, my sons, the rule of faith which is called the Creed. When you have received it, write it on your hearts; recite it daily to yourselves. Before you go to sleep, before you go forth, fortify yourselves with your Creed. No one writes the Creed so that it can be read; let your memory be your notebook that you may be able to review it if it should happen that forgetfulness effaces what diligence has given you. You will believe what you hear yourself saying, and your lips will repeat what you believe. The apostle says truly: "For with the heart a man believes unto justice, and with the mouth profession of faith is made unto salvation"; this is the Creed that you will be going over in your thoughts and repeating from memory. These words that you have heard are scattered throughout the divine Scriptures. They have been assembled and unified to facilitate the memory of dull mankind in order that everyone will be able to say the Creed and adhere to what he believes. Can it be that up to this point you have heard merely that God is all-powerful? You are beginning to hold Him as a Father when you will be born of Mother Church.

You have already received, you have meditated, and you have clung to the fruits of your meditation, so that you may say: "I believe in God, the Father Almighty." God is all-powerful, and, since He is all-powerful, He cannot die, He cannot be deceived, He cannot lie, and as the Apostle says, "he cannot disown himself." Very much He cannot do, yet He is all-powerful; because He cannot do these things for that very reason is He all-powerful; if He could die, He would not be all-powerful; if He could lie, if He could be deceived, if He could deceive, if it were possible for Him to do an injustice, He would not be omnipotent; because, if it were in Him to do any of this, such acts would not be worthy of the Almighty. Absolutely omnipotent, our Father cannot sin. He does whatsoever He wills: that in itself is omnipotence. He does whatever He wishes well, He does whatever He wishes justly, but, whatever is evil, that He does not will. No one has the power to resist the Omnipotent and not do what God wills. He made heaven and earth, the sea, and all the creatures that are in them, visible and invisible; invisible, as in heaven the Thrones, Dominions, Principalities, Powers, Archangels, Angels, all of whom will be our fellow citizens if we shall have lived rightly. He made the visible creatures of heaven the sun, moon, stars. He adorned earth with His terrestrial animals; He filled the sky with winged creatures, land with moving and creeping things, the sea with fish; he filled all regions with their proper creatures. He made the mind of man to His own image and likeness; that is where the image of God is—in the mind. That is why the soul cannot be comprehended even by itself, where the image of God is. For this purpose have we been made, to be lord and master over all other creatures, but through the sin of the first man we have fallen and have all come into the inheritance of death. We have become lowly mortals, filled with fears and errors. This is the wage of sin. Every man is born with this penalty and guilt. That is the reason, just as you have seen today, just as you know, even little children are breathed upon and exorcized, so that the hostile power of the Devil who deceived mankind in order to gain possession of men may be driven out of them. It is not, then, a creature of God that is breathed upon and exorcized in infants, but him under whose sway all are who are born with sin, for he is the prince of sinners. Now, on behalf of one who fell and thereby sent all to death there was sent into the world One without sin, who would lead back to life all who believed in Him, by liberating them from the power of sin.[3]

The mysterious element of baptism must, of course, be evaluated in terms of the influence of the pagan mystery religions, with their emphasis on an initiating rite with its mystic knowledge and revelations. St. Ambrose could address his catechumens on the mysteries to be revealed in baptism: "The moment has now come to speak to you of the mysteries and to explain to you the sacrament. If prior to your baptism one had thought it right to unveil them to you when you were as yet uninitiated this would have been more a betrayal than a revelation." The following exhortation by St. John Chrysostom beautifully summarizes in symbol and figure the central importance of Baptism in Christian Antiquity:

> Following this anointing the priest makes you go down into the sacred waters, burying the old man and at the same time raising up the new, who is renewed in the image of his Creator. It is at this moment that, through the words and the hand of the priest, the Holy Spirit descends upon you. Instead of the man who descended into the water, a different man comes forth, one who has wiped away all the filth of his sins, who has put off the old garment of sin and has put on the royal robe.
>
> In order that you may also learn from this that the substance of the Father, Son, and Holy Spirit is one, baptism is conferred in the following manner. When the priest says: "So-and-so is baptized in the name of the Father and of the Son, and of the Holy Spirit," he puts your head down into the water three times and three times he lifts it up again, preparing you by this mystic rite to receive the descent of the Spirit. For it is not only the priest who touches the head, but also the right hand of Christ, and this is shown by the very words of the one baptizing. He does not say: "I baptize so-and-so," but: "So-and-so is baptized," showing that he is only the minister of grace and merely offers his hand because he has been ordained for this purpose by the Spirit. The one fulfilling all things is the Father and the Son and the Holy

Spirit, the undivided Trinity. It is faith in this Trinity which gives the grace of remission from sin; it is this confession which gives to us the gift of filial adoption.

What follows suffices to show us from what those who have been judged worthy of this mystic rite have been set free, and what they have gained. As soon as they come forth from those sacred waters, all who are present embrace them, greet them, kiss them, rejoice with them, and congratulate them, because those who were heretofore slaves and captives have suddenly become free men and sons and have been invited to the royal table. For immediately after they come up from the waters, they are led to the awesome table heavy laden with countless favors where they taste of the Master's body and blood, and become a dwelling place for the Holy Spirit. Since they have put on Christ Himself, wherever they go they are like angels on earth, rivaling the brilliance of the rays of the sun.[4]

The teacher of the catechumen was referred to as the mystagogue, and those to be baptized were called the initiates. The so-called discipline of the secret which aimed at guarding the formulas and creeds of the Christians from those who were not baptized reached its widest use after the establishment of Christianity as the state religion. The mysterious element is an indication of how important the matter of cult was in what has been called the Golden Age. It was the manifestation of a transformation of the Roman people into a "plebs sancta," the understanding of the messianic message of a people deeply influenced by the constant ritualistic presence of a redeeming Christ. The external rite was a symbol of Christ's saving act, not a mere commemoration. The new Christian was buried in Baptism with Christ and would rise with Him. At the Eucharist he would give thanks to God for this redemption and as a member of Christ's mystical body praise and glorify Him. Withholding these practices from the neophytes and the pagans enhanced their tremondous meaning. The more important prayers were recited *sotto voce*. The practice remains even to this day in the Latin Mass: the Canon is recited secretly; the words of consecration are not audible.

Some historians feel that the mystery cults of the pagans had a decided influence on the early Christian liturgy and that their dramatic representation of the life and death of the deities was in a way preparatory to the Christian representation of the life, death, and resurrection of the Son of God. Hence they describe the liturgy as the cult-mystery of Christ and the Church. There is no doubt that many pagan rites were incorporated into Christian worship. The prostrations and genuflections of the modern Catholic Solemn Mass, as well as the use of incense, are derived from the court protocol of the divinized emperors of the East. The very expression *Mass* is derived from the *Ita missa est* used in the imperial palace and the public courts for dismissing the people. Also pagan in origin are the practices of facing east for prayer, the sunrise service, and the orientation of churches and cemeteries toward the east. The Major Litanies celebrated to this day on April 25 are traceable to the pagan feast in honor of the goddess Robigus, who was supplicated to keep wheat free from blight.

Late Christian antiquity was also characterized by a continued development of the cult of saints. A martyrology originating in Italy about the middle of the fifth century enumerates over six thousand martyrs and other confessors. Martyrdom was no longer considered the sole proof of sanctification. *Refrigerium,* or the practice of gathering at the tombs of the saints for a funeral meal, continued for many years in spite of ecclesiastical condemnation. The veneration of relics also reached new heights, and gradually legislation enforced the placing of relics in altars. The alleged discovery of the true cross by Helen, the mother of Constantine, was first related by Ambrose at the end of the fourth century, and Cyril of Jerusalem mentions that particles from it had been distributed throughout the world. A feast of the exaltation of the true cross soon spread from the East to the West. It is still celebrated on September 17.

Also evident during this period was an increased interest in religious images and pictures, which were considered by many to possess supernatural powers. The monks, many of whom made their living making icons, were inordinately attached to them. A reaction against the abuses associated with image worship culminated in the iconoclastic controversy of the eighth century and the attempted clarification of the terms of veneration and worship. At the Second Council of Nicaea (787) it was declared that

> not only the figure of the cross but also holy images whether made in colors, mosaics or other materials were to be displayed publicly in Churches or sacred vessels and vestments, on walls and pictures, in houses and by the roadsides, images of our Lord, and our undefiled Lady, the Holy God-bearer and of the honorable angels and of all saintly and holy men. For the more continually these are observed as means of such representation, so much the more will the beholders be aroused to recall the originals and to long after them giving them respected honor, but not real adoration which according to our faith is due solely to the Divine nature. He who venerates an image venerates the reality of him who is painted in it.[5]

Significantly, in the West, where the Greek language was no longer understood, the decree was mistranslated, confusing the expressions *adoration* and *veneration*. At a general council assembled in Frankfurt by Frankish bishops it was urged that the bishop of Rome excommunicate the emperor in Constantinople for worshiping icons. The stage had already been set for the tremendous changes that were to take place in Catholicism as it encountered the new races of the West. While the Greek Church concentrated on the preservation of the traditions of primitive Christianity, the Church in the West turned its attention to Christianizing the new Germano-Roman nations.

CHAPTER 2

The Conversion of
the New Peoples

The Church and the New Peoples

THE EXPRESSION "Europe was the Faith and the Faith was Europe" still fascinates many who see in medieval Catholicism the fullest expression of the Augustinian idea of the Church as a sacramental community of the faithful in constant conflict with the terrestrial city. Hence a historical consideration of the factors that tended to identify Europe with Christianity is necessary if we are to understand how it came to pass that the Church, charged by its Founder with leading men of every race and background to salvation, became identified with a small number of peoples and a limited extent of territory. How it became linked with a particular civilization and is still known primarily through a passing expression of that civilization can be understood in no other way than through the historical process.

The Middle Ages, a term that since the seventeenth century has been used to designate the period that lies between the collapse of the Roman Empire and the breakup of Catholic unity in the sixteenth century, is in many ways misleading. Popularized by the divines of Protestantism and the prophets of the Enlightenment, it implied for the former a period when the light of the Gospel was diminished by monastic obscurantism and for the latter an era when Europe was an intellectual wasteland. Research during the last century has done much to dispel this depreciation of the medieval era. Yet at the same time it has fostered a romantic nostalgia among Catholics who see this, rather than the Apostolic Age, as the Golden Age of Faith. The Middle Ages, at least in terms of the general characteristics that prevailed in the realm of religion, may be said to have extended roughly from 700 until 1700.

By the eighth century there were already in evidence those elements that were to shape the course of Catholicism for the next millennium. In spite of the decline of the papacy in the late Middle Ages and the breakup of a papal-dominated Church with the Protestant revolt of the sixteenth century, much that was the Catholic heritage of this period remained operative until the time of the Enlightenment. The emergence of the national secularized state and the scientific revolution were the chief agents in the final dissolution of the so-called medieval synthesis. As late as the peace in Utrecht in 1713, men could still speak of Christendom in a medieval sense, since the pressure from Islam was still a cogent factor in at least externally fostering a sense of unity.

The thousand-year period during which *Catholic, Christian,* and *European* became identical terms was the result of the amalgamation of the Latin Christian culture of antiquity with that of the newly converted Germanic peoples of the West. The unifying agent in this coalition was undeniably the Church of Rome. The outstanding characteristics of the millennium, as far as Catholicism was concerned, were fourfold. In the first place, there was unity of religion and world outlook, a shared *Weltanschauung.* Belief in one God and the mission of Christ as carried by His Church was uncontested. After the collapse of Arianism, belief in the Trinitarian decrees of Nicaea was never seriously threatened. No heresy was able to disrupt this unity. This does not, of course, mean to imply that there was a complete lack of individualism. Both scholasticism and mysticism later gave evidence of a more individual and subjective thought. It was an outlook that was strongly influenced by the monastic ideal of escape from the world. It was firmly believed that the finest way to serve God was to flee the world. A constant theme of religious literature was contempt for the world and preparation for death. The words of St. John, "What does the world offer? Only gratification of corrupt nature, gratification of the eye, the empty pomp of living; these things take their Being (I Jn. 2:16,17) from the world not from the Father. The World and its gratifications pass away," penetrated deeply into the thought of medieval Catholicism.

Secondly, Catholicism enjoyed a peculiar universalism evidenced in the idea that all thought and action are directed by a unitary authority which placed the community before the individual. It was a universalism that not only transcended every aspect of political, economic, and social life, it was also territorial. *Catholic* and *European* were synonymous. This universalism was most frequently evidenced in the conflicting claims to absolute domination in secular and spiritual affairs between the papacy and the restored empire, between what is called the *sacerdotium* and the *imperium*. The struggles between the papacy and the House of the Hohenstaufen were but one aspect of this collision of authoritarian aspirations. Too often the empire exchanged roles with the papacy in attempting to impose a single norm of life on the West while the temporal claims of the papacy finally undermined the prestige of both.

The third and perhaps outstanding characteristic of the period was the stratification of society as represented by feudalism. Though based on an agrarian culture and identified with land tenure, this system did not disappear with the emergence of cities. The bourgeoisie, until the French Revolution, continued to view the permanent ordering of society as something divinely ordained. The nobility, the clergy, the merchants, and the craftsmen as well as the serfs looked upon themselves as being placed in their particular social levels by divine will. At the spiritual level this stratification was idealized in *The Ecclesiastical Hierarchy* of Pseudo-Dionysius. The universe of the spirit was a vast hierarchy of laymen, monks, priests, and bishops on earth. In heaven it was an order of angelic beings. All received in a descending order whatever illumination, intellectual or sacramental, was needed for a proper functioning of society. The benefice system—the feudalized right of receiving income from Church property on a titular basis—remained unshaken until the nineteenth century. Its vestiges are still found in the canon law of the Catholic Church today insofar as they affect the administration of ecclesiastical properties.

Finally, the age was one in which the Church exercised an almost complete monopoly in the field of education. The cultural supremacy of the clergy held firm until the Renaissance of the fifteenth century.

The raw materials upon which the Church of Rome worked to form this new type of Catholicism were the Germanic peoples. The barbarians, although they had lived for centuries on the border of the empire, had been little exposed to Christianity until after the fall of the West in 476. Certain individuals and small groups had been converted, but there is no evidence of any organized missionary endeavor before this time. Most of those who embraced Christianity after entering the empire turned to Arianism.

Whereas early Christianity was forced to adapt itself to the cultural standards of the Hellenistic world—to a civilization to whose creation she had in no way contributed—the situation was now reversed. It was Christianity that was to provide the language, the culture, and the philosophy of the newer nations. The Germanic peoples, unlike the Greeks and the Romans with their highly developed political institutions, were essentially tribal and migratory. They did not possess a developed literature nor did they exhibit a lofty appreciation of the divine. Once converted, they retained many of the practices of their barbarian past. Contrary to the practice of the Church of antiquity, the convert was first baptized and only later given instructions. In many cases entire tribes were brought into the Church simply because of the conversion of their tribal leaders. The mass conversion of the Frankish tribes under Clovis is an example of this procedure. There was no intellectual preparation or antecedent moral training, so that in many cases there was a very superficial appreciation of the moral obligations of the new religion. Hence, superstitious practices and vestiges of pagan cult remained for many centuries, covered only with a thin veneer of Christianity. Divination, astrology, and nympholepsy survived in spite of frequent ecclesiastical denunciation. In family matters, the power of the father remained excessive. Even marriage did not release children from direct parental control.

In comparison with Roman society, the position of the woman was extremely low. Divorce was only gradually abolished. In legal procedure, ordeal by fire or water or by combat was given precedence over the Roman system of proof by witnesses, either oral or written. Compensation, a practice whereby money was allowed to make satisfaction for crimes, was encouraged by the Church, which saw in it a means of avoiding bloodshed. Even in the devotional sphere there was a mixing of Germanic and early feudal elements. Christ was spoken of as the *Heiland,* the mightiest son of men, the most powerful of kings, the strongest hero. The place of worship was the *Burg-Gottes,* the fortress of God. The monks were the *militia Christi,* the "warriors of Christ." The profession of faith was looked upon as an oath of fidelity to a feudal lord. The garden of Eden was a fief given to Adam by the Warrior God. The institution of kingship, or more properly of lordship, was a strong element in the new religious structure.

The practice of annual gatherings, or diets, to discuss tribal affairs and settle legal disputes is a further instance of Germanic influence on Catholicism. As early as the sixth century the Merovingian kings summoned such ecclesiastical synods. The first Germanic council of 743 promulgated ecclesiastical legislation as sovereign's ordinances. Closely associated with this practice was the annual visitation of the bishop to the various churches in his diocese. He was usually accompanied by the landgrave, or territorial ruler. By the ninth century it became customary for the trustworthy members of the parish to take part in these visitations and under oath report any irregularities.

Since the conversion of the northern lands was to a great extent the work of laymen (as witnessed by the patron saints

Olaf, Erich, Canute), it was only logical that the building and staffing of churches was carried out by laymen who looked upon the Church as their own property. Authority usually centered in the person of the warrior chief chosen from among a family thought to possess an inherited right to leadership. The anointing of kings was considered a sacramental act. The king's chief duty was to protect, to act as the guardian of the community and its unwritten laws. Hence, in contrast to the ancient Christian-Roman law, which had guarded the autonomy of the Church and the public and legal character of her functions, German law held to a more objective idea of ecclesiastical offices with little regard for the moral qualification of the incumbent of a bishopric or a monastery. Even during the Carolingian period it was considered the prerogative of the tribal leader, if he had constructed an ecclesiastical edifice, to staff it and to dispose its revenues. The Church was considered his own private property (*ecclesia propria*), and like other property it could be disposed of by sale, legacy, or exchange. The priest or abbot could be hired or released at the will of the proprietor. Should he die in office, his goods reverted to the lay proprietor. Laymen who acted as advocates for churches or monasteries in secular courts also enjoyed the same rights. By the eighth century churches of this kind far outnumbered those under the authority of the local bishops. With the development of feudalism, the system was perfected and led to the great investiture struggle which we shall touch upon in our consideration of the rise of the papacy.

The Framework of the Mass

By the end of the fifth century the framework of Eucharistic service that was to be used in the Latin West, in spite of a variety of formalities and rites, was established. The two great divisions were the North African and Gallic, with its Celtic, Mazarabic, and Ambrosian subdivisions. By the eighth century Rome had given a certain stability to the hitherto fluctuating style of the divine service and with it a definite form that could be easily transmitted to the Celtic and Germanic Catholics of the West.

It borrowed heavily from the practices of Christian Gaul. In the tenth century the liturgy that was developed in the Frankish kingdom was accepted by Rome and introduced into much of western Europe.

The language of the liturgy remained Latin, of course, since the barbarian languages were not sufficiently developed to express the contents of the divine service. The Germanic peoples naturally found the language of the people they had conquered far more practical and cultured. The use of Latin as a liturgical language also colored the prayers with a juridical overtone. This is evidenced even today in the Canon of the Roman Mass where the priest speaks of the oblation that is "approved, ratified, reasonable, and acceptable." However, since the Latin language was understood only by the clergy, there was a growing exclusion of the laity from participation in the divine service. The Mass became something to be witnessed rather than participated in. In addition to adopting the language of Rome, the Germanic peoples retained the vestments of the Roman rite, which were originally the holiday attire of imperial Rome. The alb and the cincture were a survival of the ancient tunic; the amice, a neckcloth or scarf; the chasuble, an overcoat; and the maniple, a fashionable handkerchief.

Beginning in the Carolingian period, the various parts of the Mass as well as the garments took on a symbolic meaning. The Introit referred to the Choir of Prophets announcing the coming of Christ; the Gloria alluded to the angelic hosts who heralded Christ's birth; the Gospel referred to Christ's preaching; the immersion of the host in the wine signified the return of Christ's soul to His body; the breaking of the Host, the action performed by Christ at Emmaus; the "Deliver us from evil" of the *Our Father* referred to the sorrow of the Apostles until they heard of Christ's resurrection. After the ninth century, what took place at Mass became primarily a memory of the Passion of Christ. In vesting, the priest designated the amice as the helmet of salvation; the alb made of white linen signified righteousness and purity; the maniple, a badge of honor. The outer vestment was the armor of God preparing the celebrating priest for spiritual combat.

Probably the most important change in the Eucharistic liturgy of the early Middle Ages was the evolution of the private Mass. Throughout western Europe, where the manorial estates of the nobility were scattered over large areas, each manor had a private chapel with a priest who often said Mass alone. This practice of saying a daily Mass soon became the norm, especially since the monks were required to say a specified number of Masses for the deceased brethren. By the ninth century there was also a tremendous increase in the number of Masses celebrated by individual priests. Some celebrated Mass three or four times a day; Pope Leo III is reputed to have celebrated Mass as often as nine times a day.

Unlettered and uncouth as were the new Germanic Christians, it is significant that within a few centuries the centers of Catholic intellectual life were no longer in Alexandria or Athens, but Canterbury, Paris, Oxford, and Cologne.

Influence of Early Writings

In addition to Augustine's writings, more venerated than studied, two important pieces of literature, *The Pastoral Care of Souls* and *The Consolation of Philosophy,* both composed by men who viewed with great anguish the crumbling of the ancient Roman world, came to exercise influence on the new peoples of western Europe. St. Gregory I (d. 604) may be regarded as a chief architect of the new Roman Christianity which slowly took shape as the ancient world died. It is significant that although he had been the ambassador at Constantinople, he had no knowledge of Greek and his Latin shows a definite lack of culture and refinement. A former monk, he had applied to the papacy many of the ideas that Augustine had developed in his *City of God.* He shared the Augustinian vision of an earthly society modeled upon a heavenly prototype. It was a society in which spiritual power is by nature superior to secular power and in which the Church is destined to rule through a strict hierarchical order. Gregory was the first pope to assume the title used to this day, "Servant of the Servants of God." He has been called the Father of Europe, since his notion of Christianity as a Christianized republic over which the Roman Church exercised supreme authority was a prophetic view of medieval Catholicism. Yet it was the monastic outlook of Gregory that was to give medieval Catholicism its most perduring religious element. The attitude of contempt for the world and a suspicion of all things pertaining to the flesh, including marriage itself, are in evidence in all works and sermons.

The most famous of these, and one which took on an almost sacramental aura during the following centuries, was *The Pastoral Care of Souls*. It soon became the vade mecum of the Western clergy. It was handed to bishops on their day of consecration, along with the Scriptures. It became, in fact, the guide for pastoral direction for almost all of those who labored among the newly converted races of northern Europe. The following selection shows how Gregory approached the problem that above all others perplexes the Christian pastor in his preaching to primitive peoples: the problem of sexual morality. The twenty-seventh chapter of the book is entitled "How to Admonish the Married and the Celibate."

Those who are married are to be admonished in one way, while those who are unmarried in another. Married people are to be admonished that while thinking of one another, they should endeavor to please their partners without offense to their Maker. They must act in worldly affairs so as not to fail to desire the things of God. They should be happy with present good but fear earnestly and solicitously eternal damnation. They should so grieve over temporal evils as to fix their hope with every reassurance on everlastling salvation, all the while remaining conscious that what they are now engaged in is transitory while what they hope for is permanent. The evils of this world must not destroy their courage and the hope of heaven, but should strengthen it. Nor should they be deceived by the good things of this life when they are saddened by the dreaded damnation of The Judgement.

Now then, the mind of married Christians is both weak and steadfast, since it cannot disregard temporal matters altogether, and yet is capable, in desire, of uniting itself with the eternal. Though the mind is now engaged with pleasure of the flesh it must strengthen itself with the refreshment offered by supernatural hope. Though the mind possesses worldly things for the use on the way, it should hope for the enjoyment of divine pleasures at the end. It should not be totally engrossed with its present activities lest it completely forget that which it should hope for unceasingly. St. Paul explains this concisely when he says: "They who have wives, should be as if they had none and they that weep, as though they wept not, and they that rejoice, as if they rejoice not." Now a man that has a wife as if he had none, is sexually gratified by her in such a way that he is never turned from the correctness of better intentions to sin. He who has a wife is as though he had none, views all things as transitory and endures the cares of the flesh as necessary, looking forward in his desires to everlasting spiritual happiness. The man who weeps as though not weeping, mourns outward adversities in such a way that he may yet know how to rejoice in the consolations of eternal hope. And again to rejoice as though not rejoicing is to raise the mind from things below so as never to cease to be concerned regarding things above. Paul aptly adds to the previously quoted passage: "For the fashion of the world passes away"—as if he clearly said: "Love not the world constantly since the world that you love cannot remain constant." It is futile to set your heart on something, as though you yourself remained only to have them which you love pass away.

The married are to be admonished patiently to bear those things which sometimes displease each other and to assist each other's salvation by mutual encouragement; for Scripture says: "Bear ye one another's burdens and so you shall fulfill the law of Christ." Indeed, Christ's law is love and it was this that prompted Him bountifully to bestow His blessings on us and patiently endure our sins. Therefore, we fulfill the law of Christ by our imitation of it, when we also generously share our own good possessions and lovingly endure the sins of our fellow man. The married should be instructed not to consider what they must suffer from the other but what they might cause the other to endure. If one considers what the partner must endure, then what is endured from the other is more easily borne.

The married must be warned to bear in mind that their union is for the purpose of procreation and when they allow themselves excessive intercourse, they use the occasion of procreation for the service of pleasure. They must recognize that although they do not exceed the bounds of marriage they do exceed its rights. Therefore, it is necessary to cleanse by frequent prayer the goodness of intercourse which they have soiled by the adding of pleasure to the act. Thus the Apostle, knowing heavenly prescriptions, did not so much prescribe for the healthy as for the sick, when he said, "Concerning the things whereof you wrote me," it is good for a man never to touch a woman, but for fear of fornication, let every man have his own wife and let every woman have her own husband." In his fear of sin he gave a precept to those that are strong as much as a support for those that are weak. He adds further for the weak, "Let the husband render the debt to his wife, and the wife also in like manner to the husband." So for those for whom he had made a concession to pleasure in marriage, he again adds, "But I speak this by indulgence not by commandment."

Now the mention of indulgence brings to mind the presence of sin, but sin that is more readily forgiven since the sinfulness does not lie in what is done but what is done lawfully and carried to an excess. Lot is a good example of this truth. When he fled the burning Sodom and came upon Segor, he did not immediately go up into the mountains. To flee from burning Sodom is to avoid the sinful desires of the flesh. The mountain height symbolizes the purity of the continent, that is, those, who beyond exercising sexual intercourse as far as it is required for the procreation of children, do not indulge in carnal pleasure. To stand on the mountain is to see nothing in sexual activities but the procreation of children. To stand on the mountain is to avoid clinging to sex in a worldly manner.

But since there are many, who though giving up the sins of the flesh, still do not restrict the practice of intercourse in marriage as it is due, they may be compared to Lot abandoning Sodom but not proceeding as far as the mountains. These people do give up a reprehensible life but still do not really attain the perfection of conjugal continence. For saving the weak fugitive there is the midway city of Segor: that is to say that when the married are incontinent in intercourse but avoid falling into serious sin, they are nevertheless pardoned and saved.

They find, as it were, a small city where they are protected from the fire, since the conjugal life as they practice it, is not conspicuously virtuous, it is at least safe from punishment. Thus, Lot says to the angel: "There is a city here at hand to which I may flee; it is a little one and my soul shall live?" The city is said to be near and yet is represented as a refuge of safety, because conjugal life is neither greatly separated from worldly life nor is it alien to the joys of salvation. But only the married can save their lives in this manner, that is to say in a small city, when they intercede for one another by diligent petitions. Since the angel rightly said to the same Lot: "Behold, also in this I have heard thy prayers not to destroy the city for which thou hast spoken." It is evident that when humble petition is made to God this manner of conjugal life is not condemned. In regard to such petitions, Paul also instructs saying, "Defraud not one another except, perhaps by consent for a time, that you may give yourselves to prayer."

On the other hand, those who are not married should be instructed to observe precepts more strictly since the yoke of carnal union does not make them prone to worldly concerns. Since the lawful burden of marriage does not press them down neither then should the unlawful burden of worldly cares. Indeed they should be more prepared for the final judgement because they are disengaged and more capable of performing better things. But if they neglect them they will be the more severely punished. Let them hear what the Apostle said when he wanted to instruct certain people on the grace of celibacy. He did not depreciate marriage, but condemned the cares of the world that arise from marriage. "This I speak for your profit, not to cast a snare upon you, but for that which is decent, and which may give you power to attend upon the Lord without impediment." Earthly cares arise from marriage and thus the Teacher of the Gentiles urged his listeners to do better things lest they become entwined with earthly cares. The unmarried man for whom earthly cares have become an impediment, though he is not married, has not escaped the burdens of marriage. The unmarried are to be instructed that they must not think that they may have sexual intercourse with unmarried women, without bringing damnation upon themselves. St. Paul pointed out their guilt when he included the vice of fornication among the number of abhorrent crimes, saying, "Neither fornicators nor idolaters, nor adulterers, not the effeminate, nor liars with mankind, nor thieves, nor covetous, nor drunkards, nor railers, nor extortionists shall possess the kingdom of God." And again, "For fornicators and adulterers God will judge."

They are, therefore, to be instructed to seek the harbor of marriage if they are in danger of losing salvation because of the storms of temptation. Scripture says, "It is better to marry than to be burnt." These should marry without blame, provided they have not taken vows, for one who has vowed to submit himself to a greater good, makes the lesser good, which would have been lawful for him, unlawful. Scripture states: "No man putting his hand to the plough and looking back is fit for the kingdom of God." A man therefore who had been determined for a higher aim, is convicted of looking back when he gives up the greater good and turns to the good which is less.[6]

The man who perhaps more than any other helped to form the intellectual bridge between the ancient world and the new Germanic nations of the West was the Roman magistrate Boethius (d.524). The fact that, although a Roman aristocrat educated in Athens, Boethius chose service in the Germanic court of Emperor Theodoric is in itself symbolic of the transition that was taking place. Deeply aware of the cultural heritage of the Hellenistic world, he proposed, like Albertus Magnus centuries later, to translate the great minds of ancient Greece, the philosophy of Plato and Aristotle, into Latin. Although he failed to complete the task—he translated only the *Categories* and the *De Interpretatione* of Aristotle—what he did accomplish in his effort was sufficient to supply Christendom with the vocabulary needed to preserve the thought of the now defunct Hellenistic world. The theological terminology he coined lived on through the Middle Ages and is used to this day in Catholic theological writings. The definitions he supplied for the terms and concepts that were needed to work out a speculative system of theology—"person," "nature," "eternity," "providence," and "custom"—are still basic ingredients of Catholic thought. By the creation of a new philosophical idiom, Boethius also laid the groundwork for what is known today as "scholasticism," a system which found its finest expression in the *Summa* of Aquinas. Not only the vocabulary but also the methods of analytical thought that were developed by the great theologians of the medieval period are traceable to his writings. The trivium and quadrivium, which formed the basis of the liberal arts, were, to a great extent, due to the educational writings of Boethius.

Equally influential in the shaping of Western Catholic thought was the work that he wrote while imprisoned in Pavia, *The Consolation of Philosophy*. Having risen to the position of master of the offices in the court of Theodoric, an office that put him in charge of the domestic and foreign policy of the state, he fell out with Theodoric and was imprisoned and executed. It must be remembered that Theodoric was Arian, while Boethius was a Catholic. Boethius was long regarded as a saint.

The Consolation of Philosophy was probably one of the most widely read books in medieval Europe. It was known and studied by every educated person until the time of the Reformation. From its reading were evolved the dominant Catholic ideas of God as the Creator and providential Governor of the world, the nature of eternal life, the purely negative character of evil, and particularly the reconciliation of God's foreknowledge and man's free will. Some historians believe that as a Catholic classic the *Consolation* was, after Augustine's writings, one of the most influential in the formation of the European mind. Its great theme, the idea of spiritual freedom and the domination of the Divine, still continued to attract the attention of Western philosophers as no other. The following selection from this dialogue illustrates an interest in the perennial problem of God's foreknowledge and man's free will:

"I have listened to you," I said, "and agree that it is as you say. But in this close sequence of causes, is there any freedom for our judgment, or does this destiny repress the very feelings of our minds too?"

"There seems to me," I said, "to be a great incompatibility between the existence of God's universal foreknowledge and that of any freedom of judgment. For if God foresees everything and cannot err in anything, whatever He foresees will happen must happen. Therefore, if it is already known what will happen in the future, there will be no freedom of judgment. Nothing can take place or be desired except those things foreseen in the infallible providence of God. If matters could be turned so that the results were different than as foreseen by providence, this foreknowledge would not be infallible. Rather than knowledge, it is an opinion which is uncertain; this, I feel, is not applicable to God. Furthermore, I cannot approve of that argument by which some men think that they can solve this problem: for they say that a result does not come to pass for the reason that providence has foreseen it, but rather the reverse, namely, that because it is about to come to pass, it therefore cannot be hidden from God's providence. In this way it seems to me that the argument must resolve itself into in favor of the opposite opinion. For in that case it is not necessary that what should happen is that which is foreseen, but that which is about to happen is that which should be foreseen; as though our doubt was whether God's foreknowledge is the certain cause of future events, or the certainty of future events is the cause of Providence.

But let our aim be to prove that, whatever the shape which this series of causes takes, the fulfillment of God's foreknowledge is necessary, even if this knowledge may not seem to induce the necessity for the occurrence of future events. For instance, if a man sits down, it must be that the opinion, which conjectures that he is sitting, is true; conversely, if the opinion concerning the man is true because he is sitting; he must be sitting down. Therefore, there is necessity in both cases: the man must be sitting, and the opinion must be true. However, he does not sit because the opinion is true, but rather the opinion is true because his sitting down preceded it. Thus there is a common necessity on both parts even though the cause of the truth of the opinion proceeds from the other fact. In the same manner we must reason concerning Providence and future events. For even though they are foreseen because they are about to happen, yet they are about to happen. They do not happen because they are foreseen. None the less it is necessary that what is about to happen should happen; and this alone is enough to destroy all free will.

"Yet how absurd it is that we should say that the result of temporal affairs is the cause of eternal foreknowledge! And to think that God foresees future events because they are about to happen is nothing else than to hold events of past time to be the cause of that highest Providence. In addition just as when I know a present fact, that fact must be so; so also when I know of something that will happen, that also must come to pass. Thus it follows that the fulfillment of a foreknown event must be inevitable.

"Finally if anyone believes that any matter is otherwise than the fact is, he not only has not knowledge, but his opinion is false also, and that is very far from the truth of knowledge. Therefore, if any future event is such that its fulfillment is not sure or necessary, how can it possibly be known beforehand that it will occur? For just as absolute knowledge has no taint of falsity, so also that which is conceived by knowledge cannot be otherwise than as it is conceived. That is the reason why knowledge cannot lie, because each matter must be just as knowledge knows that it is. What then? How can God know beforehand these uncertain future events? For if he thinks inevitably the fulfillment of such things as may possibly not result, He is wrong; and that we may not believe, nor even mention. But if He perceives that they will result as they do in such a manner that He only knows that they may or may not occur, how is this foreknowledge? It knows nothing for sure, nothing absolutely! How is such a foreknowledge different from the absurd prophecy which Horace puts in the mouth of Tiresias: 'Whatever I shall say, will either come to pass or will it not?' How too, would God's Providence be better than man's opinion, if as is the case with man, He only sees to be uncertain such things as have an uncertain result? But if there can be no uncertainty with God, the most certain source of all things, then the fulfillment of all that He has surely foreknown, is certain. Thus we are led to see that there is no freedom for the intentions or actions of men.

For the mind of God, foreseeing all things without error or deception, binds all together and controls their results. And when we have once admitted this, it is plain how complete is the fall of all human actions in consequence. In vain are rewards or punishments set before good or bad, for there is no free or voluntary action of the mind to deserve them; and what we just now determined was most fair, will prove to be most unfair of all, namely to punish the dishonest or reward the honest, since their own will does not put them in the way of honesty or dishonesty, but the unfailing necessity of development constrains them. Therefore, neither virtues nor vices are anything, but there is rather an indiscriminate confusion of all. And nothing could be more vicious than this; since the whole order of all comes from Providence, and nothing is left to human intention, it follows that our crimes, as well as our good actions must all be considered due to the author of all good. Hence it is unreasonable to hope for or pray against anything. If an undeviating chain links together all that we can desire, what can anyone hope for or pray against? Thus the only understanding between God and man, the right to prayer, will be taken away. We suppose that at the price of our deservedly humbling ourselves before Him we may win a right to the inestimable reward of His divine grace. This is the only manner in which men can seem to deal with God, so to speak, and by virtue of prayer to join ourselves to that inaccessible light, before it is granted to us. But if we admit the inevitability of the future, and believe that we have no power, what means shall we have to join ourselves to the Lord of all, or how can we cling to Him? Therefore, as you sang but a little while ago, the human race must be cut off from its source and ever fall away.

"What is the cause of the discord that breaks the bonds of agreement here? What heavenly power has set such strife between two truths? Thus, though separately they can be understood, they can not be combined. Is there no discord between these truths? Do they stand forever by one another? Yes, it is the mind, overwhelmed by the body's blindness, which cannot see by the light of that dimmed brightness the finest threads that bind the truth. But where does the spirit burn with so strong desire to learn the hidden signs of truth? Does it know the very object of its careful search? Then why does it seek to learn what it already knows? If it doesn't know it, why does it search blindly? For who would desire a part unwittingly? Or who could seek after that which is unknown? How should he find it, or recognize its form when found, if he doesn't know it? And when the mind of man perceived the mind of God, did it then know the whole and parts alike? Now is the mind buried in the cloudy darkness of the body, yet has not altogether forgotten its own self, and keeps the whole though it has lost the parts. Whosoever, therefore, seeks the truth, is not wholly in ignorance nor yet has complete knowledge, for he knows not all, yet is not ignorant of all. He takes thought for the whole which he keeps in memory, handling again what he saw on high, so that he may add to that which he has kept, that which he has forgotten." [7]

The Rise of the Papacy

The breakdown of the empire in the West did not immediately affect the over-all external organization of the Church. The five great patriarchates of Rome, Constantinople, Alexandria, Antioch, and Jerusalem continued to form the main divisions of Christendom, each administered independently of the other and enjoying its own particular liturgy and discipline. Even as large segments of the ancient stronghold of the faith in North Africa and Syria, already weakened by the secession of the Nestorians and Monophysites, were swept away by the forces of Islam, the two most powerful remaining patriarchates of Rome and Constantinople began to lay claim to a universal authority hitherto held in balance by the other patriarchates and metropolitanates, now vanished or shrunken in size. Little by little the two Romes, the one of the Tiber and the more recent one on the Bosphorus, began to articulate this authority with an increasing trend toward centralization.

The Council of Chalcedon had declared that the see of Constantinople was equal to that of Rome, even though the latter had been founded by the Apostles Peter and Paul. Rome's claim to universal authority was, of course, nothing novel. The bishop of Rome had, even in subapostolic times, enjoyed a position of pre-eminence in the Catholic world. In the struggle against Gnosticism, Irenaeus of Lyons could point to the Eternal City as the cornerstone of Apostolic tradition, since she had been founded by the two glorious Apostles Peter and Paul. The Jewish convert Hegesippus also wrote at an early date of the Apostolicity of the Church of Rome. In the middle of the third century a litigation involving two Spanish bishops, Basilides of Emerita and Martialis of Asturica, was settled in Rome, and during the same period the question of the validity of heretical baptism was frequently upheld by Rome with a determination that pointed to its keen awareness of a place of primacy. The expression *ship of Peter,* as referring to the entire Church, is found already in the third century. Pope Gelasius I had summed up the papal position by stating, "No one at any time or for whatever human pretext may proudly set himself above the office of him who by Christ's order was set above all and everyone and whom the universal Church has always recognized as its head." It was against the opposition to this claim that the long dormant position of bishop of Rome began to reassert itself.

Late in the fifth century, Emperor Zeno had assumed the role of the vice-regent of God in maintaining unity of faith and discipline in the Catholic and Apostolic Church. He did not hesitate to depose the bishop of Constantinople and appoint bishops in Antioch and Alexandria. For his support of the emperor, the Greek patriarch Acaius was excommunicated by the pope in Rome, an event which led to a schism between the Eastern and Western Churches that lasted until the time of Justin I in 518. Justinian I later increased his control over the Church by usurping priestly powers. It was his belief that as the Autokrator he alone represented the divinity on earth. Although in Monothelyte controversy the Roman view on the two wills of Christ had prevailed over the position of both the emperor and the patriarch, there is evidence that the emperor at that time was willing to concede to Rome in an effort to discredit his own patriarch. It was not a question of recognizing papal supremacy.

Until the end of the sixth century, however, there were few open conflicts between the sees of Rome and Constantinople involving claim to universal rule. In 595, however, the Eastern patriarch assumed the title "ecumenical," and perhaps because he misunderstood the term to signify a claim to universal jurisdiction, Pope Gregory I raised the first alarm against what he considered a usurpation of Rome's title to primacy. He pointed out that the universal jurisdiction which the term implied was reserved to Rome alone. In spite of the protest, the imperial government in the East continued to mishandle the patriarch in the old Rome, forcing the pope to look to the nations of the West for protection and support. It is significant that already at this time a mission was sent to England, a move that began a close relationship between the Holy See and the farthest outpost of Latin Christendom. It was an event which greatly assisted in bringing German and Celtic Catholics into the Roman sphere of influence.

The turning point in the decision of the papacy to emancipate itself from the encroachments of the Byzantine empire, which theoretically, at least, continued to control large areas of Italy, was the fall of the exarchate of Ravenna to the Lombards. Since the Eastern emperor was unable to assist the papacy, the pope turned to the Franks. In 754 Pepin III, who had recently usurped the kingly office from the Merovingian Childeric III, was consecrated king and given the title of patriarch of the Romans. The process was completed in the year 800, when Leo III crowned Charlemagne as emperor of the Romans and hence protector and defender of the papacy. Although Charlemagne cared little for the theoretical supremacy of the papacy, he did see to it that Roman liturgy and Roman disciplinary practices were introduced and maintained in his new empire. Like the emperors in the East, whom he emulated in many ways, Charlemagne did not hesitate to look upon himself as the Lord, Father, King, Priest, and Governor of all Christians. Not without reason has he been called a Frankish Justinian, since he appointed all bishops and abbots and summoned and presided over all synods in the empire. The pope's role, as far as he was concerned, was that of Moses praying on the mountain.

Thus the move of the papacy to exercise a control over the new Western empire it had helped to create was for the time being a complete failure. With the collapse of the Carolingian empire, the papacy was plunged into what is called the *saeculum obscurum,* the dark age. The attacks of the Normans and Saracens and the absence of strong personalities among the successors of Leo reduced the papacy to a plaything of the Roman nobility.

Three dissolute women, Theodora and her daughters Marozia and Theodora the younger, controlled the destiny of Rome for several decades in what has been called the "period of pornocracy." Order in the Eternal City was temporarily restored by the German emperor Otto I, who visited Rome twice to insure the safety of the pope. However, after his death in 973, the powerful Crescentius family assumed control of papal affairs, thus forcing the German emperors once again to appoint their own candidates. It was not until the time of Gregory VII that the papacy was again in a position to reassert its claims to universal rule.

The background of the papal claim to universal rule during the Middle Ages is best illustrated by consideration of a remarkable document known as the Donation of Constantine, which gave legal sanction to the papacy and otherwise provided the medieval world with simple answers to many complex questions relating to Church and state. Termed the most famous forgery in European history, the Donation began its eventful career by fathering the Donation of Pepin in 756. Well into the nineteenth century it continued to influence canon and civil law as well as theology. Although its authenticity was questioned in the fifteenth century, many Catholics continued to defend it until comparatively recent times. The *Syllabus of Errors* of 1864 echoes many of its assumptions.

The Donation purports to reproduce a legal document in which the emperor, Constantine the Great, rewards Pope Sylvester I (314-336) and his successors for curing Constantine's leprosy by the sacred waters of baptism. Pope Sylvester declines the offer of Constantine's crown. The pope receives, however, numerous gifts, of which the most notable are the grant of Rome, all of Italy, and the western provinces. In addition, the pontiff acquires the Lateran Palace and numerous other imperial properties and the right to the imperial diadem, tiara, and other insignia. Sylvester was decreed supreme over all clergy and churches, including the four patriarchates. The pope is declared free to consecrate regular clergy, and the Roman clergy are granted the rank and privileges of the highest Roman orders. To further honor Sylvester, Constantine recognizes the pope's superior dignity by holding the bridle of his horse. Finally, Constantine announces that he will found a new capital at Byzantium in order that the presence of an earthly emperor may not embarrass ecclesiastical authority.

The first great achievement of the Donation of Constantine came in 756 with the Donation of Pepin. This Frankish "restitution" created the Papal States, destined to endure for eleven hundred years, and by giving the pope a place in public law it strengthened papal independence.

Certainly the Donation of Constantine was the basis of Pope Stephen II's demands before Pepin, King of the Franks, to rescue him from the Lombards. Pepin's promise of unlimited help is comprehensible only if he believed the Lombards had stolen lands given by Constantine to the beloved St. Peter through Sylvester. At Pavia in 756 the Byzantine legate, Gregory, humbly asked Pepin to concede the conquered districts to imperial jurisdiction. Gregory's mildness and Pepin's refusal are best explained in the light of the Donation of Constantine. Moreover, the document containing Pepin's Donation, handing over territory to the papacy, was deposited at the Confession of St. Peter, where Constantine was said to have deposited his own Donation.

The second great service of the Donation of Constantine was in inspiring still another Donation, that of Charlemagne in 774. Einhard, the biographer of Charlemagne, calls this grant, which included Byzantine Venetia and Istria, a "restoration" and adds that Charlemagne will not rest until all stolen territories are restored. Again the authority of the Donation of Constantine exerted tangible influence on papal fortunes.

The third and most significant provision of the forgery was its justification of the "Translation of the Empire," which effectively subordinated the imperial dignity to that of its supposed source, the papacy. The pope claimed the power to transfer the imperial office from the unworthy to the worthy, in this case from the Greeks to the Franks. Allegedly, when Sylvester refused Constantine's crown, Constantine and his successors only received the crown back as sort of fief which any pope, if he so chose, could take away and give to another.

The first great manifestation of this papal theory came on Christmas Day, 800, when Pope Leo III surprised a reluctant Charlemagne with the crown of universal empire for the loyal defense of the Church. The Donation hence gave substance to papal claims to the origin and thus the finality of power.

The papal role in crowning an emperor grew from reign to reign. Eventually Innocent IV, who had Emperor Frederick II deposed, contended in 1245 that Constantine had merely restored an unlawfully possessed power. The Church had always possessed the imperium! This and similar arguments were aimed at satisfying those who considered the Donation of Constantine unconstitutional.

The original meaning of the Donation was directed not against the West, but against the East. Using the Donation as such a tool, Pope Leo IX quoted the entire Donation in a letter to the schismatic patriarch Michael Cerularius in 1054.

In papal ideology, the Donation marks a transitory stage in the development of the papal theme of temporal power. Monarchy was a benefice, not rule in its own right. In addition, the Donation had a definite fault: Sylvester received his authority and even his jurisdiction over the patriarchs from worldly hands.

Papal ceremonial was revolutionized by the Donation. As mentioned, the emperor was supposed to humble himself as *strator*. The name of the papal palace was changed to the Sacred Palace in 813. The phrygium, the cap given to Sylvester when he denied the crown, became an extraliturgical symbol. The pope donned the imperial scarlet, and imperial titles were given to papal officials.

Curiously, the popes also used the Donation as a special claim to all Christian islands. In 1091 Urban II reasserted a claim over Corsica. Adrian IV said Constantine had given the papacy Ireland, which had never even seen the eagles of Rome! On this basis Adrian gave England the island of Ireland in 1155. The Donation was also used to justify such strange practices as the German custom of permitting ecclesiastical courts to collect fines in the purely municipal jurisdiction.

Not everybody was happy about the prosperity that the Church had enjoyed since the time of Constantine. The popular view was that the Donation had corrupted the Church. Until Sylvester, the Church had been pure and spiritual. As Dante says in the *Inferno*: "Ah, Constantine! Of how much ill was mother, not the conversion, but that marriage dower, which the first wealthy Father took from thee!"

Thirteenth- and fourteenth-century heretics often appealed to the Donation. The Waldenses, or Poor Men of Lyons, contended that Constantine's gift had seduced the Church. These *Leonenses* even developed a new etymology for their name. Their founder was Leo, a disciple of Sylvester, who refused to corrupt himself with gold. Another heretical group, the Dulcinists, blamed Sylvester for letting Satan back into the world. Finally John Wycliffe in his *Trialogus* represents the Antichrist as the ultimate author of the famed Donation.

The significance of the Donation of Constantine is easy to overvalue and easy to undervalue. Little if anything that was essentially novel came through the forgery. The Donation was employed as an excuse or legal justification. As Doellinger wrote, it was a large and inexhaustible treasury from which privileges could be obtained just as they were desired.

Though the Donation was used by almost everyone, the most lasting application advanced the papal monarchy. When under Innocent III the vicarate of Christ (by which the pope exercised Christ's "fullness of powers") reached development, the Donation was relegated to nailing down a dubious privilege or adding authority to authority.

The Gregorian Reform

It is one of the ironies of history that the German emperors who rescued the papacy in the eleventh century from the domination of the corrupt Italian nobility would within a century become part of the Investiture struggle. It was the appointment of his cousin Bruno as bishop of Toul by Henry III that marked a new chapter in the history of the papacy. This act of nepotism was to have a profound effect on the entire future history of Catholicism.

The origins of the Gregorian or Hildebrandian reforms, like so much else in Catholicism, are directly traceable to monasticism, for the calling of the Tuscan-born monk Hildebrand (d.1085) to the papal court by Pope Leo IX channeled into the very heart and center of Christendom those types of reform that had been in ferment at Cluny and lesser monastic centers for over a century. Although historians still disagree as to the role of Cluny in the reform and subsequent strengthening of the papacy, it is generally recognized that the rise of the pope and the Curia to the apex of spiritual power in the thirteenth century was at least in part due to the spirit of monastic reform begun there under the monk Hildebrand. That it was also accomplished by the maturation of doctrines on the notion of authority traceable to Pope Gelasius I and the changes in canon law introduced in the eleventh century must also be admitted.

We have seen that the institution of monasticism had for five centuries determined the fate not only of religion but also of culture and civilization. By the ninth century, since most of its members were drawn almost exclusively from the nobility, it had grown to be one of the most important social institutions in medieval society. Its monastic schools were the only effective successors to the municipal schools of the late Roman Empire. Only in the great monasteries could provision be made for the teaching staffs and libraries that any continued educational effort demands. The task of preserving what was left of the classics and the Latin patristics, thus guaranteeing a literate Church, fell to the monks. They carried out even more important works. In spite of their individual vows of poverty, they had vast landholdings and agricultural enterprises which played an important role in the economy and government. After the eighth century, they were incorporated into the feudal system. Abbots were made the vassals of kings, with attendant political, judicial, and military responsibilities. In the Ottonian Empire, most of the monasteries had been brought under the control of the royal house. Their abbots were given powers in court, and in turn they supplied military levies for the imperial armies. The monks were the friends, secretaries, and confidants of kings. William the Conqueror had depended on the advice and direction of the monk Lanfranc in consolidating his conquests in England. Henry III had been educated by monks.

Yet by the mid-eleventh century there is evidence of a definite decline in the Benedictine influence. The chief cause of this decline was their loss of control over higher education. The aims of the monastic schools had become limited to little more than the preservation of literacy. By the eleventh century, political and economic growth in western Europe had advanced to a point where, for the first time since the barbarian invasions, it was possible to create an elite who could devote themselves to the study of philosophy, theology, and law. This change had the end effect of lessening the influence of the monks in the sphere of secular activity. At the same time, it engendered a desire to revert to the original ideal of the monk, which was a withdrawal from society. This return to a more strict form of life was, of course, accentuated by those who felt that the monks had rendered their historic service to Christian society in collaborating with secular leaders and that further identification with the world was detrimental to their original objective of self-sanctification. In addition, there was a danger of the monk's losing his identity in a lay society that was taking on more and more the religious practices of the monks. Men like Henry III of Germany (d.1056) and Edward the Confessor of England (d.1066) were, in a sense, monks in secular garb. The principle on which the monks had built their influence on lay society was that of him to whom more is given, more will be demanded. This maxim was in danger of losing its cogency unless a new and more exacting type of asceticism was brought forth. The clergy, especially the monks, were in danger of losing their distinctive role in society.

The first strong reaction to this situation came from those regions in Europe where there was a definite lack of strong governmental control, principally northern Italy and Lorraine. The over-all benefits of a close collaboration between the Church and the state were hardly perceptible in these provincial areas. It was from these regions, rather than from the reformed abbey of Cluny, as is often argued, that the movement stemmed to return to the spiritual ideal of the early Church. Men like Peter Damian (d.1072) and Cardinal Humbert (d.1061), dissatisfied with the secularized monasteries, carried their reforming zeal to the very apex of the Church, the papacy. The program they inaugurated, like many another, was based on a platform aimed at ecclesiastical liberty and freedom from secular control. Not content with purifying the monasteries, a process that had been repeated with short-lived success since the time of Benedict, they devised a program for the entire Christian world. The plan had its extremes. The reforming abbot Romuald eventually wanted to turn the world into a vast monastery. Pope Paschal II startled his confreres in Rome by proposing absolute poverty for all Catholics. It was the monk Hildebrand, however, who rallied the forces of ascetic reform and, after being made pope by popular acclaim in Rome in 1073, launched an attempt to establish a new world order.

Taking the lead from ideas that had been elaborated in Cardinal Humbert's work *Three Books Against the Simoniacs* (1059), Hildebrand, as Pope Gregory VII, undertook the task of imposing justice on the entire world. The Gregorian movement thus intended to create a new homogeneous situation in the form of papal domination not only over ecclesiastics but over secular rulers as well.

The three main evils that subjected the Church to lay control were simony, clerical marriage, and lay investiture. Simony, the buying or selling of an ecclesiastical office, had, of course, become commonplace as feudalism advanced, and the old Donatist heresy which denied spiritual powers to immoral clergy was resurrected to attack it. Married priests were common in the early Middle Ages, although the practice had been sporadically condemned. It was now attacked with a vengeance. The offspring of the clergy were declared illegitimate. The ideal of a completely emancipated Church was impossible, of course, if Church properties could be inherited. The removal of lay investiture, the outgrowth of the proprietary Church system whereby the temporal ruler appointed and invested the bishop with the symbols of his office, was, of course, necessary if the pope were to exercise absolute control over the entire Church.

The first sign of the triumph of the reform party in the papacy was the revolutionary decree of Nicholas II that freed the papacy from imperial control and election by riotous Roman nobility. Before this time, elections to the papacy had followed the ancient canonical rule of choice by clergy and the people of Rome. Henceforth election to the Apostolic See was to be made by the cardinals and on the initiative of the cardinal bishops. The act of election, not the consecration and enthronement, gave them full papal powers. Since the appointment of cardinals was the prerogative of the popes, an oligarchy was established. To strengthen this decision, which was unpalatable to the imperial court, the pope concluded a treaty with the Norman kingdom in Sicily, using the Donation of Constantine to enfief the territory. Hildebrand consolidated the process in 1075 by proclaiming that as the successor of Peter, the pope held supreme authority over all Christian souls. He was the supreme judge, himself subject to God. All prelates were subject to him; his powers of absolution and excommunication were unlimited.

The *Dictatus Papae* enumerates the powers now claimed by the papacy by boldly proclaiming that the Roman Church was founded by God alone:

The Roman pontiff alone can by right be called universal. He alone can depose and reinstate bishops. His legate should take precedence over all bishops in a council, even if he is of lower rank, and can pronounce the sentence of deposition against them. The pope may depose those who are absent. Among other things, we ought not to remain in the same house with those who have been excommunicated by him. To him alone is it granted, in accordance with the needs of the time, to establish new laws, to assemble new congregations, to make an abbey out of a canonry and vice versa, and to divide a wealthy bishopric and unite poor ones. He alone may use the imperial insignia. All princes should kiss the feet of the pope alone. His name is unique in the world. He alone should be allowed to depose emperors. When necessity forces him to it, he should be allowed to transfer bishops from diocese to diocese. He has the power to ordain a cleric from any church whensoever he shall wish it. The man ordained by him can preside over another church, but cannot serve it in an inferior capacity; and that he ought not accept a higher rank from any other bishop. No synod ought to be called general without his command. No chapter and no book shall be considered canonical without his authority. His sentence ought to be retracted by nobody, and he alone, of all men, can retract it. He ought to be judged by no man. No man should dare to condemn a man who appeals to the Apostolic Throne. The more important cases of each and every church should be referred to that See. The Roman Church has never erred, nor, as Scripture proclaims, will it ever err, through all eternity. The Roman pontiff, if he was canonically ordained, has undoubtedly been sanctified by the merits of the blessed Peter, as St. Ennodius, bishop of Pavia, tells us and many saintly fathers believe; just as it is stated in the decrees of the blessed Pope Symmachus. By his command and permission subordinates may be allowed to bring accusations. He can depose and reinstate bishops without calling a synod. He who does not agree with the Church of Rome should not be considered a Catholic. He can absolve vassals from their allegiance to evil men.[8]

Hand in hand with the throwing off of secular control and to a great extent responsible for its success was the development of a new system of canon law. Although Roman law had suffered an eclipse after the fall of the empire, the canons of the ancient Church, the disciplinary decrees of the general councils and legislation of earlier popes, had remained intact until the sixth century. During the ninth century, thanks to the addition of a number of forged documents drawn up by clerics in France who wished to curb the power of metropolitan bishops by appealing to Roman authority, the so-called *False Decretals* and *False Capitularies* found their way into the corpus of Church law. Since they stressed the idea of supreme authority of the See of

Peter, they formed an elaborate legal argument for the universal claims of Rome.

The rediscovery of Roman law at the school of Bologna by Irnerius (d.1125) and its elaboration by Yves de Chartres (d.1116) gave a further impetus to the systematizing of canon law. Thanks to the efforts of the monk Gratian, who attempted to eliminate the confusion and contradictions in the accumulated mass of legislation, a text appeared around 1150 entitled *The Concord of Discordant Canons*. Like the *Sentences* of Peter Lombard, which attempted to systematize theological problems through the application of dialectics, the work was to become the basic text of a new branch of theology. The decretals rather than the Gospel became the basis for moral judgments. Even the sacraments came to assume a legal complexion, and a sacramental jurisprudence developed. Baptism was now considered as a legal act through which in law the newly baptized became a member of the Christian body, itself a juristically constructed entity. Matrimony was considered as a legal contract whose validity depended on avoidance of canonical impediments drawn up by the Holy See. Ordination to the priesthood was determined by legal enactments which placed jurisdictional rights above holiness of life as qualifications. A knowledge of canon law became the requisite for ecclesiastical preferment. Throughout the remainder of the Middle Ages, canon lawyers rather than theologians dominated the papacy. The role of the papacy in medieval theological matters is incredibly unimpressive.

By 1234 all former collections of pontifical decisions were combined by Gregory IX into a single code: *The Five Books of Decretals*. The classical juridical doctrine of the Church was now complete. It defined the structure of the ecclesiastical body, the rules which Christians must obey, and the relations of the spiritual power in the world.

The administration of this ever widening area of authority fell to the Roman Curia, or court. Papal documents were no longer headed with the title *Roman Church*, but *Curia Romana*. Among the curial offices were the Papal Chancery, which drafted official documents, the Apostolic Camera, which handled financial affairs, and the Sacred Penitentiary, which dealt with the many sins not reserved to the Vatican. Many rights formerly exercised by archbishops and provincial synods were now reserved to the pope. Bishops were obliged to take an oath of obedience to the pope that closely resembled the feudal oaths binding a vassal to his lord.

The title of pope, which had hitherto been used to designate other members of the hierarchy, was now used by the bishop of Rome exclusively. The pope was no longer merely consecrated; he was crowned with a tiara, a helmet-shaped head covering used originally by the deified rulers of Persia. The selection and consecration of bishops throughout all of Christendom was now a papal prerogative. Legal cases, even down to the slightest detail, were to be settled in Rome. Whole kingdoms such as Poland, Aragon, and England were made papal fiefs.

The Hildebrandian reform, in spite of the sincerity of its leaders, did not bring peace to the Church but a sword. The city of Rome was sacked by Emperor Henry IV, and Gregory died a prisoner in Salerno, repeating the words of the psalmist: "I have loved righteousness and hated iniquity, wherefore I die in exile." The investiture struggle was to continue for many centuries until the time of Louis the Bavarian. In a way, its claims undermined the empire in the final defeat of the Hohenstaufen kings. Yet many elements of the program were accepted. Clerical celibacy, with its sharp separation of the laity from the clergy, as well as the prohibition of simony and other measures became law all over Europe. The supremacy of the papacy over earthly rulers was now embodied in the papal tradition.

The same ascetic impulse that worked so powerfully toward the reform of the central apparatus of the Church found a more natural outlet in reforming monastic life. The new monastic orders, the Cistercians, Carthusians, and Premonstratensians, raised the ideal of monasticism and, by moving into unsettled areas, helped to consolidate Christianity in eastern and northern Europe.

Chief spokesman for the new enthusiasm for withdrawal from the world was Bernard of Clairvaux (d.1153), admonisher of popes and preacher of Crusades. He is considered by many to be the greatest spokesman of the spiritual revival of the age. Bernard saw the Gregorian reform as a plan for uncompromising spiritual regeneration based on the assumption that the monastic-ascetic ideal could be applied to the whole of Christendom. Despite his high regard for the papacy, he found it stifled by the organization around it. Against the corruption of the Curia and the preoccupation with worldly power which made the pope the successor of Constantine rather than of Peter, Bernard turned to the reformer's ideal of the prophetic and apostolic mission entrusted to the Vicar of Christ. He believed that the Vicar was set over the nations to destroy and root up, to plant and build. It was a mission that suggested the dreary labor of the peasant rather than the pomp of the ruler. Bernard told the pope, "If you are to do the work of a prophet, you need a hoe rather than a sceptre." In Bernard's eyes, the secularizing tendencies of the papacy had produced a hopeless confusion between spiritual and temporal functions of the Church. Consequently, although he believed in the theory of the two swords, material and spiritual, he constantly emphasized that the power was to be used for spiritual purposes only. The pope was a minister, rather than a lord. The Church was a mother, not a mistress.

St. Bernard has been called the last of the Church Fathers. Because of his tremendous influence in every sphere of religious life, the middle decades of the twelfth century are called the Era of Bernard. His approach to spirituality has been summed up in the expression *credo ut experiar* (I believe that I might experience). In this sense his is typical of a new subjective, individualistic piety that was in evidence in Europe at the time. His mysticism is often expressed in the marriage symbol, the union between Christ and the soul.

It was especially the devotion to the Blessed Virgin that perhaps more than any other has been the lasting result of Bernard's writing and preaching. The Cistercian order he directed was devoted to Our Lady in a special way. All its churches were dedicated to the Mother of God. The Breviary, the official prayer of the priesthood, used in the Church today, shows how many of his sermons are still read on feasts of the Virgin Mary. The popular Catholic expression *ad Jesum per Mariam* (to Jesus through Mary) is ascribed to Bernard.

Bernard has bequeathed to posterity an enormous corpus of writings, sermons, and letters. The following letter addressed to the canons of the Church of Lyons, the diocese in which he was born and raised, is typical of his deep devotion to the Mother of God. At the same time it demonstrates the reserve that was so characteristic of him in his opposition to the introduction of new learning. Few theologians opposed the use of dialectics as applied to divine revelation as did Bernard.

The question of the Immaculate Conception treated here was one of the most perplexing of the medieval period. It was not solved until the nineteenth century, when Mary's Immaculate Conception was made a dogma.

> The Church of Lyons is the most renowned in all France in terms of dignity, sound learning, and laudable customs. Was there ever so strict discipline, dignified behavior, consummate advice, and so commanding a force of authority and tradition? Particularly in the offices of the Church has this body, so grounded in good judgment, avoided embracing innovations and tainting its reputation with childish frivolities. Consequently, I am amazed that some of you now wish to tarnish the lustre of your good name by introducing a new feast day, an observance of which the Church lacks knowledge, which logical reasoning disproves, and which tradition fails to support. Are we more learned or devout than the Fathers? To introduce this feast day about which they, with all their discipline and knowledge in such matters made no comment, is a most shameful effrontery. It is not as if they disregarded it without sufficient reasons, for this is an issue that could not have escaped their attention.

> You claim that our Lord's Mother should be highly honored. This is true, but "the honor of the queen loves justice." The Blessed Virgin has many legitimate titles to honor, many valid references to dignity, and needs none that are false. Let us honor her for her purity and chastity, for the holiness of her life. Let us also wonder at her fruitful virginity, and worship

her Divine Son. Let us praise her freedom from bodily lust in conception, and from pain of labor. Let us proclaim her to be honored by the angels, awaited by all people, prophesied by the patriarchs and prophets, chosen from and preferred before all. Let us glorify her as the deliverer of grace, the arbitrator of salvation, the renovator of the ages, and as glorified above the choirs of angels to the heights of heaven. This the Church sings in her honor and teaches me to sing, also. What I have learned from the Church I firmly believe and confidently teach to others; however, I must admit that I am reluctant to believe anything that I have not learned from her.

The Church, of course, has taught me to keep holy that day on which, when she was lifted from this sinful world, she brought great rejoicing to heaven. But in the Church I have also learned to commemorate the birth of the Blessed Virgin, and from the Church to regard it as a Holy Day, agreeing firmly with the Church that she entered the world already holy because she had been sanctified in the womb. I have read that Jeremias also was sanctified before he left the womb, and I believe the same of John the Baptist. Something for you to ponder is whether this is true of David, considering he said to God, "By Thee I have been confirmed from the womb, from my mother's womb Thou art my guardian, depart not from me." To Jeremias it was said: "I claimed thee for my own before ever I fashioned thee in thy mother's womb; before ever thou camest to birth, I set thee apart for myself." How beautifully the divine Word distinguishes from conception *in* the womb and birth from the womb. It manifests that the conception was merely foreseen, while the birth was blessed beforehand with the gift of sanctity, so that now one will consider the privilege of the prophet to have been merely a matter of foreknowledge or predestination.

Let us believe this in Jeremias' case. But what of John the Baptist who the angel said would be filled with the Holy Spirit while still in the mother's womb? This, I feel, certainly cannot refer only to predestination or foreknowledge. Without a doubt the words of the angel were fulfilled, as he said they would be; and one cannot doubt that he was filled with the Holy Spirit as the angel had prophesied, and in the time and place that he had foretold. Most assuredly the Holy Spirit sanctified him when he filled him. However, I am uncertain as to how far this sanctification took away original sin for John the Baptist, for the prophet, or for anyone else who was similarly impeded by grace. Still I do not hesitate to say that whom God sanctified were sanctified, and that they were born with the sanctity which they received in the womb, and that the original sin that they contracted in conception had no power at all to hinder or rob them at birth of the blessing that they had already received in the womb. Who can say that a child filled with the Holy Spirit still remained a child of wrath, and that he would receive everlasting damnation were he to die in the womb? This is very serious, but I will not, on the basis of my own opinion, attempt to explain more about it. In any case, the Church, which affirms the death but not the birth of the saint to be precious, makes a unique exception in his favor considering when the angel said, "Many will rejoice in his birth," and therefore we commemorate his birthday. And if he was able to rejoice while still in the womb, what reason is there for not celebrating his holy birth?

We cannot suppose that a privilege which has been accorded to some, though very few, mortals, was denied to the Blessed Virgin through whom all mortals have entered life. There is no doubt that the Mother of our Lord was holy before she was born. The Holy Church is definitely not mistaken in making her birthday a Holy Day and in celebrating it every year all over the world. I am of the personal opinion that she received a great blessing which not only sanctified her in the womb, but also kept her free from sin throughout her lifetime. This is a blessing which we believe has never been granted to anyone else. This unique blessing of sanctity through which she lived her whole life without sin surely glorifies the Queen of Virgins who, in giving birth to our Redeemer, obtained for us all the reward of life and righteousness. Thus, her birth was holy because great sanctity from the womb made it so.

What other honors might we add to these? That her conception which preceded her holy birth should also be honored mainly because there would have been no birth to honor had there been no conception? For this same reason might it be that a feast day should be awarded to her parents? This same reasoning could thus be used for her grandparents, and great-grandparents, and so on until there would be innumerable feast days. Such a multitude of rejoicing would be more fitting for heaven than for earth, for citizens than for exiles. Supposedly there are records of heavenly revelations; as if there could not be equally good records of how the Blessed Virgin had been seen granting the same honor for her parents, according to the commandment, "Honor thy father and thy mother." I am dubious of these supposed records which are not supported by sound reasoning or good authority. How could it follow that her conception was holy merely because her birth was holy? Is it not closer to the truth to say that, because her conception was not holy, she was sanctified after she had been conceived so that her birth would be holy? Or perhaps we might say that the conception shared in the holiness of the birth which followed. It is true that the sanctification of what had already been conceived could be transmitted to the subsequent birth, but it is impossible that the Virgin's holy birth could be retrospective, and thus sanctify the conception which preceded.

What was the source of this holy conception? Could it be that Mary was already holy before her conception so that her conception would be holy, in the same manner that her birth was holy because of the sanctification which she received while still in the womb? She could not have been holy before she existed, and before her conception she did not exist. Or was sanctity present in the act of her conception, so that she would be holy at the same time as she was conceived? This is unreasonable, for how can anything be holy without the presence of the Sanctifying Spirit, and how can there be no sin when there is carnal lust? One might say the Blessed Virgin was conceived of the Holy Spirit and not of man, but this is as yet unheard of. It is written that the Holy Spirit approached her, but it did not come with her, for the angel said, "The Holy Spirit shall come upon thee." If I may state the Church's opinion (and the Church's opinion is true), then I say that she conceived of the Holy Spirit, not that she herself was conceived of the Holy Spirit; she gave birth as a virgin, but she was not born of a virgin. Otherwise where would the unique privilege of the Mother of our Lord be, in which the

Blessed Virgin alone may glory in birth of a child and also her virginity, if we are to grant the same privilege to her mother? This would detract from the honor and glory of the Blessed Virgin. Since it was impossible for her to have been sanctified before her conception because she did not then exist, or in the act of her conception because of the presence of sin, it is obvious that she was sanctified after her conception, while she was in the womb, and that this sanctification excluded sin and made her birth, but not her conception, holy.

Thus, although a very few men have been born holy, none of them were conceived holy, so that the precedence of a holy conception was given only to Christ who sanctified all of us and, being conceived without sin, cleansed all sinners. What a certain man once humbly admitted to himself is true of all mortals: "I was born in sin; guilt was with me already when my mother conceived me."

Since these things are true, what reason can there be for a feast of the Conception? How can a feast day be introduced in honor of what was not holy? The mother of God will gladly decline a feast day in which either sin is honored or in which a false holiness seems to be implied. An innovation which is the mother of rashness, the sister of superstition, the daughter of frivolity, and regarded as against the practice of the Church, in no way can be pleasing to the Blessed Virgin. If you believed that such a feast was advisable, you should have first consulted the Holy See, and not have so hastily and so unadvisedly followed the advice of the uneducated. In fact I have also seen this fault in others, but to spare the devotion of simple hearts for the Blessed Virgin, I have overlooked it. But when I see this in learned men, members of the noble church of which I am the son, I doubt whether I can overlook it without being disgusted with you. All that I have said on this matter, I submit to the scrutiny of those wiser than myself, and I submit these words especially to the authority of the Roman Church. Upon the Church's decision in this matter I am prepared to modify anything that I have said, should it be against her teachings.[9]

CHAPTER 3

The Flowering of
the Middle Ages

The Fourth Council of the Lateran

IN MANY WAYS the Fourth Council of the Lateran can be called a watershed in the development of medieval Catholicism. The disciplinary decrees of the council provided a legal basis for a now centralized and legalized system of ecclesiastical administration. The flowering of scholasticism brought a new importance to the sacramental system. A new type of monasticism, the mendicants, who soon came to dominate the doctrinal domain of Catholicism in the universities as well as its parochial activities became the agents of this new movement, which changed the entire complexion of Catholicism. We have already seen how the rediscovery of Roman law in the early twelfth century had inspired the monk Gratian to produce his *Concord of Discordant Canons* and thus provide the Church with a normative guide in dealing with the problems affecting worship and the sacraments. The rediscovery of the complete Aristotle in the thirteenth century was to provide the means for constructing a parallel system in the theoretical domain.

The Lateran Council which was convened in 1215 was the

fourth of a series of councils that had been called by the popes in the city of Rome. The first of these had been assembled there in 1123. They were concerned for the most part with working out the details of the papal victory over the advocates of lay investiture. Hence, there was a century-old tradition of papally dominated councils by the time Innocent III summoned over four hundred bishops and eight hundred abbots from all over Europe to assemble in the Eternal City. Much of the legislation enacted there can be traced to the earlier reform movements of Hildebrand. Many of the decrees still affect Catholicism to this day.

The opening chapter of the council contains the first formal declaration of the Church of its belief in transubstantiation:

> There is one universal Church of the faithful, outside of which there is no salvation. In which there is the same priest and sacrifice, Jesus Christ, whose body and blood are truly contained in the sacrament of the altar under the forms of bread and wine; the bread in being changed (transubstantiated) by the divine power into the body, and the wine into the blood, so that to realize the mystery of unity we may receive of Him what He has received of us. And this sacrament no one can effect except the priest who has been duly ordained in accordance with the keys of the Church, which Jesus Christ gave to the Apostles and their successors.[10]

Every Christian who has attained the age of reason is obliged to receive the sacraments of Penance and the Eucharist at least once a year. Preachers and confessors are urged to see to it that instructions to the faithful are given in their mother tongue. Non-Christians, especially Jews, are obliged to wear distinctive dress and are not allowed to appear in public during Holy Week. Alienation of Church properties by laymen is forbidden. Clandestine marriage and marriage within the second and third degrees of affinity are declared illegal.

The decree on annual confession and Easter communion is indicative of the change in devotional development. In contrast to the earlier period, piety now became more individualistic and more subjective. A highly rationalized sacramental system developed, exhibiting a turn to the tangible, the concrete. The image of Christ as the Lord, the wonder worker, gave way to Christ the sufferer. An emphasis was laid on His humanity, His passion, and His death. The old Augustinian definition of a sacrament as the sign of a sacred reality gave way to a new concept which considered the sacrament not merely as a sign of grace but as a sign that actually produced or caused grace. Earlier writers had differed widely on the question of how many sacraments there were. St. Bernard, for example, enumerates ten, and other theologians included such phenomena as the sign of the cross, the invocation of the High Trinity, and the anointing of kings. By the twelfth century, following the leads of Gilbert de La Porrée and Peter Lombard, the number was reduced to seven.

Strongly evident in this clarification was the application of the Aristotelian notions of form and matter. Each sacrament was clearly delineated in terms of what constituted the rite (matter) and the accompanying formula (form). The classical summation of this development can be seen in the decree issued at the Council of Florence to explain it to the recently reconciled Armenians:

We are putting the true doctrine of the sacraments of the Church into a brief formula as an easier means for instructing the Armenians, both those of the present and those of the future. There are seven sacraments of the New Law: they are baptism, confirmation, the Eucharist, penance, extreme unction, holy orders, and matrimony; and they differ greatly from the sacraments of the Old Law. The sacraments of the Old Law did not cause grace but were only a figure of the grace that was to be given through the Passion of Christ; but our Sacraments both contain grace and confer it on those who receive the sacraments worthily. The first five of these are ordered to the interior spiritual perfection of the individual; the last two are ordered to the government and to the spread of the whole Church. For by baptism we are spiritually reborn and by confirmation we grow in grace and are strengthened in the faith; being reborn and strengthened, we are nourished with the divine food of the Eucharist. If, by sin, we become sick in soul, penance spiritually heals us; extreme unction heals us in spirit and in body as well, insofar as it is good for the soul. By holy orders the Church is governed and given spiritual growth; by matrimony she is given bodily growth. All of these sacraments are brought to completion by three components; by things as matter, by words as form, and by person of the minister effecting the sacrament with the intention of doing what the Church does. And if any one of the three is lacking, the sacrament is not effected. Among these sacraments, there are three, baptism, confirmation, and holy orders, which print on the soul an indelible character, that is, a certain spiritual sign distinguishing the recipient from the others. Hence, these are not given more than once to one person. The other four do not imprint this character and may be repeated.[11]

A changed attitude toward the question of the forgiveness of sin is clearly evident. In the early Church penance had been largely a matter of public reparation for serious violations of the commandments. Whatever indication of private penance there may have been in an earlier age was more a therapeutic measure in the spiritual direction of souls and not identified with sacramental confession. For example, St. Benedict obliged his monks to reveal their evil thoughts to the spiritual father, who was not necessarily a priest. This monastic practice spread to lay circles, and it became customary and in some places even obligatory to confess one's sins to laymen. The earlier role of the priest was that of a physician of souls, and the efficacy of his prayer was based not on a delegation of powers but rather on holiness of life. However, as public penances disappeared—that is, as penance as a means of reconciliation with the Church lost its original significance of reinstating the penitent in the Christian community —a number of radical changes appeared. Whereas until the twelfth century the formula of absolution was a deprecative prayer asking God, who alone could forgive sins, a grant of mercy, the priest now pronounced the words "I absolve you." What was once declarative now became causal. Naturally, the question arose in the minds of many as to why it was necessary to impose a penance if the words of the priest and the contrite confession of the sins had already produced forgiveness. In other words, if satisfaction for sin still remained to be done, the forgiveness already given was something different from what it had been understood as in the ancient Church. Abelard (d.1142) presents a good example of how the cause of forgiveness was now understood. He taught that, strictly speaking, contrition is the cause of forgiveness. When one is completely sincere in his sorrow for sin, that is, when he is motivated out of a pure love of God, this in itself destroys sin and eliminates the cause of eternal punishment. The role of the priest is to indicate to the sinner what he must do here on earth in order to expiate the temporal punishment still due him in purgatory. He maintained that the power of the keys, that is, the power of binding and loosing found in the commission of St. Peter (Matthew, 16:18), referred only to the lifting of excommunication. This position was condemned by the Synod of Sens in 1140. We see here that the original sense of the power of binding and loosing had been lost. To bind had originally meant to condemn or excommunicate the penitent; to loose had the meaning of restoring him to the *pax ecclesiae,* the peace of the church. It was Aquinas who sounded the death knell for the declarative notion of forgiveness by explaining that the words of the priest, "I absolve you," had the same causal effect as the words of the priest at baptism; the power of forgiveness of guilt was the same in both cases. The question of how absolution produces contrition, which was still considered necessary, was explained by making absolution retroactive. It was an explanation based on Aquinas' general description of justification as the result of the reciprocal causality of infused grace, the movement of free will toward God and the remission of sin. The inadequacy of the explanation was to lead to some disquieting results at the end of the Middle Ages, since it was the point of departure for Luther's new doctrine on the nature of justification.

The practice of private or auricular confession continues to play an important role in contemporary Catholicism. At the end of the Middle Ages it became customary for Catholics to confess their sins to the priest in an enclosed wooden frame known as a confessional. In order to secure privacy and keep his identity from the priest, the penitent and the father confessor are separated by a grille. The priest is forbidden, under threat of severe penalties, to reveal what he has heard in the confessional.

As the ancient penitential practices, fasting, wearing sackcloth and ashes, alms giving, and pilgrimages disappeared, they were replaced with the redemptive acts that often took the form of money payments. There is little doubt that the old Germanic practice of wergeld (the payment of money in recompense for an offence to the relative of the injured) was at work here. Cases of penance by proxy are recorded whereby certain wealthy individuals accomplished long penances by hiring enough men to perform the imposed penance in a short time. An English penitential work indicates how a person could finish a seven-year penance in three days by means of an equivalent number of fasts by hired men.

The medieval period also witnessed the introduction of a number of fasting regulations which continue to this day to exert a deep influence on Catholic spirituality. Every Friday throughout the year was a day of abstinence; that is, no flesh meat could be eaten. In some areas eggs and milk were also proscribed. During Lent, the forty days before Easter, reminiscent of Christ's long sojourn in the desert, all were obliged to fast. Only one full meal, not to be taken before the ninth hour, was permitted. Weddings, hunting, sexual intercourse, and sessions of civil courts were also forbidden during this period. Pope Gregory VII also enacted legislation, still current, that made fasting obligatory four different times during the year. These annual fasts, now called the ember days, are still observed by Catholics in September, December, April, and June. Other fast days are observed, depending on locality, on the vigils of great feast days.

Closely associated with the new penitential system was the practice of granting indulgences. The origin of indulgences, like that of so many other medieval religious practices, is shrouded in obscurity and controversy. The practice seems to have first appeared in southern France and northern Spain during the eleventh century. By the twelfth century it came under violent attack from theologians, who accused the bishops who granted indulgences of shameless cupidity since they exacted large monetary sums by the relaxation of penances. The opposition against them, however, gradually disappeared, once it was made clear that they were the remission of punishments of purgatory rather than the remission of ecclesiastical penalties.

The theory of indulgences was based on the belief that the Church has at its disposal a treasury of the superabundant merits of Christ and the saints. This doctrine was first formulated by the Dominican Cardinal Hugh of St. Cher (d.1263), who taught that in the blood of Christ and the martyrs, who were punished far beyond the measure of their sins, every sin has been punished. This blood, he maintains, is a treasure deposited in the shrine of the Church, of which the Church holds the keys. At her discretion she can open the shrine and by a grant of indulgence impart a share of the treasure to whomever she desires. This is not a by-passing of the punishment of sin, since it is punished in Christ and his martyrs. Thus the remission of punishment in the hereafter, which formerly had been sought through the intercession of the saints, was now granted by an act of ecclesiastical jurisdiction. Control over the treasure was reserved to the pope and the bishops. The papacy was not slow in seeing the many spiritual and temporal benefits to be found in this practice. It extended its claim of supremacy in spiritual matters from the Church militant to the Church suffering.

Since indulgences were no longer considered as the remission of ecclesiastical penances but rather as a direct remission of the punishments of purgatory, it was a logical step that they be applied to the deceased. This belief was furthered by the preachers of the Crusades, who claimed that the plenary indulgence obtained by participation in the Holy War could be applied to the dead. Originally Hugh of St. Cher rejected the notion that the power of the keys could be extended to the dead. However, later scholastics generally agreed that it was possible to release a soul from purgatory by applying merits from the treasury of the Church. The first papal indulgence for the dead, however, is not recorded until the time of Pope Callistus III in 1457. It was also taught that indulgences for the dead could be gained even by those in the state of mortal sin, so long as they provided the required monetary contribution.

Although many abuses arose from the practice of granting

indulgences, a sober consideration of the social benefits that resulted is needed if it is to be objectively evaluated. The construction of churches, money for the Crusades, the building and repair of bridges and roads, were but a few of the benefits derived from a practice that to this day is a source of scandal and ridicule for those who fail to comprehend its positive contribution to the interest of religion.

Gothic Spirituality

The decree of the Lateran insisting that the faithful be given instruction on the fundamentals of faith in the vernacular language also gave rise to an extensive literature, consisting of handbooks and manuals that were used as guides for the parochial clergy in fulfilling this task. The older penitential books were replaced with the various *summae,* or works of casuistry, that enabled the priest to delineate the various types of sins and dole out appropriate penances. The confessors were expected to cross-examine the penitents on their religious knowledge as well as their sins. Typical of this type of pastoral writing was the widely used *Oculus Sacerdotis (The Eye of the Priest)*, attributed to William of Pagula (d.1332). As a manual for confessors, it informs the priest how to interrogate the penitent concerning his religious knowledge, the Apostles' Creed, the seven virtues, and the seven vices. He is directed to take into consideration the particular status of the person questioned and the circumstances that may alter the gravity of the sin. Distinctions are made with regard to sins that are reserved to the bishop or to the pope. Such matters as marriage and sexual morality, tithing, and the fulfillment of Easter duty are treated in detail. The priest is urged to expound to the people four times a year the fourteen articles of faith, the seven sacraments, the seven works of mercy, the seven virtues, the Ten Commandments of the law and the two of the gospel, and the seven vices. Lists of sins, divided and subdivided, are the dominant feature of the book, and one seeks in vain for any reference to the nature of grace or the infused virtues. What reference there is to Scripture is clouded in allegory and numerical parallelism: Christ's forty weeks in the womb, his forty hours in death, his forty days on earth after the resurrection. Whatever lends itself to a dramatic or pictorial representation of the Bible is emphasized: Noah's flood, the fate of Nebuchadnezzar, Daniel in the lions' den, and so on. By the fourteenth century many of these works had been translated into the vernacular under such titles as the *Prick of Conscience, Handlying Synne,* and *Jacob's Well.* The *Parson's Tale* in Chaucer and *Piers Plowman* are good examples of this type of literature.

In proclaiming the doctrine of transubstantiation (that the substance of the bread became the Body of Christ and the wine His Blood) and in demanding that the faithful communicate annually, the Lateran Council greatly furthered devotion to the Real Presence. From that time on, and perhaps also influenced by the Albigensian heresy, the focus of Eucharistic speculation was on the "person" of Christ rather than the mystery of the Eucharist. It gave birth to an excessive longing on the part of the faithful to see what was hidden behind the Eucharistic veil.

Many of the legends traceable to this emphasis are evident in medieval literature. There was, for example, the story of the abbot Arsenius, who while saying Mass saw an angel over the altar ritually slaying a child and pouring his blood into a chalice. Thereupon the angel divided the members of the slain child to correspond with the division of the Host by the priest. Late medieval art also reflected this overrealistic interpretation of the Eucharist. The Precious Blood was often pictured flowing from the wounds of the crucified Christ into a challice held by a priest. Other paintings depicted Christ being ground into a mystic wine press, with his blood flowing forth from the bottom of the press into a chalice.

In addition to exaggerating the material aspect of the consecrated elements, the late Middle Ages also witnessed a flowering of Mass theology that engendered an overconfidence in the ritual itself. The practice of saying Mass privately became a norm for the secular as well as the regular clergy. In most of the monasteries it was looked upon as a private devotion. What in antiquity had been an act of public worship, in which the Christian community gathered together to hear God's word and by the Eucharistic meal to seal the new covenant, gradually became a dramatization of the Passion and Death of Christ. Eucharistic theology had come to regard the sacrament entirely under the aspect of "persona." It was a view of the Mass that was destined to obscure the all-important truth that although Christ is present in the Eucharist, the presence is by mode of substance and of sign. It tended to encourage a childish imagination which represented the Eucharistic Christ as a normally visible personage, accidentally concealed from sight by a material obstacle. To facilitate this image of the Eucharistic Lord, various formulas were devised which, nursed by allegory, fitted in with the popular eagerness to contemplate the Christ of history and His earthly appearance. Since the language used in the service was no longer intelligible to the faithful, they came to look upon it as a theatrical performance not entirely different from the morality or mystery plays that were frequently associated with the great feast days. The Mass was no longer a service that enfolded the mystery of redemption in its totality. Emphasizing the Death and Passion, it neglected the implication of the Resurrection, the communication of grace to mankind, and the consummation of all things.

The central act of Christian worship had lost sight almost entirely of the liturgy as the proclamation of God's word to all Christians to do and to become what the word of God proclaims. The disintegration of the Roman Mass during the Middle Ages and how it became increasingly misunderstood by both clergy and the laity is a historical fact no longer to be doubted. The earlier Christian view that considered the Mass as a token of man's gratitude to God and an act of reverence was entirely overshadowed by the notion of a sacrificial oblation. The Mystical Body, once a liturgical term applied to the Host and indicating the unity of redeemed mankind, now referred to the judicial body that was the Church. The *verum corpus* in contrast was now become the object of both private and personal devotion centered on a repeated miracle.

Even the vestments worn by the priest had come to symbolize some aspect of the Passion. The chasuble represented the cross;

the alb signified the gown given to Christ after the scourging; and the amice symbolized the crown of thors. The movements of the celebrant also took on this suffering symbolism. As he moved from the Epistle side of the altar to the Gospel side, the priest dramatized the journey of Christ from Pilate to Herod. The washing of the hands at the beginning of the Offertory signified Herod's cleansing of his hands before the Jews. The paten was held under the corporal to signify Our Lord's self-debasement; the priest bowed his head at the "Memento" to signify Our Lord's death; the "Nobis Quoque" was read with lifted voice, symbolic of the captain of the guard raising his voice; and at the end of the Canon, five crosses signified the five wounds Christ received. In holding his hands over the chalice and in stretching out his arms, the priest portrayed Christ suffering in the garden and on the cross. The elevation could only mean the raising of Christ on the cross. The dramatic nature of the whole service is confirmed in the expression still common today, "to hear Mass."

In addition to obscuring the real meaning of the Mass by emphasizing it as a re-enactment of the drama of Calvary, the medieval Church fostered an attitude toward the consecrated elements that tended to isolate them also from the context of the liturgy. The Host and the chalice were elevated by the priest, and the elevation rather than the consecration and the offering was considered the high point of the service. Detailed directions were issued as to the procedure to be followed in the event of a Host being dropped on the ground or the Precious Blood being spilled. They were enforced with heavy penalties. Theologians speculated on the defects and dangers that might affect the consecrated Host. Most missals contained pages of instructions on what to do should the Host suddenly appear as a child or living flesh. An entire ritual was evolved for the washing of the altar linens and the finger towels used by the priest. The laity were no longer permitted to carry viaticum to the dying, and it was considered sacrilegious for a layman to touch the chalice.

Gazing upon the sacred Host at the elevation became for many the very essence of the Mass devotion. In many cities, the populace ran from church to church to see the elevated Host as often as possible, believing that rich rewards came from such practices. There were incidents recorded of lawsuits initiated in order to insure a more favorable view of the altar.

Condemned prisoners on their way to execution were allowed to look at the Host in the monstrance, but not to receive communion. Fortesque informs us that in England, if the priest did not elevate the Host high enough, the people would cry out, "Hold up, Sir John; heave it a little higher." Berthold of Regensburg, a fourteenth-century Franciscan preacher, urged his listeners to focus their attention on the elevation of the Mass. "At the elevation of the Mass, the priest appears to say three things to you: see the Son of God Who for your sake was lifted on the cross; see the Son of God Who will come to judge the living and the dead; see the Son of God Who for your sake shows His wounds to the heavenly Father."

The Question of Apostolic Poverty

An understanding of the profound changes that were taking place in Catholicism in the thirteenth century would not be possible without some consideration of the agents of this revolution: the mendicant orders and, under their influence, the universities. We have seen that the crisis in monasticism in the tenth and eleventh centuries broke the long era of Benedictine dominance in the Western Church. In the same way as the Benedictines were a response to the social and economic needs of an unsettled and barbaric age, an era that was agrarian, unlettered, and committed to feudalism, so the mendicant movement was an answer to the transformation that occurred in Europe during the twelfth century. The emergence of urban centers, after their gradual disappearance resulting from the Islamic control of the arteries of trade in the Mediterranean, is already discernible in the late tenth century. It continued rapidly into the eleventh and twelfth centuries, especially in the Low Countries, the Rhine Valley, and northern Italy. Milan and Venice boasted populations of over 100,000. The rapid growth of commerce brought affluence unknown in earlier centuries.

The beginnings of a money economy gave rise to moral problems which simply did not exist in the less complicated society of the Carolingian and Ottonian periods. This situation had the end effect of focusing attention on the compatibility of material wealth and Christian perfection. It was not a new problem. Christ had urged poverty upon his followers, stating that it was easier for a camel to pass through the eye of a needle than a rich man to enter the kingdom of heaven. What gave the question of poverty a new urgency was the accumulation of wealth by the institutional Church. The question of apostolic poverty soon preoccupied the great saints and theologians of the day.

Even before the fall of the Western empire, the emperors, by endowing the Church with great wealth, had made it the greatest landed proprietor in the world. This wealth, which enabled the Church to survive the great migrations and invasions relatively unscathed, was increased century after century by legacies and offerings from princes and the rich. Moreover, at least from the twelfth century on, the papacy itself was again decidedly wordly. Popes tended to be primarily statesmen and administrators. The greater circulation of money and the revival of trade enabled the papacy to develop a fiscal system on a continental scale, operated by an elaborate and highly trained bureaucracy. By such means it was able to fight purely political battles by purely political means and even to buy allies and wage wars. It was also able, as a great monarchy, to maintain a court of unparalleled splendor.

There had always been individual voices protesting the accumulation of wealth in the Church. Poverty, often interpreted as an evangelical precept by the Fathers, was one of the guiding principles of both Western and Eastern monasticism. Though Augustine did not require his clerics to take a vow of poverty, he believed that "to no one . . . is it lawful to have anything of his own." As in the Church in the Acts of the Apostles, all property was to be held in common. In the Rule of St. Benedict, there is explicit legislation for the practice of poverty: "If he has any property, let him either first bestow it on the poor or by solemn deed of gift, make it over to the monastery, keeping nothing for himself as knowing that from this day forward he shall have no power even over his body." That this legislation was perpetually abused by Benedict's heirs is a well-known fact, but the witness it bears to the tradition of poverty in Christian history remains intact.

Though it had much popular appeal in the twelfth century, poverty as a means of reform always lacked sufficient direction and unity. It enjoyed only sporadic and uneven degrees of success and constantly bore the stigma of heresy. The tragedy which befell Arnold of Brescia, Peter Waldo, and others is indicative of many genuine reform movements. But orthodox or not, the various branches of the poverty movement shared a common ideal. All believed that Christian perfection lay in the renunciation of temporal possessions, since this was the example of Christ and His disciples. Consequently, the poverty movement would always be characterized by a fierce protest against the Church's wealth and luxury. The critics could never reconcile the poverty of the primitive Church with the pomp and power of the ecclesiastical organization of their own day.

One of the first attempts to disentangle the Church from unwarranted wealth was made by Paschal II. Though his plan failed, the power of its suggestion did not. It provided a measure of inspiration for the Lombard communes who by the early twelfth century were achieving some degree of liberty from both pope and emperor. It was this communal movement that saw the rise of Arnold of Brescia (d.1155). Little is known of Arnold's early life except that he was a native of Brescia and may have been a cleric. Also, he is known to have been a close associate of Peter Abelard; Arnold's condemnation by the Lateran Council of 1139 occurred in the same year as that of his more famous friend. The decree of the council gives some idea of Arnold's activities involved with the communes. According to the decree, Arnold

spread among the vulgar pernicious doctrines and filled their ears with impious words. The sacred laws, he said, did not sanction clerical possessions; the monks and priests had no right over land; nor should abbots relegate to themselves temporal power which belonged to the princes of the earth; government was the prerogative of the elected representatives of the people alone. Offerings and tithes should be tendered only for the needs of the body, not for their own pleasure. He condemned without restriction the lives of the priests . . . the splendor of their vestments, their lascivious joys and the relaxed manner of the monasteries.

In 1137, with the bishop of Brescia in Rome, the townsmen with Arnold's party took over the city and ruled it under the "two consul" system. The coup was short-lived, however, and Arnold was forced into exile through pressure from Rome.

In 1145, Arnold re-established his leadership in the communal movement, this time in Rome itself. The city had undergone a popular revolution which had almost succeeded in overthrowing the papacy. With the new pope, Eugenius III, Arnold and his party arrived at an uneasy peace. But it was not long before the continued corruption among the Roman clergy forced Arnold to renew his protest. In his eyes the possession of wealth and temporal dominions by the Church were both a negation of Christian ideals and a betrayal of Christ's teaching. For the clergy to covet worldly goods amounted to apostasy from their sacred calling. Moreover, he held that possession of property by the clergy was a barrier to salvation. Otto of Freising quotes him as saying, "The clergy who hold property, the bishops who enjoy regalia and the monks who have possessions cannot attain salvation. All these things pertain to the secular rulers and should by their beneficence be given to the clergy for their use."

Arnold continually looked to Pope Paschal's attempt to free the Church from her feudal bonds. But the hope that the papacy itself might initiate a definite program was doomed to disappointment by the mediocre and worldly popes who followed Paschal. Not even Bernard, Arnold's archenemy, or his protégé, Eugenius, could check curial ambitions for temporal affluence.

In the Roman republican movement, Arnold found what he felt was the means to purify the Church. He hoped to free Rome permanently from all priestly rule, to reduce the clergy to a condition of apostolic poverty, and limit to strictly spiritual functions the bureaucratic machinery of the Curia. With Eugenius out of the city, Arnold and his party gained control. "While dwelling in

Rome . . . he won the city to his side, and preaching all the more freely because the Lord Pope was occupied in Gaul, he built up a faction known as the sect of the Lombards. He had disciples who imitated his austerities and won favor with the populace through outward decency and austerity of life," writes John of Salisbury. But both the republic and Arnold's reform scheme were doomed to ephemeral lives. Pope Eugenius returned to Rome in 1149 and began to play the rebellious commune against the authority of Emperor Frederick Barbarossa. The death of Eugenius in 1153 did not check Arnold's decline because the new pope, Adrian IV, continued his predecessor's policy. Finally, through imperial intervention, Arnold was captured and hanged in 1155.

In some ways Arnold of Brescia shared a common fate with other medieval reformers. While his message had popular appeal, he struggled in vain to inspire ecclesiastical institutions with the will to reform. Instead, his program was crushed to that same combination of pope and emperor which he sought to dissolve.

Despite Arnold's defeat, the closing decades of the twelfth century witnessed the growing popularity of the poverty movement of the laity. The earlier efforts at reform, however admirable, left the mass of the people untouched. Yet with the ever-present antagonism of the clergy and the absence of sound direction, it was almost inevitable that these new movements tended to develop independently of the institutional Church.

Perhaps the best illustration of a potentially genuine movement driven from orthodoxy more by circumstance than conviction was the Poor Men of Lyons, founded by Peter Waldo. Waldo (d.1217) was a typical middle-class figure from the city of Lyons. His personal history and religious development are known only through the thirteenth-century chronicles seldom sympathetic to the Waldensian movement. He is said to have experienced a conversion on hearing the legend of St. Alexius, who had abandoned his riches for the sake of poverty. Waldo promptly did the same and thereby embarked on a mission which was to have ramifications for the next two centuries.

Waldo's action, about the year 1173, immediately stirred the imagination of the Lyonese, and his example attracted imitators, particularly among the lower, uneducated classes. Waldo's followers, preaching in the streets and public places throughout southern France, discoursed on poverty and called men back to the evangelical ideal. It is certain that the original aim of Waldo and his followers was conceived in a spirit of protest against corruption and negligence among the clergy. But their impulse toward evangelical poverty and their eagerness to preach the Gospel was met with suspicion by the hierarchy. Although the Waldensians justified their mission to preach by the necessity of explaining the Scriptures, the archbishop of Lyons sought to silence them, especially since they were laymen. In response to the archbishop's prohibition, Waldo said, "Judge you whether it be lawful before God to obey him who has said, 'Go ye into all the world and preach the Gospel to every creature.'" (Mark 16:15)

Banished from Lyons, Waldo journeyed into Italy to appeal his case to the pope. He arrived in Rome about 1177, on the eve of the third Lateran Council. He did secure the approval of Pope Alexander III and the council, but just five years later the new pope, Lucius III, condemned the group in words recorded by Bernard Gui: "Therefore we lay under perpetual anathema . . . those who falsely call themselves Poor Men of Lyons. . . . We include, in the same perpetual anathema, all who shall have presumed to preach, either publicly or privately, either being forbidden, or not sent, or not having the authority of the Apostolic See, or of the Bishop of the diocese." Since preaching was a crucial factor in Waldo's mission, the papal decree was the turning point for the movement. Waldo claimed that every Christian, layman or priest, was a depository of the Holy Spirit with the right of expounding on Holy Scripture. As the moorings which bound them to the Roman Church were cut loose one by one, the Waldensians drifted away from orthodox doctrine. They came to deny purgatory, indulgences, and prayers for the dead. They denounced all lying as grievous sin and refused to take oaths. All were inventions of the ecclesiastical institutions which had now abandoned the spiritual character of the early Church.

The fate of the Waldensians provided an important lesson for both the papacy and the later mendicants. Under Innocent III (d.1216), the papacy began to realize that men inspired by en-thusiasm for evangelical Christianity could not be suppressed and that multitudes would hear and follow those who were obeying literally the commands of Christ.

When one turns from the Waldensians to the Franciscans, he is immediately struck by the parallel in the careers of the two founders. Though younger than Peter Waldo, Francis (d.1226) was a member of the same economic class and attracted by the same ideal. As Waldo was inspired by the legend of St. Alexius, Francis was struck by the words of Matthew's gospel: "Going therefore to preach saying: the kingdom of God is at hand. Do not possess gold, nor silver, nor money in your purse: no scrip for your journey, nor two coats nor shoes, nor staff, for the workman is worthy of his meat. When you come into a house salute it, saying, peace be to this house." (Mat. 10:7ff.)

The ideal of evangelical perfection had the same appeal for thirteenth-century Italy as it had for twelfth-century Lyons. Be-fore long, a group of like-minded men had gathered about the youthful maverick. Although Francis did not contemplate the founding of a religious order, the old monastic organizations which he knew had a restricted apostolate which influenced fewer and fewer of the growing urban population. Like Waldo before him, Francis demanded little more of his followers than a dedication to evangelical ideals. According to St. Bonaventure's account, Francis "perceived that the number of the Brethren was gradually increasing and wrote for himself and for his Brethren a Rule for their life, in simple words. Herein the observance of the Holy Gospel was set as the inseparable foundation, and some few other points were added that seemed necessary for a con-sistent manner of life."

This, the primitive rule of the Franciscans, was the one Francis submitted to Pope Innocent III in 1209. The journey to Rome is another intriguing parallel in the career of the two religious innovators. But if Waldo and Francis followed similar paths to the papacy, their receptions were very different. Alex-ander III was willing to approve Waldo's way of life—except for preaching. Pope Innocent III hesitated at sanctioning the absolute poverty adopted by the small band from Assisi. Surprisingly, he showed less reluctance in general regarding the permission to preach. Only one or two of Francis' adherents were clerics, but Innocent ingeniously salvaged the letter of the canon which forbade laymen to preach. He ordered that "all lay Brethren that had accompanied the servant of God, Francis, wear narrow tonsures, that they might preach the word of God without hindrance."

Francis and his followers were, of course, closely attuned to the revival of the eschatological expectancy in Christendom during the twelfth and thirteenth centuries. Francis believed that he had been called to follow Christ's poverty so that he might be free to herald more effectively his coming kingdom: "I am the Herald of the Great King." He was doubtless aware of the various prophecies which foretold the imminence of the last days. Francis looked to God's kingdom as a power already working in the friars' lives and impelling them to an exercise, in their own way, of the ultimate ideals of the future. But he looked even more expectantly to the coming of that final realm which would transcend the present. He writes of the coming "Kingdom of God": "Thy Kingdom come that Thou may reign in us by grace and may make us come to Thy Kingdom, where there is the clear vision of Thee, the perfect love of Thee, the blessed company of Thee, the eternal enjoyment of Thee." Francis here does obeisance to the double sovereignty of God. One reign is by grace in the visible world through the function of Christ as mediated by the saving, sacramental Church. The other kingdom is the realm perfect and transcendent. The one is visible within the framework of the existing world, while the other is supernatural and within the cosmic frame of reference.

Francis prepares his friars for participation in both kingdoms, or rather for life in both phases of one kingdom. Their status in the existing world was necessarily one of pilgrimage and exile. In this manner only could they enjoy deliverance from the fleeting present and attachment to the abiding future. True friars, contemptuous of all worldly affairs, would pass without danger from the temporal to the eternal. They could claim the coming kingdom because they were not fettered by the existing order. Francis' ideal was simple: "The followers of most holy poverty, having nothing, loved nothing, and therefore had no fear of losing anything."

Poverty and the kingdom were linked from the first to last in the thinking of Francis. Poverty was the special means which his unique followers were to employ in announcing the coming of the kingdom. Francis may at certain times have questioned the reaction of the Church to his way of Gospel poverty. But he never doubted that the Church would ultimately and inevitably defend that special renunciation of the friars which was likewise Christ's will for them. He did not hesitate, therefore, to pledge his loyalty to the Church, to her pope, and to her institutional procedure. The Second Rule contains this passage: "Brother Francis promises obedience and reverence to the Lord Pope Honorius and to his successors canonically elected and to the order of the holy Roman Church."

Francis sought, finally, to subordinate his life and brethren to the historic Church as to the authoritative guardian of his Christ-inspired poverty. The pope was to be asked "to assign them one of the Cardinals of the Holy Roman Church to be governor, protector, and corrector of this brotherhood, so that being always subject and submissive at the feet of the same Holy Church, grounded in the Catholic faith, we may observe poverty and humility and the Holy Gospel of our Lord Jesus Christ, which we have firmly promised." By the year 1223, when the Second Rule was approved by Pope Honorius III, the Franciscan brotherhood was definitely a religious order.

The influence of St. Francis on subsequent centuries is incalculable. Even to this day, his cult has made him one of the most admired and familiar figures in the Christian world. Unlike other religious reformers who attempted to improve the Church by means of legal codes and a more rational examination of the Gospel and the Fathers, Francis injected into Catholicism a new ideal. It was an ideal that found the essence of Christianity in the simple following of Christ—a Christ who is not a goal but rather a holy way of life. Theological *summae* and formularies of law were for him not the way to a knowledge of Christ. This was to be found rather in a heartfelt imitation of the Master as seen in the Gospel narrative.

Perhaps one of the most important features of the mendicant movement was that it gave a new meaning to what is today called the apostolate, or pastoral care of souls. In the older monasticism the faithful came to the monastery for spiritual consolation; the purpose of these orders was the glory of God through the personal sanctification of its members. Benedict warned his followers, "Place nothing before the *opus dei,* the chanting of divine office, and the celebration of the Eucharist." The mendicants centered their activities in the work of preaching and caring for the welfare of the laity. In the case of the followers of Francis, this apostolate was to be achieved chiefly through moral example. In the case of the other great mendicant order of the Middle Ages, the Dominicans, this activity turned more toward the preaching of the word of God. It was the appearance of the Dominicans that shifted the mendicant movement into the academic world.

The Dominicans, or the Order of Preachers, came into existence during the Church's struggle with the most formidable of the medieval heresies, the Albigensians, or Cathari. Like the Waldensians, they stood in opposition to the overorganized Church, and yet in preaching a more subtle doctrine which was strongly reminiscent of earlier Manichaeism they appealed to the educated classes, especially in southern France. Hence their suppression demanded a highly centralized but mobile organization that would have the preaching of true Catholic doctrine as its chief objective. This project necessitated the training of an elite corps of teachers and brought the mendicant movement into close association with the universities. Founded by the Spaniard Dominic de Guzmán (d.1221), the order that bears his name perfected in many ways the changes in monasticism that had been inaugurated by Francis. Whereas the Franciscan rules and regulations, which were the result of an almost spontaneous movement, were in fact devised in opposition to the ideal of their founder, who wished "to have nothing to do with the rules and regulations of Augustine, Benedict, or Citeaux," the rule of St. Dominic was a calculated and well thought out constitution which through a devolution of authority would insure flexibility in the more external and diversified activity that was its aim. Rejected was the monastic attitude of the monk who, as the member of a family, looked to his abbot as a father.

This patriarchal approach was replaced by a constitution that envisioned the friar as a member of a great company not bound by a vow of stability but at the disposal of a general, duly elected by his fellow friars. The appearance of the Dominican rule, with its departure from a patriarchal to a more democratically regulated life, marks the beginning of the history of religious institutional legislation that exerted a profound influence on the spiritual and intellectual life of Catholicism until the time of the Reformation. It may be compared to the role that was played by the constitution of the Society of Jesus from the sixteenth century to the present.

What distinguished this Order of Preachers from all previous orders was its emphasis on the election and constituting of authority by stressing the functions of commissioners rather than religious superiors. The over-all government of the order was in the hands of men elected directly by the friars, who acted as electors at the discretion of local boards. The legislative and juridical power of the order was invested in a group of men who were elected for short periods of time by men chosen ad hoc for this purpose. In addition to the general administration, the order was divided into regional and local groups, provinces, and individual convents, the latter restricted in numbers. At all three levels—general, provincial, and conventual—there was a single executive officer. The local prior was elected by the members of his own community, the provincial by delegates from the various houses of the province, and the general by an electoral board or general chapter consisting of representatives from the provinces. No legislation affecting the order could be put into effect until it had been approved by three consecutive annual chapters. The most remarkable feature of the Dominican legislation was that it put supreme authority in the hands of the friars not necessarily holding important positions as ruling superiors. The end result was a radical change in the notion of authority. The monks had been totally submissive to the direction of the abbot as a son to his father. The authority was personal and monarchical and lasted for the lifetime of the abbot. For Dominic and his followers, superiors were constituted for a short time and solely for the purpose of directing the entire order toward its chief aim, which was the salvation not of the individual member but of the entire body of Christians. The superior was not, as with earlier monasticism, intended to guide the individual friar to salvation. This separation of authority was, of course, aimed at implementing the real end of the order, which was the defense of Catholic truth by preaching. In brief, the order was founded to combat ignorance and heresy. Every individual house was to have a doctor of theology, and from the very beginning schools of the order were founded in the great university centers of Paris, Oxford, Cologne, Montpellier, and Bologna.

The Mendicants and Scholasticism

It was this close association of the mendicant Dominicans with the universities, soon followed by the other mendicants, that enabled the Church to put at its disposal the fruits of scholasticism. Thanks to this, the great wave of Greco-Arabic learning became the ally rather than the enemy of Catholicism. Perhaps the most important aspect of the new type of religious institution founded by Francis and Dominic was, in spite of their internal democratic structure, their direct control by the papacy. With generals resident in the Eternal City and a mythical ownership of all their possessions by the pope—a fiction to insure their claim of absolute poverty—the mendicant orders, especially the Dominicans, became the trusted agents of papal policy throughout the remainder of the Middle Ages. Thus, the extremely dangerous movements that accompanied the reorganization of society in the twelfth and thirteenth centuries—eschatological poverty and the Greco-Arabian philosophy with its deterministic and pantheistic tendencies—were brought under control.

In this respect the mendicant orders contributed greatly to the furthering of Catholic unity, which reached its fullest expression in the thirteenth century. Yet in the over-all picture, it is questionable whether they fulfilled their main objective of reforming the Church. Unlike the Hilderbrandian reform, which was so successful in emancipating the Church from secular control and in which the spirit of monasticism took hold of the very center of the papal government, the poverty movement never entrenched itself in the papacy. The spirit of Christ the poor man was little in evidence in the papal Curia. Further, the involvement of the friars in parish work, especially since they enjoyed privileges of immunity from local episcopal and parochial control, brought them into competition and conflict with the diocesan clergy. Many saw in them a genuine threat to the established ecclesiastical order. William of St. Amour wrote in 1255 a widely read book entitled *On the Perils of the Last Time,* which described the friars as "those ungodly men whose appearance had been foretold by the Apostle as the immediate sign of the coming of the Antichrist and the end of the world." A famous theologian in Prague, Matthew of Janov (d.1394), called them the third arm on the body of Christ that had crippled the other two and reduced the secular clergy to a state of uselessness. Until well into the fifteenth century their presence at the universities was a constant source of strife, and their bickering over the nature of true poverty and the question of the Immaculate Conception was a fount of open scandal for the laity. Jean de Gerson, Chancellor of the University of Paris during the time of the Great Schism, ascribes many of the woes of Christendom to the friars, especially the general denigration of theology resulting from the fruitless quarrels between the Dominican and the Franciscan schools of theology.

In addition to the Friars Minor (Franciscans) and the Order of Preachers, two other mendicant orders, less numerous and influential but nonetheless formative forces in the devotional and religious life of Catholicism in the Middle Ages, must be mentioned.

The origin of the Carmelites, or Order of Our Lady of Mount

Carmel, is surrounded with obscurity. Once believed to have been founded by the prophet Elias, it was, as far as can be historically ascertained, originally a group of hermits settled near Mount Carmel in the Holy Land during the crusades. Driven from Palestine by the Moslem reconquest in the thirteenth century, the order was organized and soon established houses in Italy, Spain, and England. One Simon Stock, an Englishman about whom little is known, appears to have changed the constitution of the order which, in contrast to the other mendicants, was extremely severe in prohibiting the eating of meat or the wearing of shoes, and remodeled it after the Dominican constitution. A fifteenth-century legend attributes to Stock, who is not mentioned in the official category of the saints, a miraculous scapular which even to this day is highly revered in some dark corners of Catholicism. According to the legend, the Blessed Virgin appeared to St. Simon at Cambridge on July 16, 1251, and gave him a scapular with the promise that whoever wore it would be assured of salvation. Later in the fifteenth century a forged papal bull attributed to Pope John XXII, entitled the *Sabbatina*, represented the pope as declaring that the Virgin Mary had appeared to him in a vision and promised to release from purgatory on the Saturday following his death anyone who died wearing the scapular. A number of popes in modern times have approved this pious practice and the conditions laid down in the apocryphal bull.

The fourth of the great mendicant orders of the Middle Ages was that of the Friars Hermits of St. Augustine. Like that of the Carmelites, its origin is obscured. Certainly it was not founded by St. Augustine. It appears to have originated with the uniting of a number of hermitical groups already established in Italy in the twelfth century. Its incorporation into an order was the result of a general policy of the papacy of bringing all religious communities under its control. Like the Carmelites, it was given a modified Dominican rule and gradually followed the latter order by moving into urban centers and the academic world. From those who followed the Augustinian rule came some of the most important figures in the reform of the sixteenth century, including Erasmus of Rotterdam and Martin Luther.

All the mendicant orders were, of course, associated with lay organizations called second and third orders. The former were generally groups of nuns who adapted themselves to the rules of the Franciscans or the Dominicans. The latter were composed of laymen living in the world who, though not taking vows, nevertheless attempted to follow out the ideals of their respective founders. Thus the mendicants exhibited a greater influence on the laity than the older orders. Popular devotion to the Passion of Christ (Francis had borne the stigmata, or the five wounds of Christ) and to our Blessed Lady was sponsored by them. The rosary, which is in the popular mind associated with St. Dominic, owes its origin to practices going back to the twelfth century. In its present form, consisting of fifteen decades corresponding to the like number of meditations on the life of the Virgin, it is traceable to the late sixteenth century. The popular Catholic prayer, the Hail Mary, or Ave Maria, appears late in the twelfth century in an abridged form. The second component, a petition for help in the hour of death, was not known until the fifteenth century. As a prayer, it did not gain popularity until the seventeenth century. Mention might also be made of the Stations of the Cross, since they are also associated with the mendicants. The practice of following the *Via Crucis* in Jerusalem was given great popularity by the Crusades, but it was not until the fifteenth century that the stations were erected outside of Palestine. They varied greatly in number. The present number of fourteen is traced to the seventeenth century, when the devotion was again popularized by the Franciscans. The mendicants still form the largest group of the religious in the Catholic world today, and they exert a wide influence in determining popular piety. Most Catholic missions are in their control.

The New Theology

By directing the activities of the mendicant orders into the world of learning, the Church was able to put in its service one of the most perduring of medieval Catholicism's contributions to Western thought: scholasticism. Although some of its partisans trace this system of thought to the sermon of St. Paul on the Areopagus and see it reflected in a steady growth down through Boethius and Anselm, it was not until the thirteenth century that it began to exert a profound influence on Catholic theology. This was due to the development of the universities and the concomitant rediscovery of Aristotle. The latter provided the first complete philosophical system that the Church in the West had ever encountered, and the former provided the apparatus with which to project the new learning into the life of the Church. The great problem which confronted Catholicism after the intellectual revival of the twelfth century was the accommodation of the new learning to an integrated explanation of the plan of redemption.

Earlier attempts to formulate a system that could adapt the results of Greek logic and dialectic to the data of revealed truth had been sporadic and often disastrous. Tertullian had voiced the general antipathy of the Latin Church to speculative theology when he had inveighed against "Unhappy Aristotle! who invented for these men dialectic, the art of building up and pulling down, an art so evasive in its propositions, so far fetched in its conjectures, so harsh in its arguments, so productive of contentions, embarrassing even to itself, retracting everything, and really treating nothing." The monk Gottschalk in the ninth century was described as a destroyer of the faith and condemned to life imprisonment for toying with the question of grace and free will in terms of dialectics. Bérenger in the eleventh century was summoned to Rome and forced to recant publicly his application of Aristotelian logic to the question of Real Presence. The opposition to a too rationalistic explanation of doctrinal truth continued throughout the following centuries. Both Peter Abelard and Gilbert de La Porrée, generally regarded as heralders of scholasticism, incurred the wrath of Bernard of Clairvaux for allegedly subverting Christian doctrine with dialectics by harnessing a highly sophisticated and delicately balanced system of metaphysics to elucidate the simple message of the Gospel.

The introduction and appropriation of Aristotle was a long and complicated process. It can be traced not only to the intense interest in speculative matters that marked the entire twelfth century but also to the projection of northern European interests into the Arabian world in Spain, Syria, and Sicily. Aristotle's works had been taken up, studied, and translated by Moslem and Jewish philosophers as early as the ninth century. Paradoxically, it was the schismatic Christian Nestorians who had preserved many of the writings of the Greek philosopher for transmission to the Arabs. Al-farabi in the tenth and Avicenna in the eleventh century were the great pioneers in translating and interpreting his metaphysical writings, but it was the Spanish Moslem Averroës who takes the credit for presenting Aristotle whole and entire in the Christian West, soon to share his enthusiasm for the Stagirite as representing the highest achievement of the human mind. Between 1170 and 1180, Gerard of Cremona had translated most of Aristotle's works on physical sciences, while James of Venice translated the *De Anima* and the *Metaphysics*. The ethical and political works of Aristotle were not in translation until the 1250's.

Although the Dominican Albertus Magnus (d.1280) was the first theologian to write commentaries on the complete writings of Aristotle, it was his pupil Thomas Aquinas (d.1274) who molded the entire corpus into what has been acclaimed the greatest synthesis of the medieval world and the finest example of scholastic theology. For this reason Aquinas is not only considered the perennial and common universal Doctor of Catholicism but also called the Angelic Doctor and has been officially proclaimed the patron of Catholic theology.

There can be no doubt that his thought dominates a great and powerful segment of Catholic theologians to this day. Yet from a historical point of view it must be borne in mind that Aquinas and the system he perfected were never universally accepted during the Middle Ages and were often condemned. His system formed a small section, and at times a very small section, of general Catholic theological thought in Europe until quite recent times. The revival of Thomism in the sixteenth century as a weapon in the Counter Reformation was of dubious success, and it would be presumptuous to point to the adulation given Aquinas since the times of Leo XIII in the nineteenth century as an indication that his was the most intellectually satisfying and influential system of the medieval period. Much of the reputation Aquinas enjoyed during the Age of Faith was due more to the position given him by Dante in the *Divine Comedy* than to any universal acclaim from the Church. Nor can it be correctly stated, as many claim, that in accepting Aristotle—baptizing him as it were—he departed from a long tradition of Catholic theological thought that had been hitherto dominated by Augustinian Platonism. An examination of his writings demonstrates a heavy reliance on Platonism, especially his treatment of the virtues and his idea of the Supreme Being as reflected in a graduation of creatures.

What gives the system of Aquinas a perduring, perennial value is not so much his reconciling of faith and reason by the use of analogical concepts as the lucid and succinct manner in which he constructs an all-embracing edifice on a few simple principles. His treatment of the Trinity, the Incarnation, the nature of grace, and the Eucharist represents some of the most precise thinking in the entire history of Catholic dogma. It is for this reason that the papacy for the last four centuries has reiterated the claim that his is the perennial and communal philosophy and has indicated that his teaching is to be considered as the official doctrine of the Catholic Church.

Since his explanation of the Eucharist is officially recognized as the Church's own, it may be cited as an example of the scholastic method of collecting diverse statements on a given subject and sifting them through repeated distinctions, thus sharpening their truth content. By posing doubts, the method leads to inquiry and from inquiry to truth. Thomas first states a succession of negative arguments and then a contrary proposition from Scripture or the Fathers. Then with clear logic he arrives at the true conclusion, which is in accordance with the authority he has last adduced as proof. The selection taken from *Summa Theologica* also represents the completion of the doctrinal development on the Eucharist. The question discussed is whether the body of Christ is in the sacrament in a real or only in a figurative sense:

It seems that the body of Christ is not in this sacrament in a real sense but only figuratively. It is written in John 5.54 that when Christ uttered the words: "Except you eat the flesh of the Son of Man and drink his blood, etc. Many of His disciples on hearing it said: this is a hard saying:" to whom He rejoined: "It is the spirit that enlivens, the flesh profiteth nothing:" as if he were to say, according to St. Augustine: "Give a spiritual meaning to what I have said. You are not to eat this body which you see, nor to drink the blood which they who crucify Me are to spill. It is a mystery that I put before you, in its spiritual sense it will quicken you, but the flesh profiteth nothing."

Christ said (Math. 38,20): "Behold I am with you all days even to the consummation of the world." Now Augustine makes this observation (Tract. 30 in Joan) "The Lord is on high until the world is ended, nevertheless the truth of the Lord is here with us, for the body in which he rose again must be in one place, but His truth is everywhere. Therefore, the body of Christ is not really in this sacrament but only figuratively.

No body can be in several places at the same time. This is not even possible for the angels since they could then be everywhere. Christ is a true body, therefore, it seems that it is not the Eucharist in a real sense but only figuratively.

The Church's sacraments are for the profit of the faithful, but according to Gregory, in a certain homily (28 in Evang.) the ruler is rebuked for demanding Christ's bodily presence, as Augustine says on John 16,7: "Except I go the paraclete will not come to you." (Tract. xciv in Joan) Therefore, Christ is not in the sacrament of the altar according to His bodily presence.

"On the contrary," says Hillary (de Trin. 8): "There is no room for doubt regarding the truth of Christ's body and blood; for now by our Lord's own declaring and by our faith His flesh is truly drink. And Ambrose says (De Sacram. 6): As the Lord Jesus Christ is God's true Son, so it is Christ's true flesh which we take, and His true blood which we drink."

I answer that, the presence of Christ's true body and blood in this sacrament cannot be detected by sense nor understanding, but by faith alone, which rests upon Divine authority.

Hence, on Luke 22,19: "This is My body which shall be delivered up for you." Cyril says: "Doubt not whether this be true; but take rather the Saviour's words for faith; for since He is the Truth He lieth not." According to John 14,1: "You believe in God, believe also in Me." And since faith is of things unseen, as Christ shows us His Godhead invisibly, so also in this sacrament He shows us His flesh invisibly.

Some men have contended that Christ's body and blood are not in this sacrament in a real sense but only figuratively. This is contrary to Christ's words and is heretical. Berergar, who first devised this heresy, was forced to withdraw his error and acknowledge the truth of the faith.

From this authority the heretics are wrong because of a misunderstanding of St. Augustine's words. When Augustine says "You are not to eat this body which you see," he means not to exclude the truth of Christ's body, but that it would not be eaten in the form in which it was seen by them. And by the words: "It is a mystery that I put before you; in its spiritual sense it will quicken you," he does not mean that His body is in the sacrament merely according to mystical signification, but spiritually, invisibly, and by the power of the spirit. Expounding John 64, "The flesh profiteth nothing," he says: "Yea, but as they understood it, for they understood that the flesh was to be eaten as it is divided piecemeal in a dead body, or sold in the shambles, not as it is quickened by the spirit. Let the spirit draw nigh to the flesh then the flesh profiteth very much; for if the flesh profiteth nothing then the word had not been made flesh that it might dwell among us."

Now this is suitable, first for the perfection of the New Law. For, the sacrifices of the Old Law contained only in figure that true sacrifice of Christ's Passion, according to Heb. 10,1: "For the law having a shadow of the good things to come, not the very image of things." For this reason it was necessary that the sacrifice of the New Law instituted by Christ should have something more, namely, that it should contain Christ Himself crucified not merely figuratively but in a very real sense. Therefore, this sacrament which contains Christ Himself, as Dionysius says (Eccl. Hier. 3), is perfective of all the other sacraments in which Christ's virtue is participated.

Secondly, this belongs belongs to Christ's love, out of which for our salvation He assumed a true body of our nature. And because it is the special feature of friendship to live together with friends, as the philosopher says (Ethic. 9), He promises us His bodily presence as a reward, saying (Math. 24,28): "Where the body is there shall the eagles be gathered together." Yet He does not deprive us of His bodily presence but unites us with Himself in this sacrament through the truth of His body and blood. Hence, He says (John 57): "He that eateth My flesh and drinketh My blood abideth in Me and I in him." Therefore this sacrament is the sign of supreme charity, and the uplifter of our hope, from such familiar union of Christ with us.

Thirdly, it belongs to the perfection of faith which concerns His humanity just as it does His Godhead.

That saying of Augustine and all others like it is to be understood of Christ's body as it is seen in its proper form; according as Christ Himself says (Math. 26,2): "But Me you have not always." Nonetheless He is invisibly in the form of this sacrament wherever it is performed.

Christ's body is not in this sacrament as a body is in a place, by dimensions commensurate with the place, but in a special manner proper to this sacrament. Therefore, we say that Christ's body is on many altars, not as in different places but sacramentally: and therefore we do not say that Christ is there only as a sign even though a sacrament is a kind of sign; but that Christ's body is sacramentally present as stated above.

This argument is true of Christ's bodily presence in its visible appearance, but not as it is spiritually, that is invisibly, after the manner and by the virtue of the spirit. Augustine says, "If thou hast understood Christ's words spiritually concerning His flesh, they are the spirit and life to thee; if thou hast understood them carnally, they are also spirit and life, but not to thee." [12]

It would be impossible to conceive of the tremendous impact of scholasticism and the direction given it by the mendicant theologians without the newly evolving universities. In a way they are one of the most unique contributions of Catholicism to the Western culture. Nothing quite like them existed in antiquity, and they are still not to be found in the cultures and civilizations of the Orient. Historians still dispute among themselves on their precise origin. Certainly they must be considered in the context of the general development of a corporate consciousness evident since the twelfth century in European society as reflected in the guilds as well as the mendicant orders. For the medieval university was not as it is often believed to be, that is, an institution of higher learning so named because it purported to offer a universal knowledge; it was basically an association or corporation between students and faculty. During the eleventh and twelfth centuries, as the older monastic and cathedral schools, traceable to the reforms of Charles the Great, began to decline, they were replaced by new-school scholars who banded together and drew up constitutions to protect themselves and their students from the encroachments of the local clergy and the civil authorities. These corporations were empowered to give to those who passed through the required course of studies a license to teach anywhere in the growing network of similar institutions. Two types of universities emerged: the northern with its prototype in Paris, which was largely a corporation of scholars, and the southern with Bologna as the prototype, with the control of the university in the hands of the student corporation. The northern universities tended to emphasize theology, whereas the southern types were more interested in legal and scientific studies. Although the University of Paris was not founded by the papacy, in its struggle to liberate itself from the control of the catherdral clergy represented by the chancellor of Notre Dame, it turned to papal protection. Thus the papacy exercised an early control over the university and later founded or chartered twenty-one similar institutions throughout Europe. For almost three centuries the University of Paris was looked upon, along with the papacy and the empire, as the third great power in Western Christendom, and it was the arbitrator of all important moral, social, and theological questions.

The course of theological studies was a long and arduous one. After a six-year study of the trivium—grammar, logic, and rhetoric—and the quadrivium, now reduced to a study of the ethics of Aristotle, the student was given a licentiate and thus qualified to begin the long years of theological study which consisted in a perusal of Scripture and commentaries on the four books of *Sentences* of Peter Lombard. Seldom was the graduate course finished before the age of thirty-five. Actually less than 1 per cent of the clergy finished the entire program.

By the end of the thirtcenth century a number of specific schools based on membership in one or another of the mendicant orders had evolved. The Franciscan, traditionally more in the Augustinian-Platonic tradition, was dominated by men like Alexander of Hales (d.1245), John of La Rochelle (d.1254), Bonaventure (d.1274), and Raymond Lull (d.1316). The Dominicans, in addition to Albertus Magnus and his pupil Aquinas, filled distinguished chairs of theology in the persons of Robert Kilwardby (d.1279) and Deitrich of Vrieberg (d.1310). For the most part they remained under the influence of Aristotle.

Late Medieval Mysticism

The dangers of developing a highly complicated and abstract system of speculative theology are, of course, obvious. The interorder quarrels on the questions of grace, predestination, the relative merits of poverty, and the nature of the beatific vision found their way from the lecture hall to the pulpit. Yet it would be unfair to claim that the mendicants, by plunging so deeply into the intricate explanation of seemingly nonessential theological matters, lost sight of their role as preachers and directors of souls. The Dominicans, especially in the Rhineland, an ever fertile soil for new ideas, produced a number of theologians who stand in striking contrast to many of their confreres in combining the intellectual life with a deeply spiritual mysticism which they preached to others. The Rhenish mystics Meister Eckhart (d.1310), Johannes Tauler (d.1361), and Heinrich Suso (d.1336) may be cited as oustanding examples of late medieval mysticism.

In contrast to the extremely complicated and abstract theology of the schoolmen, they fostered a more direct approach to the divine. Their sermons and writings reflect a strong element of Neo-Platonism reminiscent of the early Fathers. The emancipation of man from himself and his surroundings and the inexpressibility of the divine were underlying themes.

The following sermon delivered by Tauler to a group of Dominican nuns shows the stirrings of an interest in a spirituality unfettered by juridical and dialectical terminology. It is a commentary on the parable found in the fifteenth chapter of St. Luke's Gospel:

> Today's Gospel tells of a woman who lost a coin, and lit a lantern and searched for the coin. This woman is God's divinity, the lantern is His sacred humanity, and the coin is the soul of man.
>
> There are three characteristics which any coin must have if it is to be genuine. It must be of the right weight, it must be made of the proper metal, and it must bear the right stamp and image. All three qualities are indispensable.
>
> First, it must be made of gold or silver, the required metals for coins. My dear children, what a marvelous coin the human soul is! It is in fact a golden coin! We can never really appreciate or understand its worth. Furthermore, a coin must be of the right weight; but how can we weigh this coin, the soul, which weighs more than heaven and earth and everything in them? God Himself is in this coin, so it must weigh as much as God. Then there is the image on this coin, which is the image of God's divinity. He has infused this into man's soul supernaturally out of His inexpressible love, at the same time completely absorbing and engulfing the soul into Himself. If this is to happen to you, be sure that you will need to seek Him by a more perfect, more direct and much higher way than any by which the outer man could seek Him. You will need something far above all the pious exercises of the external man, all his sufferings and activities and the rest of it, all the images and performances he may devise for himself. How are we to do this? See what this woman did: she lit a lantern and ransacked her house.
>
> It was Eternal Wisdom who lit this lantern, and it was

lit with God's true love; for a lantern should be lit and should burn. Dear children, you do not know what love of God is. You think that you have found the love of God when you think fine thoughts and find joy and delight in Him; but this is not love at all. This is not how love acts. When we have love we burn, wanting God, lacking God, feeling ourselves forsaken by God, in continual torment, yet content to be tormented. In this torment we are melted and consumed by the fire of our need for God, and still, through it all, we remain content. This is love, for love is not what you imagine it to be; and this is the light of the lantern.

The woman searching for the coin ransacked her house. When we search for God, we must be both active and passive. We must be active, seeking; and we must seek in two different ways, one exterior and one interior. The interior way is quite different from the exterior, and is far above it as heaven is above the earth. We seek God exteriorly when we carry out good external works of various kinds, as we are commanded or inspired by God and advised by those who love Him; especially in the exercise of virtues which we practice or can practice.

But the other way is far superior to this: we go into our own souls, into the very depths, and seek the Lord there, as He counselled us when He said: "The kingdom of God is within you." Anyone who wants to find this kingdom—that is, to find God, with all His riches and in His own being and nature—must look for it where it is, in the very depths of his soul, where God is infinitely closer to the soul and more integral to it than is the soul itself.

We must seek for the depths of our souls and we must find them. We must go into our house, our souls; and all our senses, everything to do with them, and everything which comes to us through them must all be left outside. When we go into our house and look for God there, God in His turn looks for us and searches the house. He behaves just as we do when we are searching for something, throwing aside one thing after another until we find what we are looking for. This is just what He does to us. When we have gone into our house, when we have searched for Him in the depths of our souls, God comes and searches for us in every part of our house.

Not everyone will understand what I am saying, though I always speak plain German. Those who have experienced something of what I am talking about and have been enlightened by it will understand what I mean; but no one else will. When I speak of "going in," I do not mean entering into one's soul occasionally, only to come out again and occupy oneself entirely with created things. And when I say that God seeks man in his house and ransacks it, I mean that in this house, in the depths of our souls, we are completely deprived of all the ideas and conceptions of God by which we have ever thought of Him before. Our house is ransacked; it is as if we had never known anything about God. As He seeks for us, this happens again and again; every idea that we ever had of Him, every manifestation of Him that we have ever known, every conception and revelation of Him which we ever had will be taken away from us as He searches to find us.

If our natures could endure to have this process of deprivation repeated, day and night, a thousand times over, and if we could endure it with resignation, this would be of more benefit to us than all the understanding and all the spiritual favors which we could receive. When we are searched in this way, if we will suffer it with resignation, we are led infinitely higher than we could ever be brought by all the good works and practices and ideas which we could ever perform or receive. Those who really achieve this become the most blessed of men, because this trial becomes so easy to them that they can retreat at will into the depths of their souls in an instant, and ascend far above their natural limitations.

However, the majority of people are only too inclined to cling to the earth; they must always have some created thing to hold on to tightly. Some people are completely unresigned, completely attached to creatures. They are like a barn floor which has to be prepared for the threshing, and is so rough and uneven that it needs scrubbing with a strong, stiff broom to make it smooth and even. If a threshing floor is already smooth, it only needs a feather duster over it to make it ready. Men who have no resignation are rugged and uneven, and they need God's strong, stiff broom, temptations and sufferings of many kinds, to teach them to resign themselves to Him.

These happy ones who have resignation, who are smooth, have no need of this; they go from happiness to happiness; every created thing which could hinder them dies away from them; they go more deeply into the depths of their souls, clinging to nothing as they progress, possessing their spirits in poverty and nakedness and true resignation.

Dear child, when your spirit is naked and blind and resigned as the Lord would have it, when it is exactly as He wants it to be, when you have let Him seek you and ransack your house, then the lost coin is found; and that finding will be more to you than any man can think or know. Oh, my dear children, if we let ourselves be sought for in this way, it will take us much farther than all the ideas, good works, and practices which human intelligence can devise. Our Lord assured us of this when He said: "If anyone wants to follow Me, let him deny himself and come to Me." We deny ourselves when we refuse to cling to anything which could hinder our progress to God.

People who cannot resign themselves encounter great temptations; they are burnished with God's strong, stiff broom. Then they give up hope, and their temptations become worse and they fall into despair and dreadful fear. They come and say: "It is all useless, Father. God has taken all His light and grace away from me." If such people could only be smooth and even, if they could be resigned, they would never be happier than when the Lord searches for them, and in His searching they would find true peace. So, whether God wishes to find you in blindness, darkness and coldness, or whether He wants to find you in fervor, whatever His will may be, resign yourself to it, and let Him find you there.[13]

CHAPTER 4

The Breakdown of
the Catholic Synthesis

The Autumn of the Middle Ages

THE PERIOD following the high-water mark of Catholicism in the thirteenth century which witnessed the breakup of universalism, the decadence of scholasticism, and the transition to a world-wide mission activity is often called the Autumn of the Middle Ages. Yet the term must not be understood solely as implying complete dissolution. In a way, it was a period that harvested many of the high ideals of the monastic Church. Thus it gave men an opportunity to reappraise the role of Catholicism in a new world that was rapidly changing and liberating itself from the narrow confines of feudalism.

There had been a brief break in this isolationism during the Crusades and the Mongolian invasions which severed for a time the encircling ring of the Moslem world. Franciscan and Dominican friars had made contact with the court of the Great Khan in the mid-thirteenth century, and there were high hopes in papal circles that the leader of the Mongolians would embrace Christianity. The Franciscan John of Plano informed the pope that the Nestorian Christians in the household of the Mongolian leader were convinced that this leader was about to convert to Catholicism. St. Louis, King of France, sent the Flemish friar William of Rubruck to the heart of Mongolia with the same expectations and with the hope that a Christianized Khan would co-operate with the crusaders in crushing the Seljuk Turks; this event came close to realization with the capture of Baghdad in 1258. In 1273, Gregory X invited the Great Khan, Abaga, to the second Council of Lyons.

One of the most interesting episodes in this East-West exchange was the visit of the Ongut Turk Rabban Sauma to Rome in 1287. Born in Peking of Christian parents, he had journeyed to the Eternal City to visit the leader of Western Christendom and the tombs of the Apostles. It is recorded that he celebrated Mass in Bordeaux and that King Edward I of England received communion from him. The journeys of Marco Polo also aroused a new interest in the East later in the fourteenth century. Pope Nicholas IV sent the Franciscan John of Monte Corvino to Peking, and by 1305 he had established a number of churches and baptized over six thousand converts. Enthusiasm in Rome was so great that the pope decided to establish a Western hierarchy for China. Seven Franciscan friars were consecrated bishops and sent there as missionaries. John was made the first Latin archbishop of the Far East. It is recorded that he translated the New Testament and the Psalms, and he also celebrated Mass in the native tongue. The recapture of the Mongolian capital by the Chinese in 1362 marked the end of the mission.

The western hemisphere was also the scene of missionary activity. A bishop was sent to the Norse colony in Greenland in the early twelfth century, and a diocese was established at Gardar, near present-day Julianhaab. All in all, some twelve bishops resided here during the years from 1124 to 1377, and there is strong evidence of sporadic missionary activity in North America. Papal tax collections from the diocese of Gardar are recorded in the Vatican, and the ruins of the Cathedral of St. Nicholas are still extant. A number of monasteries were also set up in this outpost of medieval Catholicism which mysteriously disappeared in the fifteenth century.

Yet the dream of a world dominated by Roman Catholicism, succinctly expressed by Innocent III, "The Lord gave Saint Peter not only the Church to rule, but the entire world," was to prove illusory. The equilibrium between the papacy and the empire was rendered impossible by the emergence of national states. The central apparatus of the Church became more and more secularized as a result of its triumph in the investiture strife. The syntheses between reason and revelation and between philosophy and theology were undermined by nominalism, and finally the struggle concerning the constitution of the Church led to schism and the eventual dissolution of the Christian Republic of the Middle Ages.

The political imbalance created by the defeat of the Hohenstaufens after the middle of the thirteenth century soon brought the triumphant papacy into open conflict with the now dominant power in western Europe, Capetian France. In the conflict between Pope Boniface VIII and Philip the Fair the papacy was to suffer a setback from which it never recovered. French influence on the papacy had been at work for some time before the claim of the royal power to tax the Church was attacked by Boniface in a papal bull entitled *Clericos Laicos.* The bull threatened with excommunication any interference from the state in the collection of papal revenues. The situation was further inflamed when Philip demanded the degradation of the bishop of Pamiers, an open affront to ecclesiastical authority. In response, Boniface issued his famous bull *Unam Sanctam,* which has been described as the most absolute theocratic doctrine ever formulated. In 1303 the pope himself was apprehended at Anagni by the agents of Philip and died soon after. The shock to Catholic Europe was, of course, immeasurable, but it was a prognostication of events to come. The bull, which has been the object of various apologetical interpretations, is as follows:

We are compelled by the true faith to believe and hold that there is one, holy, Catholic and Apostolic Church. This we firmly believe and simply confess. And outside of this Church there is neither salvation nor remission of sins; as the bridegroom announces in the song of Solomon "My dove, my undefiled is but one; she is the only one of her mother, the chosen one of her who bore her," which represents the mystic body, the head of which is Christ, and indeed Christ's head is God. In this Church is one God, one faith, and one baptism. For in the time of the flood there was one ark prophesying the one Church. This ark was completed in one cubit and had one helmsman and master—that is Noah. And we read that all things existing on the earth outside this ark were destroyed. This Church we venerate as unique because the Lord said through the prophet: "May God deliver my soul from the sword and my unique one from the power of the dog." He prayed for the soul, that is for himself as the head and for the body. And he called this body the unique Church because of the unity of the bridegroom, the faith, the sacraments, and the charity of the Church. This is that seamless tunic of the Lord which was not cut but given by lot. Therefore there is one body of the one, unique Church and one head, not two heads, as if it were a monster. This head is Christ, Christ's vicar, Peter, and Peter's successor. For the Lord said to this Peter, "Feed my sheep," sheep in general, not any particular sheep or group of sheep. From this it is known that everything was entrusted to Peter. If therefore the Greeks or anyone else say that they were not entrusted to Peter and his successors, they necessarily admit that they are not Christ's sheep. For the Lord says in the gospel of John that there is one fold and one shepherd. We are taught by the evangelical works that there are two swords, the spiritual and the temporal, in the control of the Church. For when the Apostles said: "Behold there are two swords," which as the Apostles were speaking meant two swords in the Church, the Lord did not reply that it was too many but that it was enough. Certainly he who denies that the temporal sword was under the control of Peter, misunderstands the word of the Lord when he said: "Put your sword into the sheath." Therefore, both the spiritual and material sword are under the control of the Church, but the latter is used for the Church and the former by the Church. One is used by the hand of the priest, the other by the hand of the kings and knights at the command and with the permission of the priest. Moreover, one sword ought to be subjected to the spiritual. For the Apostle says, "There is no power unless from God and it must be ordained by God." Moreover, the powers would not be properly ordered unless one sword was under the other sword and as it were the lower made the higher by the other. *According to Dionysius, the divine law is that the lowest is made the highest by the medium.* . . . Moreover, we ought the more clearly to admit that the spiritual power exceeds the temporal in both dignity and nobility as spiritual things surpass temporal ones. And this we are clearly taught by the giving of tithes, benediction, sanctification, the acceptance of this power, and the governing of these things. For as the truth testifies, the spiritual power has established the temporal power and judged it if it were not good. So the prophecy of Jeremiah concerning the Church and the ecclesiastical power is confirmed. "See, I have this day set thee over the nations and over the kingdoms to root out and to pull down and to destroy, and to throw down, to build, and to plant." Therefore if the temporal errs, it will be judged by the spiritual power. But if the spiritual power errs, the minor will be judged by the superior—the supreme spiritual power can be judged by God alone, not by man. For the Apostle testifies, "The spiritual man judges all things and he himself is judged by no-one." Moreover, this authority, even though it is given to a man and is exercised by a man, is not human but divine. For by the divine command it was given to St. Peter and the rock was made firm for him and his successors in Christ whom he had confessed. The Lord said to Peter, "Whatsoever thou shalt bind on earth shall be bound in heaven; and whatsoever thou shalt loose on earth shall be loosed in heaven. . . ." We therefore declare, say, affirm, and announce that for every human creature to be submissive to the Roman pontiff is absolutely necessary for salvation.[14]

Boniface's successors Benedict XI and Clement V came more and more under French influence until the latter moved the papacy to Avignon, where it remained until 1378. This period, known as the Babylonian Captivity of the Church, was not as dark as is often depicted. The papacy, as we have seen, took a great interest in Christian missionary activity. The Council of Vienne in 1311, although disgraced by the condemnation of the Knights Templar, exhibited a lively interest in reform measures.

It attempted to strengthen episcopal control while simultaneously curtailing papal powers. The reintroduction of synods modeled on the ancient Church and a raising of the level of clerical training were also matters proposed at the council.

The Church and High Finance

What did lessen the already damaged prestige of the papacy during the Avignon period was the perfection of a fiscal system that soon made the Church the most powerful financial body in Europe. Since the monetary policy of the Church has had a direct bearing on its inner and spiritual life, it may be well to look at the complicated machinery that was perfected by the popes at Avignon.

It was the abuse associated with this practice that perhaps more than any other led to the breakdown of medieval Catholicism. The Church, whose office it was to save souls from perdition, tended to make this salvation a merely external appliance. The remission of sins and the certainty of the soul's peace with God were associated too closely with money. We have already seen that as a temporal ruler the medieval papacy was the largest landowner in Italy. From the beginning of the patrimonies, as these properties were called, the popes received various revenues that were used for household expenses, the construction and maintenance of Church property, and the various charities. Following the Donation of Pepin, the patrimonies were merged into the states of the Church, and as temporal rulers the popes began to receive dues and taxes. However, it was not until later in the eleventh century that a well organized financial administration appeared.

Until the close of the Middle Ages, the financial administration of the papacy was centralized in the Camera, an office which grew ever more important and efficient, while the Camerarious, its chief agent, became one of the most important officials of the Roman court, subject only to the pope. Subordinate officials in the bureau included a treasurer, depository, and advisory college, auditor, vice-auditor, fiscal proctor, advocates of the Camera, keeper of the auditor's seal, scribes, notaries, couriers, and numerous collectors. Besides the apostolic Camera, the College of Cardinals organized a Camera for their common income, and in addition, many popes maintained a private purse.

In transferring the revenues to Rome, various methods were employed. Special messengers of the collectors themselves brought the receipts at first, but by the thirteenth century the papacy employed methods of merchants and deposited the money in banking institutions. Later, Italian bankers, designated *mercatores camerae*, were ordinarily employed, and they reaped immense benefits from their association with the Holy See. Other familiar banking devices soon developed in the form of bills of exchange, interest, money changing, and loans on taxes to be collected, all of which were in common use by the rising commercial class.

The census, originally a rent paid for leased portions of the papal domain, came in time to include three other types of revenue: payments made by exempt ecclesiastical bodies, tribute from temporal rulers, and Peter's Pence. The first of these originated in the ninth century when monasteries sought from the Holy See the protection no longer provided them by the declining Carolingian empire. The monastery gave to the pope theoretical ownership of its property and paid an annual sum in return for protection from royal intervention in monastic affairs and for exemption from the temporal and financial jurisdiction of the local bishop. With the passage of time, spiritual exemption was also included, an aspect which became the primary purpose of the payment and which contributed much to the laxity of monasteries in the later Middle Ages.

Similarly, a number of civil rulers, seeking protection for their temporal possessions, sent annual tribute to the Holy See in payment for this protection. In times of political uncertainty, the lay lord would voluntarily surrender his lands to the pope in order to receive them back as papal fiefs; thus he recognized the eminent domain of the pope over his property, of which he received back the usufruct. The lord could then employ ecclesiastical censures against his enemies. Under Pope Innocent III and his successors in the thirteenth century, when papal supremacy throughout Christendom was undisputed, the kingdoms of Castile, Aragon, Portugal, Sicily, and England were papal fiefs, along with many lesser lands. A famous example is the tribute of one thousand marks annually which King John of England promised in 1213 as acknowledgment of his vassalage to the pope.

The third kind of census, commonly known as Peter's Pence, originated in England as a voluntary contribution but was also paid by Norway, Denmark, Sweden, and Poland. With time, the Pence lost its voluntary aspect and came to be regarded by the popes as a mark of dependency on the Holy See. Traditionally each household was assessed one penny, and all money in excess of the amount levied for the diocese was retained by the bishops and archdeacons. Although the Pence never constituted a major source of revenue, nevertheless payment continued to be made by the Scandinavian countries until the Protestant Reformation.

Pope Innocent III, to meet the problem of financing the Crusades, began in 1199 the practice of taxing clerical incomes. The original levy was one-fortieth of the annual income. Later popes imposed the tax more frequently, for less worthy projects and at a higher rate, usually one-tenth. To insure payment, a virtual army of assessors and collectors was employed by the Camera, empowered with severe ecclesiastical censures to be invoked against negligent clerics. In countries that developed strong central monarchies, the popes usually found it expedient to share proceeds with the rulers, the latter often receiving the lion's share. In 1302, for example, the king of England was granted one-half the collection, and in 1309 he received one-fourth the total.

A further revenue, called subsidies, consisted of occasional requests made to the bishops and clergy by the pope, asking for charitable contributions toward some matter of immediate concern, such as the defense of the Church against the attacks of Italian rebels and heretics which increased with the passage of time. Theoretically the ecclesiastics were free to comply or refuse these requests, but by the thirteenth century this liberty affected only the size of contribution, and occasionally the amount to be collected was determined in advance, in which case the usual ecclesiastic censures could be invoked for nonpayment.

When the popes assumed the right of confirming or even appointing all archbishops and many bishops as well, a benefice tax began to supply the papal coffers with another major source of income, and the tax also provided Christendom with a tradition that was to grow to scandalous proportions. During the papal residence at Avignon, it became the mainstay of the Camera, and any prelate who received appointment to office paid for it dearly. The benefice taxes were basically of two kinds: common services and petty services. The separate Camerae of the pope and the Curia divided the common services (the amount of service being fixed at one-third the annual income of the benefice), and their officials and servants received the petty services. In addition to the services, the prelate had to pay the sacra, which was divided among the officials of the papal Camera and amounted to one-twentieth the amount of common service.

A fixed list of the income of the various benefices was maintained by the Camera, and the amount of services was reckoned from this, being raised or lowered as the value of the benefice fluctuated. The total amount for common services between the years 1334 and 1378 was 1,097,957 gold florins, or an average of nearly 25,000 florins annually. In the ten-year period from 1316 to 1326, the total number of obligations recorded was 669, and these yielded the enormous sum of 897,545 gold florins. The largest amount promised was 168,105 florins in 1317. In the event that an incumbent to a benefice died before paying the tax in full, his successor was charged with the deficit. In 1370, Archbishop Frederick Scarweden promised Urban V the sum of 123,-000 gulden, a sum which included the services of his four predecessors.

In 1328, John XXII in public audience announced that excommunication, suspension, or interdict had been imposed on one patriarch, five archbishops, thirty bishops, and forty-six abbots for failure to make "servitia" payments. Between the years 1365 and 1368, seven archbishops, forty-nine bishops, one hundred and twenty-five abbots, and some minor officials were excommunicated for failure to pay.

The common services constituted the largest source of income for the Avignon popes. The burden bore heavily on the higher clergy, and it became customary for them to borrow large sums of money to meet their payments. Pluralities, absenteeism, reservations, and simony are some of the major abuses which, aside from the scandal of the excessive rates, arose from the practice of paying for benefices. The evil was denounced by the best men in the Church as contributing generously to the moral degeneration of the papacy and the higher clergy. Another charge that fell directly upon the prelates was the visitation tax rendered to the Apostolic and curial Camera on the occasion of an ad limina visit to Rome. This tax was not a large amount, nor was payment required for every visit.

In the fourteenth century and thereafter, the annates became significant papal revenues. Briefly, in their final form they were designated as a portion of the first year's revenues from a benefice after its vacancy was filled by the pope. The annates were thus confined to benefices filled by papal provision. John XXII (called the Father of Annates) in 1317 reserved for the papacy for a space of three years the first year's income of all vacant benefices which yielded an annual income of over six silver marks. The same pope systematized the collection of annates by sending his own official collectors to all Christian lands to gather the tax under pain of papal censure.

Closely associated with the annates was the *fructus medii temporis,* income from vacant bishoprics and abbacies, which by prior custom had been appropriated by prelates and kings. This tax was to be reserved for the papal treasury as long as the benefices remained vacant.

Some of the Avignon pontiffs wished to curb both the annates and the *fructus medii,* while others exploited them to the full. For instance, it often happended that a bishopric might become vacant two or three times during a year, an abuse exemplified in 1374 when Gregory XI, by a series of shifts, was able to collect annates four different times from the same benefice. At other times a bishopric might remain vacant for even longer periods. In this way, Benedict XII is reported to have realized an enormous income, allowing some benefices to be unoccupied during his entire pontificate. At one time he was receiving the *fructus medii* from three hundred and thirty benefices.

The *jus spolii*, like the annates and *fructus medii,* also developed during the so-called Babylonian Captivity at Avignon and was steered away from the bishoprics and into the papal coffers. It was the right of the prelate to appropriate all or a portion of the personal property of deceased ecclesiastics who had been under his jurisdiction. At first the pontiffs reserved the right to confiscate the temporal goods only of the clerics who died in the state of the Holy See, but the right of spoils was gradually extended, and in 1362 Urban V reserved for his entire pontificate the right of appropriating "all movable goods and credits of prelates, rectors and other ecclesiastical persons who died anywhere except in France and England." His successors made no exceptions, and during the fourteenth century spoils constituted one of the most considerable sources of revenue and also one of the most odious.

Another source of income was the payment of procurations. Originally a form of hospitality given to bishops, papal nuncios, legates, and other dignitaries when they visited an area under their jurisdiction, the practice developed a mercenary aspect. With the advent of money, it became a system of cash payments. The papacy profited when it granted prelates the privilege of collecting procurations by deputies. From the amount received, a portion, usually one-half, was given to the pope. Innocent VI, in 1355, ordered papal collectors in several countries to visit the Churches, make any needed reforms, and collect the procurations which would have been due the bishop for each visit. Procurations from certain districts were also reserved for the popes. Such practices led to laxity in clerical discipline because bishops, since they no longer received procurations, ceased visiting their dioceses.

In the later Middle Ages, recipients of certain kinds of absolutions, dispensations, and indulgences made payments, called compositions, to the pope for these favors. The amount of composition was reached by an agreement struck between the Cameral official and the petitioner. The compositions were associated with penitential discipline, excommunications, interdictions, dispensations from vows, and restitution for ill-gotten goods.

Such were the scope and variety of the papal revenues. Although there is some justification in the fact that the pope was temporal ruler of an extensive state and governments do not function without revenue, unquestionably the papal demands were at times excessive and burdensome. The vast and efficient system of financial operations drew resentment from many quarters.

From the descriptions of the revenues given above, it is evident that most of the burden fell on the clergy; however, the taxes came ultimately out of the pockets of the faithful. Both shared a common hatred for the numerous extractions, with the result that in the later Middle Ages we find an anticlerical laity and a national-minded clergy.

The Question of the Church's Constitution

Of the Church during the Avignon period, it was said that every spiritual favor, every privilege, exacted a fee and every service and appointment required a payment, for each had a current market value in gold. As Tawney says, "Men felt with considerable justice that the papacy was too little interested in the business of saving souls and too much concerned with that of extracting money from its constituents." The abuses associated with the deep involvement of the papacy in fiscal matters was one of the causes of the Protestant Revolution.

Two voices were raised against the secularization of the papacy during the Avignon period, both of which were to shake the medieval church to its very foundations: the English Franciscan William of Occam (d.1350) and a former chancellor of the University of Paris, Marsilius of Padua (d.1343). Both entertained views of the Church that were in opposition to prevailing concepts.

For William of Occam, the Church was a community of believers, with a basic structure that is outlined in the Church of the Apostles. Rejecting the claim of canon lawyers as true interpreters of the Gospel, he relegated the role of the pope to that of an executor of laws already approved by the universal Church. He can in no way create a new article of faith. "No truth," he writes, "is Catholic unless it has been divinely revealed, either by it being inserted into the Scriptures or because it has become known through the certainty of the universal Church." Placing the pope above all positive law in temporal matters is tantamount to reducing Christian law, the law of liberty, to a binding custom of slavery. Such an interpretation of papal power would bring about greater servitude than did the law of Moses. Occam insisted that the choice of the pope actually rested with the entire body of the faithful, especially with the people of Rome. His election by the College of Cardinals was nothing more than the exercise of delegated authority, justified by its usefulness and hence revocable in case of emergency.

Although Occam accepted the monarchic authority of the pope over the Church as necessary for securing the salvation of souls and the government of the faithful, he maintained that the pope's power was ministerial rather than dominational in that it was to serve only the spiritual needs of the faithful. The popes, he claimed, had overextended the rights they falsely attributed to the Petrine commission. The difficulties afflicting the Church of his day had arisen from the fact that the Roman pontiffs had gone beyond their own province of operation and, as he saw it, had even stretched out their hands to what was not rightfully theirs. The "whatever you bind" phrase in the words to St. Peter had to be understood with limitations and exceptions.

Far more revolutionary in his denunciation of the medieval Church was Marsilius of Padua. The *Defensor Pacis,* which he published in 1324, has been described as the most remarkable literary product of the Middle Ages and hailed as comprising "the whole essence of the political and religious theory which separates modern times from the Middle Ages." Supported with arguments from Aristotle and the Scripture, Marsilius contends that the papal claims to complete ecclesiastical jurisdiction are actually a perversion of the ideas of the state as an autonomous body.

For Marsilius, the Church is a purely spiritual and sacramental community, its members united in a common faith and the sharing of sacramental rites. Like the state, it is dependent on a meshing of various parts and functions. Relying heavily on Aristotelian concepts of the state, Marsilius attacks the sharp dichotomy of the papalists between the lay and the cleric. Each cleric or layman is a citizen with inherent rights to participate in those affairs that affect society as a whole. The important question is not whether a person is ordained, but whether he is a citizen using his reasoning powers in matters affecting his religious belief. The choice of laymen to serve in councils would permit their superior intellectual and moral qualities to offset the ignorance and selfishness of certain members of the clergy. As a multitude of persons, the Church really demands no supreme leader, but it is advantageous to have an arbiter in matters of theology. Practical government should be relegated to local bishops and priests, and religious sanctions such as excommunication and suspension should be ignored, since the priesthood has no coercive power.

For Marsilius, coercive jurisdiction over all men, whether priests or laymen, the appointment and approval of persons, and the institution of all offices belong to the authority of the faithful human legislator and certainly not to any individual priest or college of priests as such. The Roman bishop's position in his system is that of an administrator executing the wishes of the general body of Christians. A representative council of all Christians would be the supreme authority in the definition and prescription of secular and religious matters as well. The principal authority (mediate or immediate) to determine the meaning of ambiguous statements in Holy Scripture belongs only to a general council or to those to whom it has been delegated by the corporation of faithful Christians.

The reluctant return of the pope to Rome in 1378 did little to alleviate the troubles that were now affecting Christianity.

In April of that year, the College of Cardinals, still predominately French, elected the archbishop of Bari, Bartolomeo Prignano, to the chair of Peter. Yet within a few months the same body declared his election null and void and proclaimed a new pope, who took the name of Clement VII. Historians still dispute the cause of the Great Schism that followed. Some see it as the result of the two contending forces of the later Middle Ages, the new spirit of nationalism and the old spirit of international solidarity which had formed the basis of Catholicism. Others trace it to the general decadence and lack of spiritual ideals that had characterized the papal court at Avignon—a court that St. Catherine of Siena had described as having a stench worse than that of hell. Yet the basic issue that was raised by the schism grew directly out of the extreme claims to the fullness of power that went back to the Hildebrandian reform. The problem was one of conflicting ideologies as to the correct governing of the Church. Was it—as had been so often declared by Gregory and his successors—an absolute rule, or was it a limited and constitutional oligarchy? Were the cardinals merely an advisory and electoral body, or did they constitute the real government of the Church, with the pope merely an executive officer?

With the dilemma of two popes whose claim to absolute authority kept them above the authority of any other power and a college of aristocratic cardinals whose oligarchical orientation would countenance submission to none outside their own ranks, churchmen faced a difficult problem. They turned to a theory which, since the twelfth century, had been developed by canon lawyers, that of conciliarism. It was basically a theory that envisioned the Church as a vast corporation composed of head and members which performed joint functions, but each of which possessed its own rights and duties. According to this theory, the pope is not the sole depository of all power in the Church, but rather authority extends also to the members. The entire body of the faithful, through the election of the pope by cardinals, transfer this right to these representatives, who, should the pope fail in matters of faith, are obliged to rescind this transfer.

The term *Church,* then, has both a general and a special

meaning. There is a distinction between the Universal and the Apostolic Church. The Universal Church is made up of various members: Greeks, Latins, men and women, cleric and lay, constituting one body which is called Catholic. The head of the body, the Universal Church, is Christ alone. In the Church are the seven sacraments and man's entire salvation. It has never erred, never suffered schism, and can neither deceive nor be deceived. The other Church is the Apostolic or private Church which is included in the Catholic Church. This Church has far less authority than the Universal Church. It embodies the instrumental and the operative functions of the Church Universal and exercises its power of binding and loosing. It cannot, however, have greater authority than that which is granted to it by the Universal Church.

A number of theologians—Henry Langenstein, Dietrich von Niem, and Jean de Gerson among them—refined this theory to the point of subjecting the pope to the judgment and legislation of the only true representative of the Universal Church, a general council.

It was the conciliarist group that finally solved the great dilemma of having two papal claimants by electing at the Council of Constance, in a compromise method which included lay voters, Martin V as the new pope. Two important pieces of legislation, aimed at avoiding future schisms by curtailing the authority of the pope, were proclaimed by the council. The decree *Haec Sancta* of April 6, 1415, expresses the views of the conciliarist movement:

This holy synod of Constance, constituting a general council, lawfully assembled to bring about the end of the present schism and the union and reformation of the Church of God in the Holy Spirit, in order that it may achieve more readily, safely, amply, and freely, the union and reformation of the Church of God, does hereby ordain, ratify, enact, decree, and declare the following: It declares that being lawfully assembled in the Holy Spirit, constituting a general council and representing the Catholic Church militant, it has its power directly from Christ, and that all persons of whatever rank, even the pope, are bound to obey it in matters relating to faith and the end of the schism, and the general reformation of the Church of God in head and members.[15]

A cursory examination of this famous document shows that the expression *represent* as taken in context had neither a dogmatic nor a judicial meaning. Rather it strongly implied the notion as the Church vicariously present, in the more primitive sense as the assembly of the elect of God, the Biblical Holy People. The extreme monarchial view of the papalists who had come to identify the pope with the Church, as well as entirely spiritual notions of the Church as recently advocated by Wycliffe and Huss, were avoided. Nor was the Church here envisioned as a purely democratic institution. The corporate nature of the Church as composed of body and members is explicitly stated, although led by the Holy Spirit; in her external and organizational form she is directed by the assembled council with its episcopal make-up. Perhaps the most important feature of this decree is that it not only emphasizes the importance of the episcopate but also silently rules out the theory of the cardinals' constituting the governing body of the Church. The notion of the collegiality of bishops would find adherents again in the seventeenth century in France. It would be revised in the Second Vatican Council of our own day.

In order to establish within the framework of the Church's constitution a permanent instrument of conciliar control, the council also issued a decree entitled *Frequens*. Its purpose was to subject the central apparatus of the Church to periodically convened assemblies which would keep in check the unreasonable claims of the papacy as well as insure reform. In other words, the decree gave to the general council the same type of parliamentary control over the pope that was emerging at that time in the national states of Europe. It read as follows:

> The frequent holding of general councils is the best method of cultivating the field of the Lord, for they root out the briars, thorns, and thistles of heresies, errors, and schisms, correct abuses, make crooked things straight, and prepare the Lord's vineyard for fruitfulness and rich fertility. Neglect of general

councils sows the seeds of these evils and encourages their growth. This truth is borne in upon us as we recall times past and survey the present.

Therefore by perpetual edict we affirm, enact, decree, and ordain that henceforth general councils shall be held as follows: the first within five years immediately following the end of the present council, the second within seven years from the end of the council next after this, and subsequently every ten years forever, in places which the supreme pontiff a month before the close of the previous council with the council's approval and consent, shall name, or failing him, the council itself shall appoint and designate. Thus there will always be a certain continuity. Either a council will be in session or one will be expected at the end of a fixed period. This period, the supreme pontiff, on the advice of his bretheren, the cardinals of the Holy Roman Church, may shorten in case of emergency but on no account prolong. Nor may he change the place set for the meeting of the approaching council, except for reasons of obvious necessity.

In case of an emergency, such as siege, war, pestilence, or something similar, when it seems imperative to change this place, then the supreme pontiff, with the signed consent of his said brethren or two-thirds of them, may substitute another place near the spot first selected, convenient and inside the same nation, unless the same or a similar calamity affects the whole nation. In that event he may call the council at some near and convenient place inside another nation. The prelates and others who are habitually summoned to a council shall be required to attend just as if that place had been the fixed one from the beginning. Any change of place or shortening of the period must be legally and formally published and announced by the supreme pontiff a year before the data set for the council, so that members can assemble to hold it at the time he appoints.[16]

Although the new pope, Martin V, approved of the decrees of Constance insofar as "they favored the faith and salvation of souls" and did in compliance with the decree *Frequens* call for a council at Pavia in 1423, it was obvious that the papacy was determined to carry on its struggle against conciliarism.

Because of pestilence, the new council was poorly attended and terminated the following year. In 1431 Martin's successor suspended the next general council at Basel and transferred it to Florence. It was at Basel, however, that conciliarism reached its highest development, and perhaps the finest expression of this theory of the Church as the people of God was drawn up by the German cleric Nicholas of Cusa (d.1464). He was one of the greatest minds of the fifteenth century and is often heralded as the founder of modern philosophical thought. In a work published during the council entitled *De Concordantia Catholica* (*On Catholic Concord*), Cusa outlined a theory which viewed the Church as a divine cosmos from the head of which, Christ, grace flowed into humanity through the hierarchy.

The hierarchy is a general priesthood in which the pope, bishops, and even simple priests participate. However, since men are by nature free, it is only with their consent that ecclesiastical leaders and their laws can have any acceptance. It is by this consent of the faithful that bishops represent the diocese and the council represents the entire Church. The pope and the bishops are equally the successors of Peter and have essentially the same power; the graduation of powers in the Church is thus a matter of use or execution. The primacy of the pope is, for Cusa, not a matter of jurisdiction. The pope is not a universal bishop, but rather takes precedence over bishops as an administrator who acts for the good of the entire body of the faithful. Infallibility and supreme power belong therefore to a general council which in turn derives its authority from Christ when it represents the unanimous agreement of all Christians. Hence the council, although convened by the pope, does not depend on him and may in fact depose him if he is guilty of heresy. The decisions of the council do not demand the approval of the pope, but on the contrary are binding upon him. The basic difference between the legislation of a council and the decrees of the pope is that the former is already law, while the latter demand conciliar approval to give them validity. Since Cusa shared the current opinion that many of the abuses in the Church were due to the usurpation of authority by the pope, it was his plan to render this misuse impossible by giving wider powers to the College of Cardinals. The college was to be more international in its make-up, and it was to be chosen with the consent of the bishops. As a further curtailment of papal power, he recommended the restoration of the rights of the metropolitans and the patriarchies of the early Church.

In spite of the abortive attempts of the conciliarists to reform the constitution of the Church, the fifteenth century witnessed a continual struggle between those who had defended the extreme monarchist view of the papacy and those who had wished to democratize and federalize it. In 1460 Pope Pius II published a decree aimed at eliminating the "deadly poison" of conciliarism from the Church's organism by forbidding under pain of excommunication any future appeal from the pope to a council. The prohibition was repeated by Pope Sixtus IV in 1483 and by Pope Julius II in 1509. Ironically, it was from among the members of the reformed monastic groups, especially the Carthusians, that the loudest denunciation of the pope's refusal to submit to a council arose. The Carthusian Vincent of Aggsbach urged that the bishops of the Church convene a council in spite of the pope's opposition. He argued that it is not right that the wickedness of a small party should be a hindrance to the general good of the Church. "The experience of fifty years teaches us that the Roman Curia avoids the idea of the council as a plague, for it will be called to account for its evil practices." Even more strongly worded was the complaint of another Carthusian, Jacob of Jutterbog, who wrote in 1449:

From the reform councils, it is quite clear that the doctrine of papal supremacy is only a shield behind which the Italians and their party shelter themselves from reform. Even were the pope well intentioned, one can honestly say that the resistance of the people who surround him often is such that a reform of the Church cannot be accomplished by the pope alone. It demands an effort by the entire Church convened in a council. Everything must be done to insure the execution of the decree *Frequens*. By this means the injury inflicted on the Church by Eugene IV may perhaps be healed.

The popular piety of the century before the Reformation reflects the anxiety of a Catholic world dismayed by the schism and by the struggle between the conciliarists and the curialists and grown tired of the intricate, complicated arguments of the schoolmen. For many, religion had become a matter of urgency and pathos. In a sort of anguished uncertainty, the faithful clutched at whatever external object they could identify with temporal and spiritual security. The very elaboration and multiplication of devotional practices led many to lose sight of what underlay them. The result was a strange mixture of faith and irreverence, ceremonial usage and immorality. There was an overdose of what the great spiritual writer of the century, Jean de Gerson, called melancholy imagination. In art, the central themes were the sufferings of Christ, the Last Judgment, and the sorrowing Virgin. The paintings of Grünewald and Bosch reflect an almost brutal realism in delineating sufferings. The Dance of Death was a constant reminder to the faithful of the imminence of death and the swift passage of worldly honors. In many cases, rather than turning to what the imagery in painting and sculpture only symbolized, the people venerated the representation of the objects themselves.

It was against this background that one of the most influential religious movements in the late medieval period, the *Devotio Moderna,* or New Devotion, developed. Identified with the Flemish priest Gerhard Groot and spread by the community he founded, the Brothers of the Common Life, the devotion was fundamentally a living protest against the decadent monasticism and sterile theology of the times. The Brothers and their disciples nurtured a more personal faith in Christ, the Christ of the Bible, and a more rational approach to self-discipline. Rejecting the need for monastic vows and scorning religious formalism, the movement was to a great extent aimed at what would be called today a lay apostolate. The schools conducted by the Brothers influenced many of the great religious reformers of the following century: Erasmus, Luther, Calvin, and Loyola. Perhaps the finest example of the spirituality fostered by the New Devotion is the *Imitation of Christ* by Thomas a Kempis. The following excerpts from this work, which, next to the Bible, has been over the centuries since its composition one of the most widely read treatises on lay piety, will show how its author scorns the dialectics of the schoolmen and urges his reader to a more intimate and personal relationship with the Almighty. Nowhere in the work is there reference to religious vows, and the institutional Church is generally ignored:

A happy man is one whom truth teaches by itself, not by figures and words that pass, but as it is in itself. (Ps. 17:36; Is. 28:26)

Our opinion and sense often deceive us and we learn little. Of what use are great disputes about deep and obscure matters when we shall not be questioned concerning them on judgment day? It makes little sense for us to neglect profitable and necessary things and willingly concern ourselves with those things which are curious and harmful. We have eyes, but do not perceive clearly. (Ps. 65)

Why should we concern ourselves about philosophical terms? He to whom the eternal Word speaks is set at liberty from many opinions. All things are from one Word, and all things speak of this Word, and this Word is the beginning which speaks to us. Without this Word no one understands or judges rightly. He to whom all things are one, and draws all things to one and sees all things in one, may have a peaceful heart and repose peaceably in God. (1 Cor.:22) O Truth! My God make me one with you in eternal love. (John 17:22) I am wearied by the frequent reading and hearing of many things; in you are all things I want and desire. Let all teachers hold their peace, and let all creatures be silent in your presence, and may only you speak to me.

The more a man is one and simple within himself, the more he is able to understand more higher things without labor because he receives understanding from above. A pure, simple, steady spirit is not wasted away by many affairs because he does them for the honor of God, and tries to be at peace within himself, and free from all selfishness.

What can be a greater hindrance and trouble to you than your own unmortified affection of heart? A good and devout man first disposes inwardly the works which he is to do externally. Neither do they draw him to the desires of many temptations, but he turns them to the rule of right reason. Who could have a stronger conflict than one who strives to overcome himself? And this should be our task to overcome ourselves, and daily gain strength over ourselves, and steadily improve each day.

All perfections in this life bring with them some imperfections, and all our speculations have some obscurity. Humble knowledge of oneself is a surer way to God than the deepest search for science. Neither learning, nor the mere knowledge of anything which is good in itself and ordained by God is to be blamed. But a good conscience and a virtuous life are always preferable. But because many people concern themselves with knowledge rather than living well, they are often deceived, and bring forth little or no fruit at all. If men would use as much diligence in rooting out vices and planting virtues as they do in proposing questions, there would not be so many great evils committed, and so much scandal among people, nor so much laziness in monasteries.

Truthfully then, at the day of the Last Judgment we shall not be examined on what we read, but on what we have done. Neither will we be judged on how learnedly we have spoken, but on how religiously we have lived. Tell me, where are all those great doctors you knew while they were living and flourishing in their learning? Now their places are filled by others, and I doubt if they even remember those that went before them. While they lived they seemed to be important, but now they are not spoken of.

Oh, how quickly the glory of the world passes away! (1 John 2:17) If their lives had been answerable to their learning, they would have studied and learned well. How many people in the world perish because of vain learning and little care for the service of God! Many are lost in their own imagination because they chose to be great instead of humble. He who is great in charity is truly great.

He who is small in his own eyes, and does not seek glory is truly great. He who is truly prudent looks upon all earthly things as naught compared to gaining Christ. (Phil. 3:8) And he who renounces his own will and does God's will is truly learned.[17]

The Reformation

The Reformation of the sixteenth century can be said to mark the greatest crisis that Catholicism had faced since the persecutions of Diocletian and Decius. For the first time since its victory over Arianism, the idea of Catholic as interchangeable with Church was successfully challenged. By the middle of the sixteenth century that part of Christian Europe that could still be called Catholic embraced less territory than that ruled by Gregory the Great almost a thousand years before. Not a few, even among those who still gave allegiance to the Church of Rome, looked to the religious upheaval as marking the end of Catholicism as a universal religion.

Although the causes of the Protestant Reformation have been more discussed by historians than the Reformation itself, it must be admitted that the events that separated most of northern Europe from Rome were to be found more in an antecedent breakdown of charity than in divergencies concerning matters of faith. To define the Reformation as the breakup of a universal Christian faith overlooks the fact that a division had already occurred because of a collapse of faith's first fruit, fraternal charity.

The Great Schism, the immorality and secular interests of the Renaissance papacy, the rise of the national state, may all be listed as causes of the Reformation. Yet what underlay them was the undeniable fact that the Catholicism of the late Middle Ages became the object of a growing scrutiny that questioned whether the form it had taken, as a result of the medieval synthesis, was the form intended by Christ. It was not only a challenge to the Constantinian concept of the Church, which had envisioned itself as a political entity, but also a questioning of the entire theological direction that, with the introduction of Greek and Arabian philosophy, had severed much of its dogmatic thought from earlier Christological moorings. For many it seemed that the institution formed in response to the needs of the violent barbarian age was no longer fulfilling its role as a mediator between Christ and man. A preoccupation with rights and privileges rather than spiritual needs and evangelical values had paralyzed the institutional Church from top to bottom. For others—and this had been and continues to be to the present day the complaint of the Byzantine Church—the Church in the West had sacrificed the inner realities of the Christian message to the interests of a particular civilization. It had failed to perceive that Christianity has a horizontal as well as a vertical dimension.

The increase in population, the advent of technology, the strengthening of national governments, and the emergence of a new money economy were changes that the official Church often seemed to ignore. The Renaissance papacy, in spite of abortive efforts to arouse Europe to the threat of advancing Islam, seemed to have withdrawn from the real issues of the day.

Yet the revolt that occurred cannot be placed entirely at the feet of the papacy. Its causes are attributable to the tensions that pervaded the entire superstructure of Catholicism long before Luther sounded the call to reform. There were tensions between the College of Cardinals and the pope and between the higher and the lower clergy. Strained relations between the secular clergy and the religious orders were surpassed only by the growing and scandalous enmity between the various religious orders themselves, especially the Dominicans and the Franciscans. In addition, an ever increasing anticlericalism was reaching a breaking point. Finally there was a widespread feeling of anti-Romanism in all of northern Europe that identified the recent vicissitudes of Catholicism, the Babylonian Captivity, the Great Schism, and the obnoxious fiscal policies of the papacy with the Italian and Latin element in the Church. Since the return of the popes to Rome, the central apparatus of the Church had become increasingly Latinized and commercialized.

Even when the break did occur with the appearance of the Augustinian monk Martin Luther (d.1546), his action was welcomed by many sincere Catholics as the only alternative to avoiding the complete destruction of Christendom in the West. A cursory glance at some of the proposals of his first reformatory writing may startle the modern-day Catholic. In his condemning of the widespread belief that indulgence be understood as the forgiveness of sin, he was in complete agreement with many contemporary theologians, including his first papal adversary, the Dominican General Cajetan. His recommendation that the College of Cardinals be reduced to twelve in number and that the Roman Curia be limited to one-hundredth of its present size were but echoes of the suggestions of the fifteenth-century reformers. The abolition of papal taxes and reservations also has a familiar ring to anyone acquainted with the reform proposals of the conciliarists. The liturgical changes he advanced, namely, the use of the vernacular, the abolition of the private Mass, and the granting of the Chalice to the laity, were also recommended by many sincere Catholics of the time. Even more in agreement with him were were those who recommended the abolition of enforced clerical celibacy, since it was the greatest single cause of sacerdotal immorality.

Yet his eventual rejection of the papacy and his new doctrine on the nature of justification and the role of Scripture in the economy of salvation gave birth to a concept of the Church which rendered papal supremacy, the authority of the hierarchy, and a distinct priesthood superfluous. Justification was no longer considered an objective transformation of the soul, but rather an ethical process. Man as a sinner was accepted by God in view of the merits of Christ without any objective sanctification through sanctifying grace. It was a view of faith that deprived good works of merit and reduced the sacraments to mere symbols. For Luther, justification, man's salvation, was the result of faith, an experience of which God alone was the author. It was an awareness of the forgiveness of sin by a merciful God because of Christ's merits and without any necessary dependence on a sacrament.

The problem of how man was justified was not a new one. Since the time of Augustine, when in opposition to the Pelagians he had worked out the gratuitousness of man's salvation, the theme of justification had never ceased to occupy the theologians of the West. For the early scholastics, the justifying element consisted in faith and charity, and these concepts were understood by them in a purely Biblical sense. However, after the introduction of

Aristotle, the scholastics formulated a concept of grace as a supernatural habitus of the soul—in other words, a quality within the soul that produces a wholly supernatural participation in the divine nature. For the reformer, however, grace was to be understood simply as the favor of God, a complete gratuity. Thus Luther writes, commenting on St. Paul's letter to the Romans: "The scholastic theologians imagine that original sin is like actual sin, entirely removed, as if sins were something that could be moved in the flick of an eyelash as darkness is by light. They followed the method of Aristotle in his *Ethics* and he bases sinfulness and justification and the extent on their actualization on what a person does."

Evident in Luther's rejection of the traditional doctrine of the Church is the influence of nominalism. This system of theology, often referred to as the *via moderna* (the modern method), as opposed to the older scholasticism, was in many ways an evangelical reaction against the influence of Aristotelian thought in Christian doctrine. It urged the reform of theology conceived more as a discipline of faith founded on the Bible and the tradition of the early Fathers. Its basic tenet was that the omnipotence of God, if properly understood, renders deductive theology impossible. The absolute power of God goes beyond any route that theologians, using a few scraps of revealed information, may devise to circumscribe it. It questioned the sacramental system as the only way that God could confer grace. It reopened the whole problem of the relationship between the Gospel and tradition as understood in antiquity. As a consequence, the idea that the Church could create doctrine independently of what was contained in the New Testament came under criticism.

For William of Occam and Gabriel Biel (d.1495), both of whom influenced Luther, there can be no direct proportion between God's reward and the status of man. God is in no way obliged to reward man. He can in no way be any man's debtor, as this would deny His absolute omnipotence. Since God accepts man and his works as worthy of heaven, there is no need for a habitus. God can accept man without this particular quality. In short, God can take the sinner as a sinner into His favor and justify him. Christ's justice alone is capable of filling the chasm that separates God and the sinner. Since man is utterly corrupt, justification is exclusively God's work. Flowing from this assumption is a denial of the treasury of the Church and its role as a dispenser of sacramental graces.

The incredible rapidity with which this doctrine, modified by men like Calvin and Zwingli, spread throughout all of northern Europe in itself attests to the dissatisfaction of so many with the practices of late medieval Catholicism. Political intervention, it is true, played a significant role in this diffusion, but the alluring simplicity of the Protestant message, and especially its answer to the doubts and anxieties entertained by many religious-minded Catholics, must be considered a factor in explaining its immediate success. By the fourth decade of the sixteenth century, all of Scandinavia, the British Isles, and much of Germany, Austria, and France had separated from the communion of Rome. Yet in spite of the fact that Luther had called for a general council of the Church to examine his doctrine and as late as 1535 had informed the papal legate Vergerio that he would not attend such a council to defend it, it was not until 1545 that the pope finally convened a general council to counter the spread of this new heresy.

The reasons for the delay on the part of the papacy were for the most part political. The pope as a temporal ruler was caught between the territorial aspirations of the Hapsburgs and the king of France. Conciliarism, the threat of convening a council independently of the pope, was still a strong weapon in the hands of the European powers. There were good grounds for believing that should a council be successfully summoned by the heads of the national governments, the Roman Curia and eventually the papacy itself would be abolished. The possibility that a temporal power might reduce the pope to a mere court chaplain was as great under Charles V as it had been under the earlier Hohenstaufen emperors.

A further cause for delay was that the new ideas preached by Luther and his followers were not at first diagnosed as being radically opposed to traditional Catholic doctrine. They were all the outgrowth of late medieval speculation on grace, Scripture, and the role of the political papacy in man's redemption. Luther was looked upon as a sincere reformer who was merely voicing a dissatisfaction with contemporary Catholicism that had been in vogue for centuries.

It was not until the election of Pope Paul III in 1534 that any real hope for the convocation of a council to arrest the spread of Protestantism was realized. Paul soon gathered about him a group of sincere reformers, for the most part humanists—Contarini, Caraffa, Sadoleto, and Pole—whom he commissioned to draw up a plan for the elimination of ecclesiastical abuse. The resulting document, entitled *Consilum de Emendanda Ecclesia,* largely the work of Gaspar Contarini, a layman recently made cardinal, shows how deeply Catholics of the time, even in the College of Cardinals, felt that the future of Catholicism depended on the cleansing of the Roman Curia.

The document attacked the fiscal policies of the Roman Curia and insisted that the realization of the Apostolic ideal of pastoral office would remain an impossibility unless there was a radical change in the Curia's administrative system. The abuses in the Church, it pointed out, were due to the fact that the pope had surrounded himself with a group of flatterers who had exaggerated the notion of papal power. "Certain popes had been led to imagine that their will was law." It also recommended that for the good of the Christian religion the number of mendicant orders be reduced or allowed to die out. So radical were the proposals that one of the leading figures in the Curia protested that they would lead not to the reform of the Church but to her disruption. They would produce revolution rather than reformation. Yet a revolution had already taken place in the Christian commonwealth of the Middle Ages. Another decade was to pass before a general council was successfully summoned. By this time the protestantization of much of northern Europe was an accomplished fact.

When the much-delayed council finally convened in the city of Trent in 1545, its attendance was hardly impressive. There were less than forty bishops present, and most of these were Italians. There was a long debate over whether the council was "representative of the universal Church." There was a fear that the formula still smacked of conciliarism. Also hotly argued was the issue of whether the council should give priority treatment to disciplinary matters rather than dogmatic questions. To define new dogma rather than reform the Church ran the risk of permanently separating most of northern Europe from Catholicism. A compromise was finally reached which led to a decision early in 1546 to deal simultaneously with the two main tasks before the council: the redefinition of Catholic dogma and the reform of the Church.

Among the twenty-one general councils of the Church, if we include the Second Vatican Council, the Council of Trent is unquestionably the most important in the shaping of Catholicism. By comparison with previous and subsequent councils its numerical strength is not an important factor. The Council of Chalcedon numbered 630 participants, the first Vatican over 700, and the third session of the second Vatican over 2,000 participants. Even the duration of the council from 1545 to 1563 is not as impressive as it may seem, since it was suspended from 1548 to 1551 and from 1552 to 1561. Yet in terms of disciplinary decrees and its clarification of Catholic dogma, it did more to refine and articulate what is today held as the basic doctrine of Catholicism than any other council in the history of the Church.

Its decrees on faith were the definitive and authoritative answers of the Catholic Church to the erroneous doctrines of Luther, Zwingli, Calvin, and their disciples. The nature of the sacraments, especially Confession and the Sacrifice of the Mass, which form the backbone of present Catholic religious practices, also found their final exposition and definition at Trent. There is a great deal of truth in the observation that had Trent's decree on justification been decreed at the Lateran Council at the beginning of the sixteenth century, the Reformation would not have occurred and the religious unity of the Middle Ages would have endured.

The decrees on justification are unique in the history of dogma for their brevity and completeness. They have been described as the most impressive codification of the teaching on grace of the Golden Age of Scholasticism, handed down as a precious heritage of the Middle Ages. One searches in vain in earlier patristic or scholastic literature for a more definite or more satisfactory explanation of the most important question in the Christian religion: How is man saved? Furthermore, the decrees countered the Renaissance notion of man as the center of the universe with the more traditional conviction which assigns that position to God. They avoid both the danger of Pelagianism, excluding the supernatural action of God's grace from the process of salvation, and the extreme position fostered by Protestantism, which excludes the co-operation of man.

The decrees were in fact largely the work of the Augustinian humanist Seripando, who had often been suspected by his colleagues of being a Lutheran. However, it is unfair to describe them as the lowest multiple of scholastic thought. They avoid the scholastic jargon detested by the reformers and thus open the gate for a possible compromise with Protestantism.

The decrees serve a threefold purpose. They expose the sinner's incapacity to save himself by his own efforts and the absolute gratuitousness of the first justification for which Baptism is required. They then explain the manner of man's co-operation and lay bare the core of Catholic doctrine on justification, namely, that the remission of sin is also a sanctification and renewal of the whole man. Finally they underscore the fact that a union of the justified with Christ is the basis for the meritoriousness of man's good works. They thus dispel once and for all the misunderstanding that the Catholic concept of faith prejudiced the mediatorship of Christ and his universal efficaciousness.

The following excerpts from Trent sum up the present position of the Church on justification:

> Herewith is given a brief description of the justification of the sinner, as being a translation from that state in which man is born a child of the first Adam, to the state of grace and the adoption of the sons of God through the second Adam, Jesus Christ, our Savior. However, this translation cannot, since the promulgation of the Gospel, be effected except through the cleansing water of regeneration or its desire as it is written:

Unless a man be born again of water and the Holy Spirit, he cannot enter into the kingdom of God.

Furthermore, it is declared that the beginning of that justification in adults must proceed from the predisposing grace of God through Jesus Christ, from his vocation, whereby without any merits on their part, they are called; that they who by their sins had been cut off from God may be disposed through His enlivening and helping grace to convert themselves to their own justification by freely assenting to and cooperating with that grace; so that, while God touches the heart of man through the illumination of the Holy Spirit, man himself while receiving that inspiration, neither does absolutely nothing since he can reject it, nor is he able by his own free will and without the grace of God to move himself to justice in His sight. Hence when it is said in the sacred writings: Turn ye to me, and I will turn to you, we are reminded of our liberty; and when we reply: Convert us, O Lord, to thee and we shall be converted; we confess that we need the grace of God.

This disposition or preparation is followed by justification itself, which is not only a remission of sin, but also the sanctification and renewal of the inward man through the voluntary reception of the grace and gifts whereby an unjust man becomes just, and from being an enemy becomes a friend, that he may become an heir according to hope of life everlasting. The causes of the justification are: the final cause, which is the glory of God, Christ and life everlasting; the efficient cause, which is the merciful God who washes and sanctifies gratuitously, and who signs and anoints with the Holy Spirit of promise, who is also the pledge of our inheritance; the meritorious cause is His most beloved only begotton, our Lord Jesus Christ, who when we were enemies, for the exceeding charity wherewith He loved us, merited for us justification and charity. Whence also they hear immediately the words of Christ: "If thou wilt enter into life, keep the commandments." Wherefore when receiving true Christian justice and immediately on being born again, they are commanded to preserve it pure and spotless, as the first robe given through Christ Jesus in place of that which Adam by his disobedience lost for himself and for us, so that they may bear it before the tribunal of our Lord Jesus Christ and may have life eternal.

But when the Apostle says that man is justified by faith and freely, these words are to be understood in that sense in which the uninterrupted unanimity of the Catholic Church has held and expressed them, namely that we are said to be justified by faith, in that faith is the beginning of human salvation, the root and foundation of all justification, without which it is impossible to please God and to join the fellowship of His sons; and we are thus said to be justified gratuitously, because none of these things that precede justification, whether faith or works, merit the grace of justification. For, if by grace, it is not now by works, otherwise, as the Apostle says, grace is no more grace.[18]

The question of the number and nature of the sacraments was not difficult for the council Fathers to explain since it had a long-standing tradition dating back to the early Middle Ages and was formulated in the decree for the Armenians at the Council of Florence in 1439. Their septenary number had been stabilized since about the year 1150.

Unlike the decree for the Armenians, which divided the seven sacraments between those that look to the needs of the individual and those that were concerned with the community (Holy Orders and Matrimony), the Tridentine decree merely gives a brief description of the function of the sacraments in the life of the Church as a whole.

There was little new in the exposition on the sacraments. However, the decree on Christian Marriage, *Tametsi*, demanding that Matrimony be performed before a priest and two witnesses and holding invalid any marriages between Protestants and Catholics, gave rise to sociological problems that to this day remain unsolved.

The position of Trent on the nature of the Mass also exhibits a cautious and conservative mentality. Since there was little speculation in the medieval period on the Mass as a sacrifice, it limited itself to merely declaring that it was a sacrifice propitiatory for both the living and the dead:

And inasmuch as in this divine sacrifice which is celebrated in the Mass is contained and immolated in an unbloody manner the same Christ who once offered Himself in a bloody manner on the altar of the cross, the holy council teaches that this is truly propitiatory and has this effect; that if we, contrite and penitent, with sincere heart and upright faith, with fear and reverence, draw nigh to God, we obtain mercy and find grace in seasonable aid. For, appeased by this sacrifice, the Lord grants the grace and gift of penitence and pardons even the gravest crimes and sins. For the victim is one and the same, the same now offering by the ministry of the priests who then offered Himself on the cross, the manner alone of offering being different. The fruits of that bloody sacrifice, it is well understood, are received most abundantly through this unbloody one, so far is the latter from derogating in any way from the former. Wherefore, according to the tradition of the Apostles, it is rightly offered not only for the sins, punishments, satisfactions, and other necessities of the faithful who are living, but also for those departed in Christ but not yet fully purified.

Though the Mass contains much instruction for the faithful, it has, nevertheless, not been deemed advisable by the Fathers that it should be celebrated everywhere in the vernacular tongue. Wherefore, the ancient rite of each Church, approved by the Holy Roman Church, the mother and mistress of all churches, being everywhere retained, that the sheep of Christ may not suffer hunger, or the little ones ask for bread and there is none to break it unto them, the holy council commands pastors and all who have the *cura animarum,* that they either through themselves or through others explain frequently during the celebration of the Mass some of the things read during the Mass, and that among other things they explain some mystery of this most holy sacrifice, especially on Sundays and festival days.[19]

In declaring the objective character of the Sacrifice as something more than just a memorial of the Sacrifice of the Cross and a mere Communion rite, the Council of Trent secured the foundations for later liturgical development. Yet it was a development that was for many centuries the victim of papal conservatism. In 1570 a decree of Pope Pius V binding on the entire Western Church standardized the Mass liturgy. But as the great historian of the Roman Mass, Josef Jungmann, remarks: "The forces of further evolution were often channeled into the narrow bed of a very inadequate devotional life instead of gathering strength for new forms of life." Thus the Roman Mass entered into a condition of rigidity and fixation, and a living liturgy was replaced by rubrics. It was to remain so until the mid-twentieth century.

In addition to its doctrinal decrees, Trent also exercised a profound influence on the future of Catholicism by promulgating a series of regulations aimed at protecting the faithful from the erroneous doctrines of Protestantism, namely, the Index of Forbidden Books and the erection of seminaries for the training of future priests. Although both were intended as temporary measures to prevent the spread of heretical doctrine and to insure a better-educated clergy, both had the end result of cutting off the laity and especially the clergy from the two main streams of intellectual activity, the world of books and the universities. More, perhaps, than the dogmatic formulations of Trent, these protective laws have perpetuated the division in Christianity that began in the sixteenth century.

It is significant that, in the spirit of Trent, St. Thomas Aquinas was in 1567 declared a Doctor of the Church. Scholasticism, which had borne the brunt of the attack from the reformers, was now firmly entrenched. The *Summa* replaced the *Sentences of Peter Lombard* as the basis for theological studies. In the papal bull establishing the perennial philosophy of the great Dominican theologian, not only did the Church herself (as the historian of the popes, Pastor, remarks) "take the science of the Middle Ages under her protection against the hostility of Protestants and even some Catholics, but she also recognized the teachings of Aquinas as the richest fruit of an earlier evolution and as an unperishable treasure. At the same time, she proclaimed that she recognized her own doctrines as that of the Great Schoolman." His doctrine, as Pope Pius V remarked, was, in contrast to all others, "more safe and secure."

The Counter Reformation

Historians still debate whether the Council of Trent was either ecumenical or reformatory, whether it was a final surrender of the episcopacy to the papacy or a return to the true concept of the Church. There can be no doubt, however, that it was in the eyes of those who remained in the papal camp the victorious conclusion of a great antiecclesiastical war that had raged against the papacy since the thirteenth century. It was a triumph over both Conciliarism and Protestantism. Its enactments clearly rejected the collegiality of bishops, on the one hand, and the idea of a spiritual Church with the Sricpture alone as the sole rule of faith, on the other. Its principal enunciations, that traditions as well as Scripture are sources of belief and that the Church alone can interpret both, formed the Magna Charta of future Catholicism. Its insistence that the Church possess a sacramental priesthood with seven Sacraments as efficacious sources of grace, with the Mass at the center, forms what continues to this day to be the basis of most Catholic religious practices.

Perhaps the most powerful means of implementing the decrees of Trent was the newly established order of the Jesuits. Founded by the former soldier Ignatius of Loyola (d.1556) and approved by Pope Paul III in 1540, the Society of Jesus soon became the chief instrument of the Counter Reformation, or, as it is sometimes called, the Catholic Restoration. The order was but one of several new communities formed during the period. Yet it was distinguished from all the others by its rapid expansion, its concept of military obedience, and its complete allegiance to the direction and authority of the papacy. Much more than the monastic and mendicant orders, it was dedicated to a life of activity. The order displayed an almost relentless concern for the salvation of souls. Within fifty years after the death of its founder, the Jesuits numbered over 13,000 members, and the Catholic education of youth as well as candidates for the priesthood in most of Catholic Europe was entrusted to its direction. It is impossible to conceive of the Counter Reformation without the heroic self-sacrifice of its members, who penetrated almost every corner of Christendom to restore and revitalize Catholicism. The Jesuits constitute the largest and most influential religious order in the Catholic Church today.

The price that was paid for the triumph of Trent was a heavy one for Catholicism. Although the papacy was strengthened and centralized—it stood higher at the beginning of the seventeenth century than at any time since the thirteenth century—nevertheless, the loss of most of northern Europe to Protestantism was immeasurable. For it had been the Germanic peoples who had made the greatest contribution to the theology and devotional practice of the medieval Church.

Yet a centrifugal movement toward nationalism and subjectivism continued unabated even in the areas that had remained loyal to the papacy. The two dominant Catholic powers in western Europe, Spain and France, continued to foster particularist interests in opposition to the universal aims of the Church. Gallicanism, a modified form of Conciliarism, reigned supreme in France. Spain, unaffected by the reformers, preferred to go its own way at home and in its New World colonial possessions.

Content in the conviction it had emerged triumphant from its struggle with Protestant sectarianism, Catholicism, during the century after Trent, followed a policy of indifference, if not open hostility, to the mighty intellectual changes that resulted from the new scientific discoveries. Its mood is best described as "triumphalism." It was only gradually that Church officialdom accepted the new cosmologies developed by Kepler and Newton. The condemnation of Galileo and the disapproval of the religious aspects of the Peace of Westphalia are typical of this determination to resist change.

In the realm of theology, the question of the relationship between grace and freedom raised by the reformers remained in the forefront. There are a number of reasons for this. Since the decrees of Trent had set a limit on the range of theological speculation in the dogmatic field, attention was now focused on ethics and casuistry. Furthermore the Tridentine decrees on Confession, with their insistence that all mortal sins be confessed according to their number and species, intensified an interest in moral problems. In directing the clergy to a more pastoral concern for souls and making the confession and forgiveness of sins an important feature of this care, Trent demanded a more precise knowledge of Christian morality. The old schools of philosophical theology—

Scotism, Occamism, and Thomism—were now replaced by a number of moralistic schools identified according to the extent to which they favored human liberty over ecclesiastical law. There was a proliferation of moral systems, entitled absolute tutiorism, mitigated tutiorism, probabilism or aequiprobabilism, compensationism, and laxism, to name a few. Probabilism was and is to this day the most widely accepted of them all.

Since the confessor was concerned primarily with passing judgment on his penitent, it was necessary for him to find a group of principles that would enable him to do so according to universal moral norms while at the same time protecting the freedom of conscience of the penitent. The result was that controversies on the question of what system to choose led to the sterility of the whole moral theological endeavor and to a general disregard for the unique character of Christian morality. Dogma and ethics were gradually separated from their Christological foundations.

The basic principle of probabilism was simple. In all cases where a definite decision was required under conditions which did not admit of full certainty regarding the existence of a law or obligation, a person was allowed to act according to what was termed a *probable* conscience. Yet by many this procedure was seen as a rationalism that tended to attenuate the discrepancy between the ordinary pleasures and practices of the world and the requirements of Christianity. It offered to the man of the world the maximum of indulgence which was compatible with submission to the minimum requirements of the Church. It was often criticized as leading to a relaxation of morals by advocating a double standard of morality. Many non-Catholics saw in it what they considered an intrinsically immoral doctrine of making a fundamental distinction between two classes of sin, mortal and venial—a distinction dependent on the nature of the external act and not the moral guilt it implied.

One of this system's bitterest critics was the French author Blaise Pascal (d.1662), who in his *Provincial Letters* ridiculed the system as being inconsistent with Christianity itself: "We read little of the Fathers. We quote only the new casuists. When you Jesuits arrive, we put away St. Augustine, St. Chrysostom, St.

Jerome and others." In the uncertain political atmosphere of the time, Catholics, and especially the Jesuits, were accused of advocating a system wherein the end justifies the means. The Spanish Jesuit Juan de Mariana startled many of his fellow Catholics by openly advocating tyrannicide on a basis of this principle. In his work *On the Nature of Kingship,* he wrote:

The prince who has seized power with force of arms, and with no legal right or public approval, may be killed by anyone and deprived of his life and position. Since he is a public enemy and afflicts his fatherland with every evil, since he is truly clothed with the title and character of a tyrant, he may be removed by any means and gotten rid of by as much violence as he used in seizing power.

There was an amazing outpouring of texts and manuals that weighed the moral implications of almost every conceivable human act. One casuist of the period, Antonine of Diania, solved over twenty thousand cases in his work on moral principles. Treated by the casuists were such questions as the quantity of meat that could be eaten on Friday without committing a mortal sin, how much of the Mass one could miss on a day of obligation, whether an oath to a Protestant was binding, and so on. A standard manual on moral theology used in present-day Catholicism is typical of this continuing trend. The following treats Mass attendance:

A venial sin is committed by voluntarily omitting an unimportant part of the Mass, e.g., from the beginning of the Mass to the Offertory exclusive, or the part that follows the Communion, or even the part which precedes the Epistle together with that which follows the Communion.

A mortal sin is committed by missing an important part voluntarily, e.g., that which precedes the Gospel together with what follows Holy Communion, the part extending from the beginning of the Mass to the Offertory inclusively, the part of the Canon that precedes the Consecration, or the part between the Consecration and the *Pater Noster,* or the Consecration alone; but probably not the Communion alone. It is held that momentary and necessary withdrawal during the Consecration would be excusable.—Whoever misses an important part must supply this part in a later Mass on the same day.

The obligation to hear Mass is not fulfilled by him who is not present at the Consecration. But if one is present at the entire Mass except the Consecration, it may be presumed that the Church would not oblige him to attend another Mass.— If one, even though he be late for Mass arrives before the Consecration he must remain for the rest of the Mass in case he can not assist at a later Mass, since he can still essentially fulfill his Sunday obligation; but if one were so late as to miss the Consecration he would not be obliged to remain for the rest of the Mass.

Only he can satisfy his Sunday obligation in a domestic oratory who has received an indult to that effect; such an indult includes all relatives by blood or marriage to the fourth degree who live with him; furthermore his guests and those servants that are necessary for himself or the priest during the Mass.— Canon Law allows anyone to fulfill his Sunday obligation at a Mass said in the private chapel of a cemetery as also in a domestic oratory of a cardinal or a bishop.—He does not comply with his Sunday duty who attends a Mass said by a priest in a private home or a cabin on board a ship by virtue of a purely personal privilege. It would be otherwise, however, if the privilege is not purely personal, e.g., if the Holy See grants permission to say Mass in any becoming place in the missions or in non-Christian territory.

Wherefore, one satisfies his Sunday obligation by being present in church even if he cannot see the priest; so, too, if one is in the sacristy or close to the church, provided always that he is able to follow the main parts of the Mass.—Whoever is more than sixty feet distant from the church can no longer hear Mass even if he is still able to follow the priest at the altar, e.g., by means of a radio. An exception is allowed in the case where he is united to the church by a large crowd of people.

The intention to hear Mass is sufficient. The intention to fulfill one's Sunday obligation is not necessary. At least that degree of attention is required that one is aware of the progress of the Mass or of its principal parts.—Thus, one does not fulfill his obligation if he sleeps soundly during the Mass;

whereas, he does who plays the organ, sings, or takes up the collection or who makes his Confession during Mass; providing in each instance, however, that the person can in some way advert to the Mass, especially during the Consecration and Communion. Priests hearing Confessions during Mass should pause for a while at the Elevation and Communion.[20]

This system led on one hand to a morbid preoccupation with sin and scrupulosity and on the other to laxism. No question of ethical behavior was too small to escape the scrutiny of the probing confessors.

Much more detrimental to the Catholicism of the post-Reformation era than the quarrels among the casuists and related to it was the heresy of Jansenism. Although Trent had definitely stated that good works meritorious for salvation are tied in with both grace and the will of man, it had left as an open question the manner in which these two factors co-operated. Nor had it explained whether or not or to what degree grace works infallibly and to what extent it was to be reconciled with man's freedom.

Cornelis Jansen, after whom the heresy is named, was born in 1585 in Holland and pursued his theological studies at the University of Louvain. Here he came under the influence of the writings of one Michael Baius, who during the late sixteenth century had taught, among other erroneous doctrines condemned by Pope Pius V in 1570, that God was obliged by justice and a right possessed by the creature to create man for eternal happiness. He contended that sanctifying grace and all other gifts called gratuitous and supernatural by the Church were actually due to man. Hence it was possible for man to attain his salvation by strength of his own nature. The Protestant overtones were obvious.

Jansen became professor of theology at Louvain in 1630 and five years later was appointed bishop of Ypres. During the years before his death, he composed a work in defense of Baius entitled *Augustinus*, in which he severely attacked Thomism and the theology of the Jesuits. Lamenting the ignorance of Rome on theological matters, he pointed out that the Thomists and the Jesuits could continue their sterile disputes till Judgment Day and still stand further from the truth than they already were.

Augustine, not Thomas, is the true champion of genuine Christianity. The book was published in 1640 after his death, and the reaction was startling. Many Protestants declared that if the pope had approved the book, the unity of Christendom would have been restored. Other theologians acclaimed the work as a clearcut exposé of the Pelagian doctrine of Rome. The Vatican reaction was otherwise.

In August, 1641, Pope Urban VIII put the book on the Index. Ten years later a group of Jansenists led by Saint Amour, a professor at the Sorbonne, presented their case before the Holy See. After a long deliberation five of its basic positions were condemned as heretical. The issues as drawn up and defended by the Jansenists are contained in the following propositions:

> Some of God's precepts are completely and proximately impossible to certain of the just; that is, they cannot be fulfilled by these just ones, no matter how these may wish and endeavor to fulfill them, according to their present weak ability, they being destitute of the efficacious aid necessary to full will and operation. They lack the efficacious grace which could make said precepts possible: that is, they lack that special aid without which the justified man, according to the Council of Trent, cannot persevere in his received justice, that is in the observance of God's commands.
>
> The grace of Christ, necessary to every act of piety, is never resisted; that is, the effect, for which it is proximately given by God, is never frustrated.
>
> For meriting or demeriting in the state of fallen nature, freedom from a necessity of infallibility is not required; but freedom from coercion is sufficient, if the essence of liberty and of merit be precisely considered; although, because of man's condition, there be always found an indifference as to power, by which the will, even when subject to grace proximately necessary and of itself efficacious, may not wish (to correspond)—but the will can never not wish (to correspond) at the time it is subject to grace.
>
> The semi-Pelagians admitted the necessity of antecedent grace for all imperfect acts, even for the beginning of faith; and they were heretics inasmuch as they taught that grace is

such that the will may or may not assent to it, that is, that grace is not of itself efficacious.

It is semi-Pelagian to say that Christ died for all men, or that all without exception, receive through His death, the grace necessary for salvation, which grace it is in the power of man's free will to acquire, without the aid of grace of itself efficacious.[21]

The condemnation, however, had little effect on the spread of heresy. Large segments of the French clergy continued to foster its doctrine on predestination and its condemnation of laxism. Since its disciples advocated a more intelligible liturgy and a return to primitive penitential methods, it was popular with the educated laity. Members of the French Parliament, many of whom were influenced by the Cistercian nuns of Port Royal near Paris and their spiritual director Antoine Arnauld, claimed that the Holy See had unjustly condemned the doctrines of Jansen. The Vatican, they claimed, had right to pass judgment on heretical theories but not on dogmatic facts. Vestiges of Jansenism are still evident in modern Catholicism, especially in its conservative attitude toward the relationship between art and morality.

Constant condemnation of the heresy by the official Church only fed fuel to the growing resentment of the French clergy to the interference of the papacy. In 1682 they declared that the pope was possessed of only spiritual powers, that is, he is subject to the decrees of Constance, and hence his pronouncements were to be approved by the consent of the entire Church. Gallicanism, as this was called, continued in France until the time of the Revolution.

In the devotional area, the post-Tridentine Church, in response to the challenge of Protestantism, continued to emphasize those practices most severely attacked by the reformers. These included the veneration of the saints, especially the Virgin, and the worship of the Eucharist.

In the liturgy, stress was placed on the Real Presence of Christ in the Eucharist. The spirit of the time pushed into the background any idea that the laity had a part to play in the prayer of the priest or that they should co-offer with him at Mass. Since the reformers had emphasized the priesthood of all the faithful and denied a special priesthood, it was now deemed necessary to underline what distinguished and separated the layman from the priest rather than stress those functions they shared in common.

One looks in vain in the spiritual writings of the time for any reference to a participation in the Mass that would foster a deeper appreciation of divine cult. Any attempt to translate the liturgy into the vernacular was frustrated by Rome. In 1661 Alexander VII condemned a translation of the Missal under pain of excommunication. It was firmly believed that the faithful would have a greater reverence for the liturgy of the Mass if it were enshrouded in a veil of mystery. Although the allegorizing so common in the late medieval period was gradually dropped, its place was taken by the use of prayers aimed at preparing the soul for the Elevation of the Host through acts of faith, hope, and charity.

Meditations on the Passion and Death of Our Lord continued to play an important role in Catholic prayer formula. Although the spread of printing helped to encourage this sort of participation for the educated, it was necessary to stimulate the illiterate masses with other means. Following the example of the Protestants, common prayers and singing were encouraged. The recitation of the Rosary at Mass, with its contemplation of the Mysteries of the Redemption, became widespread. Preaching, when it did occur during the Mass, generally had little connection with the Gospel reading of the liturgy. Even the pulpit no longer stood near the altar, but was moved into the center of the Church. The reception of Communion, although much more frequent than during the Middle Ages, took place after the Mass and, because of the strict law of fasting, usually after an earlier nonparochial Mass.

Communion was looked upon as an independent and self-contained exercise, and not as a participation in the Sacrifice, but as a reception of Christ present continuously in the Sacrament. The altar furnishings, the tabernacle where the Host was preserved, and its splendiferous surroundings eclipsed the meaning of the altar as a table, a mensa, for a divine banquet. The adoration and glorification of the Real Presence remained the central act of the Mass. In a catechism published in 1734, the author lists the Mass as one of five ways in which Christ is to be worshiped in the Blessed Sacrament. The faithful were urged when attending Mass to say their daily prayers until the time of the Elevation and thereafter to worship the Divine Lamb. In many places, the grand procession of the Blessed Sacrament during missions and Forty Hour devotion was considered more important than the Mass liturgy. The practice of Benediction, or exposing the sacrament for devotion and adoration, was also widespread, especially in convents of nuns. Guilds and confraternities dedicated to the Holy Eucharist abounded.

It was during this period also that the baroque architecture, with its rich and flamboyant style, flourished. Its counterpart is evidenced in the polyphonic music of the time and the great compositions of Mozart, Haydn, and Beethoven. At the consecration of the Cathedral of Salzburg in 1628 a festival Mass, requiring two eighty-member choirs and an orchestra, was sung. Generally the liturgy took on all the coloring of the superlative court ceremonial of the age of absolutism. The faithful were there to admire dimly and from afar the dramatization of this unapproachable magnificence.

Yet, in spite of the fact that the liturgy and theology of the period remained sterile and unproductive, the seventeenth and eighteenth centuries were rich in religious enthusiasm and sanctity of life. The seventeenth century has been called the century of saints, an age of spiritual grandeur. St. Vincent de Paul, St. Jean Eudes, Jean Jacques Olier, Bossuet, and Fénelon are certainly examples of the new life and militancy that were evident in the Church at the time. Paradoxically, however, piety flourished most widely in those areas where the decrees of Trent were never wholly accepted. It is now generally admitted that the Counter Reform, which attempted to extract the very essence of Catholicism from its late medieval form, was overly negative. As a movement, it failed to affirm consciously the totality of Catholic dogma.

Perhaps the outstanding saint of the post-Reformation period was the holy bishop of Geneva, Francis of Sales (d.1622). Heir to the Catholic humanism of the sixteenth century as represented by such men as Jacop Sadoleto, Erasmus, and Reginald Pole, a group whom the Tridentine reform tactfully ignored, he might be called the prototype of modern as opposed to medieval spirituality. His career as a bishop was characterized by his conciliatory attitude toward Protestantism, his care for individual souls, and his secularized asceticism. Like Erasmus in the previous century, he envisioned a Catholicism in which the laity were to play an important role. His constant aim was to make piety attractive not by couching it in the ideals of monastic withdrawal but by projecting it into the affairs of everyday life. Spirituality was not to be the prerogative of the cloister. It had a place in the company of soldiers, in the workshop of craftsmen, and in the domestic life of the married. His writings translated the abstract notions of sin and grace into a working psychology, thus reducing to irrelevance the theory concerning the nature of grace and its effects on the soul that plagued his period of history. It is for this reason that Francis of Sales has been credited with laying the foundations of that modern Catholic spirituality which is still practiced to this day.

His most famous work, *Introduction to the Devout Life,* was one of the most widely read works of the seventeenth and eighteenth centuries. During the nineteenth century it was revived, and it continues today to furnish spiritual inspiration to a large Catholic reading public. The book first appeared in 1690, and it was soon translated into Italian, Latin, Spanish, Flemish, and German. An English translation appeared in 1613. It has also appeared in modern Greek, Armenian, and Chinese. The book presents the Saint's method for dealing with one of the great problems of the Catholicism of his time: transforming external observance to inward experience and participation. The selection on marriage, which was deleted from some of the later editions, offers a good example of how humanism was gradually breaking down some of the monastic prejudices against the marriage state:

> Marriage is a great sacrament; but I speak in Christ and in the Church. To all persons and in all things, that is in all its

parts, marriage is honorable. For all persons, because even virgins should honor it with humility; for all persons because it is equally holy in the rich and poor; in all things because its beginning, its end, its advantages, its form, and its matter are all holy. It is the nursery of Christianity which is providing for the earth, faithful souls to complete the number of elect in heaven. Therefore, the preservation of the holy state of matrimony is of the greatest importance to the state because it is both the origin and source of all its streams.

If only the Son of God were invited to all weddings as He was to that of Cana. Then the wine of His consolation and blessing would never be lacking. The most important reason why there is commonly little of it at the beginning is that instead of our Lord, Adonis, and instead of our Lady, Venus are invited. He that would have his lambs fair and spotted, as Jacob's were, must like him set fair rods of divers colors before the sheep when they meet to couple. The man who desires a happy married life should in his espousals consider the sanctity and dignity of the sacrament. Instead, there are a thousand offensive things done in play, feasting, and speaking. How can we be so surprised to see its disorderly effects?

Above all things, I exhort married people to that mutual love which the Holy Spirit of the Scripture recommends so highly to them. I entreat you who are married! It means nothing to say: Love one another with a natural love; two turtle doves make such love. Nor does it mean anything to say: Love one another with a human love; heathens have practiced such love. Husbands, love your wives, as Christ also loved His Church; and wives, love your husbands as the Church loved her Son. It was God who brought Eve to our first father, Adam, and united them in marriage. It is also God, my friends, who with His invisible hand has joined together the holy bond of your marriage and has given you each other. Why then can you not cherish one another with the most sacred, and most holy kind of love?

This love will cause, first of all, a permanent union of your hearts. If the glue is lasting, two pieces of fir glued together will break more easily in any other place than at the band. God joins the husband and wife by His own blood. Therefore, this union is so strong that the soul must separate from the body of one of the two rather than the husband from his wife. This union is not understood through the body, but through the heart, of the affection, and of love.

The second effect must be the inviolable fidelity of the couple united in this love and marriage. Formerly seals of fidelity were engraved upon the rings that were worn on the fingers. Then, the secret meaning of this ceremony in marriage is in this. The Church blesses a ring by a priest's hand. First by giving it to the man, she admits that by this sacrament she puts a seal and a sign upon his heart to the end that henceforward no love for any other woman should enter therein as long as his wife shall live. Then, the bridegroom puts the ring on the hand of his bride, that her heart must never hold the affection for another man, so long as he whom our Lord gives her shall live upon the earth.

Husbands, preserve a tender, constant, and heartfelt love for your wives. Woman was taken from that side of the first man which was nearest his heart to the end that she must be loved cordially and tenderly by him. The weakness and infirmity of your wives, in body or in mind, ought not to lead you to any kind of disdain, but rather to a mild and affectionate compassion. God has created them in a way that they should be dependent upon you, and you should receive from them more honor and respect. You should also have them as your companions although remaining their superiors and head. And you, wives, love your husbands tenderly to whom God has given you, but with a love of respect and full of reverence. God created them as a sex more vigorous and commanding and was pleased to ordain that the woman should be dependent upon the man, being bone of his bone and flesh of his flesh; and that she be taken from a bone of his removed from under his arm to show that she should be under the will and guidance of her husband. Holy Scripture recommends this submission to you. Yet the Scripture provides that not only should you accommodate yourselves to it, but that your husband exercise it over you with great charity, kindness, and mildness.

Saint Peter says that husbands likewise dwelling with your wives according to knowledge, give honor to the woman as the weaker vessel. While I exhort you to advance more and more in this mutual love in which you are indebted, take care that it does not regenerate into any kind of jealousy. Just as the worm often grows in the most delicate and ripest apple, so often does jealousy grow in the deepest and most sincere married love. As a result it breaks down and destroys the essence of this love, and causes dissension, arguing, and divorce. However, it is true jealousy does not enter where friendship is built on true virtue in both persons. Jealousy to a great extent leaves an infallible mark on love that is somewhat crude and sensual. It shows an imperfect and inconstant virtue which is subject to distrust. While it may prove the size and importance of a friendship, it never proves its goodness, purity, and perfection. The perfection of friendship presupposes an assurance of the virtue of those whom we love; and jealousy presupposes a doubt.

Should you married men desire that your wife be loyal to you, let your example be one of faithfulness and loyalty. How can you require of them that which you do not give them? Is it fidelity you wish of them? Then behave yourself in this manner. If instead, you yourselves teach them evil ways, do not be disgraced by their fall.

Wives, work tirelessly to keep your honor, and allow no misconduct to injure the perfection of your reputation since your honor is inseparably joined with purity and modesty. Avoid all improper advances, no matter how slight; and never permit any evil intentions to tempt you. Suspect anyone who appears to praise your beauty and charm, because a man who praises what he cannot buy is strongly tempted to steal it. If to praise you he adds the dispraise of your husband, he offers you a heinous injury. Obviously, he wants not only to ruin you but already considers you half ruined. The bargain is half-made with the second merchant when one is disgusted with the first.[22]

CHAPTER 5

World-wide Catholicism
in the Industrial Age

Features of 19th and 20th Century Catholicism

THERE ARE FOUR discernible tendencies in Catholicism of the nineteenth and twentieth centuries. In the first place, the separation of the Church from the laicized state accentuated the contrast between Catholic and modern thought and forced a reappraisal of its relationship to constitutional and democratic government and the social question. The beginnings of a liturgical movement produced a new method of pastoral work which offered greater participation on the part of the laity. The definition of the First Vatican Council on papal infallibility marked an increase in the pope's religious and moral authority. Finally, a world-wide mission activity which in the nineteenth century had followed colonial expansion was in the twentieth forced to come to terms with non-Christian religions and atheistic Communism. The resultant confrontation produced a strong trend toward the re-establishment of Christian unity, or ecumenism.

Just as France, through its political and cultural hegemony, exercised the greatest influence on Catholicism during the seventeenth century, so it was through this eldest daughter of the

Church that those destructive forces that continued to harass the Church in the eighteenth and nineteenth centuries were channeled. Two important, interrelated movements—the Enlightenment and the French Revolution—form the background in the struggle of Catholicism to reassert itself and once again dominate the religious thought of Europe as it had done during the Middle Ages.

The Enlightenment was in many ways more opposed to Catholicism than was the Protestant revolt, for it struck at the very roots of revealed religion by denying the authenticity of the Scriptures and the existence of the supernatural. It involved on an unprecedented scale the substitution of the natural for the supernatural and of science for theology. In exalting and at times deifying human reason, it looked to the laws of nature rather than ecclesiastical legislation for moral direction. With the assumption that man would use his reason to obey the natural law, the Enlightenment gave birth to the idea of progress.

It advocated a new concept of religious freedom and a scientific humanitarianism which operated independently of institutionalized Christianity. In attempting to reappraise Western civilization without sectarian prejudice or ulterior purpose, the Enlightenment also fathered the main feature of modern liberalism often inimical to Catholicism. The Church was accused of fostering an otherworldly morality of standing in opposition to the findings of the new social sciences, economics, politics, and critical history. Imbued with the new enthusiasm for scientific discovery, the leading minds of Europe taught basic philosophies that were often at variance with the scholastic system inherited from an age when the physical sciences were little regarded by theologians. The lack of harmony between faith and science did not imply a repudiation of the notion of God, but since it was based entirely on reason it had the disastrous effect of undermining the mysterious content of Christianity. The discoveries made by Newton, Boyle, and others gave the impression that everything, including religion, could be determined with geometric precision. The political writers of the period, in advocating religious tolerance, fostered another notion diametrically opposed to the Catholicism of the times: the equality of all religions.

Deism, as the religion of the Enlightenment was called, was largely a British creation. It did not find its way into Catholic Europe until well into the eighteenth century. When it did appear it was identified with Free Masonry. Originally a society that opposed the growth of atheism and irreligious libertinism, Masonry advocated religious tolerance and the improved moral conduct of its members. It specifically excluded the altercations of politics and theology from its meetings and welcomed membership from among the Catholic clergy. However, in 1738 Clement XII condemned the organization in the bull *In Eminenti Apostolatus Specula*. Thus was inaugurated a series of papal denunciations that were to continue until modern times. The chief reasons alleged for the condemnation of Masonry were that it fostered clandestine political sedition, was a secret society, and as an indiscriminate asociation of men of different faiths imperiled the purity of the Catholic religion. The conflict between Catholicism and Free Masonry, especially in Latin countries, was intensified over the centuries since Masonry was often the only refuge for those who, for political or other reasons, had fallen out with the Church. Until quite recent times Masonry was considered by Catholic officialdom as one of its most subversive and dangerous antagonists. Membership in Masonic societies is still forbidden for Catholics, under pain of excommunication.

The French Revolution projected the ideas of the Enlightenment into the political sphere and brought about the final dissolution of the feudal, stratified society that was so much a constituent element of medieval Catholicism. Its violent attack upon the Church was not, however, directed solely against its feudal vestiges. In destroying the close ties between the episcopacy and the state, it also attempted to uproot Christianity itself. Thus it is no exaggeration to say that Catholicism in the nineteenth century lived in the shadow of the French Revolution.

Yet it was this very extremism that turned the intellectuals of Europe once again to the basic principles of Catholicism. By destroying the old regime and wiping out the remnants of the Holy Roman Empire, it laid the ax to Gallicanism and forced the clergy of Europe to look once more to the papacy for direction. In proclaiming a complete separation of Church and state it provided Catholicism with opportunities for expansion unknown in the ancient regime. More importantly, the reaction against the extreme rationalism of the Enlightenment and the Revolution turned men's minds once again to the religion of their forebears. Romanticism, especially as represented by men like Chateaubriand and Ozanam in France and Görres and Sailer in Germany, extolled Catholicism as the mother of the highest art and the custodian of patriotism.

The French priest Félicité Lamennais (d.1854) was probably the most influential of the new breed of Catholic intellectuals who wished to make the Church the beneficiary of the new liberties of the Revolution. "Instead of trembling before liberalism," he urged, "let us Catholicize it." However, since he advocated too strongly that the cause of the Church no longer be identified with the restored monarchies, he fell out with the Holy See. Gregory XVI, the pope at this time, regarded any idea of an alliance between the Church and the liberals as unthinkable. It was the Dominican Jean Lacordaire (d.1861), the greatest pulpit orator of the nineteenth century, who carried the cause of Catholic liberalism to the very heart of the French nation in the Cathedral of Notre Dame. Like Lamennais, he wished to reconcile the Catholic faith and modern freedoms. Between 1835 and 1850 his dramatic sermons, extolling Catholicism because of her social and moral contributions to civilization, were the rage of Europe. Thousands who had lost their faith, including the aging Talleyrand, returned to the Catholic fold.

Apologetic in tone, his sermons reflected much of the romantic spirit of restored Catholicism. Their reassuring messages continued into the twentieth century and are reflected in the apologetic writings of Chesterton and Belloc. The following selection from one of his sermons illustrates the attempt of nineteenth-century Catholicism to reassert itself by extolling the Church as the perennial guardian of law and authority:

Since then order exists somewhere in the world of ideas, since,—notwithstanding the frightful fermentations of discord which disturb and divide it,—a public society of minds has succeeded in founding itself, it is then true that there exists also, an intellectual sovereignty, a sovereignty of which Catholic doctrine is alone in possession, since alone it has triumphed over schismatic force which keeps intelligent beings in hostility and in dissolution. Just as there is no civil society without a civil government, nor any civil government without a civil sovereignty, so there no more exists any society of minds without a government of minds, neither any government of minds without an intellectual sovereignty,—a sovereignty which no more destroys the liberty of the intelligence than civil sovereignty destroys civil liberty, but which, on the contrary, establishes it, by delivering souls from the disorderly yoke of schismatic force. This is that intellectual sovereignty which all the authors of schisms have sought, and which they still seek, together with all those who aspire, whether from ambition or from love of mankind, to found the public unity of minds. When a philosopher ascends his rostrum, he simply makes a throne of it for himself; he places himself as a sovereign; he seeks in his science and in his genius for the secret of that superiority *par excellence* which produces unity; and he is right in so doing, up to the point when, alarmed at his powerlessness, he recognizes and adores the hand by which all kings reign, and which, having given the empire of earth to conquerors, has refused to sages and philosophers the empire of truth, to give it to Jesus Christ, and by Jesus Christ to the Catholic Church.

Let us progress still further, Gentlemen, and endeavor to find in what intellectual sovereignty consists; for, as long as we do not know this, something will be wanting to the evidence of our deductions.

Intellectual sovereignty can only reside in the ideas or the mind. It is impossible to take it elsewhere, for all that which is intellectual is either idea or mind, the object of thought, or the subject of thinking. Now, intellectual sovereignty does not reside in the object or in the idea; the idea is not living independently of the mind which receives it, it is capable of change by entering there, may lose its rectitude and its force, and not emerge therefrom to pass into another mind, without a cold and fruitless energy, like an arrow weakly thrown by an archer without vigor.

You have before you illustrous examples of this. The Greek Church has all the ideas of the Catholic Church, or very nearly, and yet the Greek Church exists inanimately, possessing no more unity than that of a corpse bound round with bands by the cruel hands of the Russian autocracy. The Bible also contains catholic ideas, and the Protestants have lighted upon them in the hope of deriving life, unity, and intellectual sovereignty from them: have they succeeded in accomplishing this? Much less than the Greeks; immobility has preserved to these some appearance of a body; action has reduced those to the consistency of a heap of ashes. What is then the virtue of ideas beyond the mind, in which they take their form, their power, their immortality? But what is the mind itself, that the intellectual sovereignty should have in it its throne and its action? What are the minds of which the Catholic Church is composed? Alas! they are men: You, myself, the first child who, on leaving this assembly, will go to confess his sins. It is then our intelligence, taken singly or in common, which possesses intellectual sovereignty, that formidable sovereignty which, during eighteen centuries, in spite of all the schismatic force of which the world disposes, captivates a hundred and fifty millions of men around one and the same dogma. And around what dogma? Around a dogma which does not satisfy their innate thirst for light, which irritates their passion for darkness, which wounds their spiritual individuality to the quick, and demands from their free-will a humiliating acception. What! you and I, all of us together, a thousand men, a hundred thousand men, are capable by their own minds of such an act of sovereignty? Do not believe a word of it; beware of believing it; it is not possible. As men, we possess nothing more than the philosophers and the intellectuals, who have been able to do nothing and who have done nothing, because radically all minds are equal, because no mind is the sovereign of another mind.

Do you wish to return to ideas? Do you wish to conclude that intellectual sovereignty resides in ideas, and that the world is subject to us by their energy? But why do not ideas become corrupted in our intelligence of the Greeks and the Protestants? Who or what, then, has given them another character with us? Why are they so vain elsewhere, why so powerful in the Church? You see clearly that the circle is closed, and that logic leaves no haven open to us!

Yet Catholic unity exists; it exists alone in the world; it supposes a power of unity, an intellectual sovereignty. Who has imparted this to us, since ideas do not impart it, and the mind of man does not possess it? Evidently another mind than our own is within us, another power animates us, another spirit protects us, another spirit speaks to us,—the spirit which departed from man at Babel, and which returned on the day of Pentecost. If God is not in the Church, it may be some other thing, but very certainly it is not man.

Rationalism often reproaches us with being wanting in justice with regard to itself. It appears to think that we contest the entire domain of truth with it, as if it were incapable of ever disclosing a single true idea; we do not go so far. But, however it may be on this point, the question between rationalism and ourselves is also a question of sovereignty. We say rationalism, that even if it possessed the entire truth, had it even, if it were possible, more truth than the Church possesses, it would not rally minds into any stable unity, such as is necessary to the existence of mankind; because the most sincere and the most religious rationalism is but an effort of man in favour of man, an attempt at sovereignty which is destined always to be shattered in pieces against the immense schismatic force which is unfortunately in activity in the moral world. We do not even claim for ourselves, as men, that which, during six thousand years, has escaped from the hands of rationalism; we know that no mind is the sovereign of another mind. We profess that it is impossible even for Socrates and Plato to make a single subject. The unity of the Church is for us a divine phenomenon, which is only to be explained by the perpetual presence of the spirit of God in the midst of us. We believe that God has reserved the intellectual sovereignty to himself, and that every attempt to obtain it will invariably end either in the enslaving of souls by autocracy, or in their ruin by doubt and negation. These two proofs, indeed, are necessary to the glorification of Catholic unity, so that, assailed always by imitators armed with science or with the sword, the Church may pass through the midst of their designs without failing to fulfill her destiny, ever virgin, ever mother, ever queen, and seeming to vanish in smoke the hopes of a rivalry which pursues her always only to become her perpetual crown.[23]

In England, John Henry Newman also appeared as the great apologist of Catholicism, as the Oxford movement led many from the Church of England to the ancient religion. Newman was not, however, a victim of Romanticism, as were so many among continental Catholics. Although he expresses the view that during the course of time Catholic inquiry had taken certain definite shapes and had thrown itself into the form of a science, with a method and phraseology of its own, he was no herald of neo-Thomism. In his later years he wrote:

> For myself, hopeless as you consider it, I am not ashamed still to take my stand upon the Fathers, and do not mean to budge. The history of their times is not yet an old almanac to me. Of course I maintain the value and authority of the *Schola* as one of the *Loci Theologici;* nevertheless I sympathize with Petavius in preferring to the contentious and subtle theology of the Middle Ages; that more elegant and fruitful teaching which is moulded after the image of erudite antiquity. The Fathers made me a Catholic, and I am not going to kick down the ladder by which I ascended into the Church.

The position of Newman as an intellectual has not been duly assessed. In many ways he stands at the beginning of a new Christian philosophy that is only now being appreciated. By attempting to reconstruct philosophy in an age of excessive rationalism, he centered his interests on the problems of religious belief as they are actually experienced by men in the modern world. Problems of faith led to problems of individuals, for only individuals can believe. It was Newman's thesis that a philosophical system was not a substitute for personal thinking. For him, all philosophical systems are approximations to, and thus inadequate statements of, objective truth.

The Struggle with Liberalism

In spite of the brief Catholic revival in Europe during the era of Metternich, the Church was soon confronted with a series of problems that once again strained its defensive efforts to the limit. Liberalism in political theory, modernism in theology, and the apostasy of the masses as a result of the Industrial Revolution were the three fronts where the Church attempted to check the assault of a modern secularized society grown increasingly antagonistic to its claims.

The *Syllabus of the Chief Errors of Our Times* of Pope Pius IX is perhaps the clearest manifestation of the growing gap between the ideals of papal Christianity and the world of the nineteenth century. This list of modern errors that had been reprobated and condemned in some thirty allocutions, letters, and encyclicals of the pope during the previous eighteen years of his pontificate raised a storm of unprecedented fury in all quarters hostile to Catholicism. For many Catholics it seemed an embarrassing reversal of the pope's earlier espousal of liberalism. For others it appeared as the definitive divorce of Catholicism from modern civilization. However radical the propositions may appear, they must be taken in the context of the various documents from which they were extracted. Although later modified by Pope Leo XIII, who as bishop of Perugia had exerted a great influence on Pius in drawing up the eighty propositions, many of them are still representative of the Catholic position in the continuing struggle between nature and supernature, between religion and secularism.

It must be borne in mind that the *Syllabus* was not a dogmatic statement but rather an enumeration of errors concerning the relationship between the Catholic Church and the state. It was an attempt to check an uninhibited belief in human progress and the exaggerated expectations of those who assumed the complete perfectibility of secular life. Since the famous document still forms the basis of a widespread fear that Rome continues to harbor sentiments inimical to modern society, we give it in its entirety:

There exists no supreme, all-wise, all provident divine being, distinct from the universe, and God is identical with the nature of things, and is, therefore, subject to changes. In effect, God is produced in man and in the world, and all things are God and have the very substance of God, and God is one and the same thing with the world, and, therefore, spirit with matter, necessity with liberty, good with evil, justice with injustice.

All the action of God upon man and the world is to be denied.

Human reason, without any reference whatsoever to God, is the sole arbiter of truth and falsehood, and of good and evil; it is law to itself, and suffices, by its natural force, to secure the welfare of men and of nations.

All the truths of religion proceed from the innate strength of human reason; hence reason is the ultimate standard by which man can and ought to arrive at the knowledge of all truths of every kind.

Divine revelation is imperfect, and therefore subject to a continual and indefinite progress, corresponding with the advancement of human reason.

The faith of Christ is in opposition to human reason, and divine revelation not only is not useful, but is even hurtful to the perfection of man.

The prophecies and miracles set forth and recorded in the sacred Scriptures are the fiction of poets, and the mysteries of the Christian faith the result of philosophical investigations. In the books of the Old and New Testament there are contained mythical inventions, and Jesus Christ is himself a myth.

As human reason is placed on a level with religion itself, so theological science must be treated in the same manner as philosophical sciences.

All dogmas of the Christian religion are discriminately the object of natural science or philosophy; and human reason, enlightened solely in an historical way, is able by its own natural strength and principles, to attain to the true science of even the most abstruse dogmas; provided only that such dogmas be proposed to reason itself as its object.

As the philosopher is one thing, and philosophy another, so it is the right and duty of the philosopher to subject himself to the authority which he shall have proved to be true; but philosophy neither can nor ought to submit to any such authority. The Church not only ought never to pass judgment on philosophy, but ought to tolerate the errors of philosophy, leaving it to correct itself.

The decrees of the Apostolic See and of the Roman Congregations impede the true progress of science.

The method and principles by which the old scholastic doctors cultivated theology are no longer suitable to the demands of our times and to the progress of the sciences.

Philosophy is to be treated without taking any account of supernatural revelation.

Every man is free to embrace and profess that religion which, guided by the light of reason, he shall consider true.

Man may in the observance of any religion whatever, find the way of eternal salvation, and arrive at eternal salvation.

Good hope at least is to be entertained of eternal salvation of all those who are not all in the Church of Christ. Protestantism is nothing more than another form of the same true Christian religion, in which form it is given to please God equally as in the Catholic Church.

The Church is not a true and perfect Society, entirely free; nor is she endowed with proper and perpetual rights of her own, conferred upon her by her divine Founder; but it appertains to the civil power to define what are the rights of the Church, and the limits within which she may exercise these rights.

The ecclesiastical power ought not to exercise its authority without the permission and assent of the civil government.

The Church has not the power of defining dogmatically that the religion of the Catholic Church is the only true religion.

The obligation by which Catholic teachers and authors are strictly bound, is confirmed to those things only which are proposed to universal belief as dogmas of faith by the infallible judgment of the Church.

Roman pontiffs and ecumenical councils have wandered outside the limits of their powers, have usurped the rights of princes, and have erred in defining matters of faith and morals.

The Church has not the power of using force, nor has she any temporal power, direct or indirect.

Beside the power inherent in the episcopate, other temporal power has been attributed to it by civil authority, granted either expressly or tacitly, which on that account is revocable by the civil authority whenever it thinks fit.

The Church has no innate and legitimate right of acquiring and possessing property.

The sacred ministers of the Church and the Roman Pontiff are to be absolutely excluded from every charge and dominion over temporal affairs.

It is not lawful for bishops to publish even letters apostolic without the permission of government.

Favors granted by the Roman Pontiff ought to be considered null, unless they have been sought for through the civil government.

The immunity of the Church and of ecclesiastic persons derived its origin from civil law.

The ecclesiastical forum or tribunal for the temporal causes, whether civil or criminal, of clerics, ought by all means to be abolished, even without consulting and against the protest of the Holy See.

The personal immunity by which clerics are exonerated from military conscription and service in the army may be abolished without violation either of natural right or of equity. Its abolition is called for by civil progress, especially in a society framed on the model of a liberal government.

It does not appertain exclusively to the power of ecclesiastical jurisdiction by right, proper and innate, to direct the teaching of theological questions.

The teaching of those who compare the Sovereign Pontiff to a prince, free, and acting in the universal Church, is a doctrine which prevailed in the middle ages.

There is nothing to prevent the decree of a General Council, or the act of all peoples, from transferring the Supreme Pontificate from the Bishop and City of Rome to another bishop and another city.

The definition of a national council does not admit of any

subsequent discussion, and the civil authority can assume this principle as the basis of its acts.

National churches, withdrawn from the authority of the Roman Pontiff and altogether separated, can be established.

The Roman pontiffs have, by their too arbitrary conduct, contributed to the division of the church into Eastern and Western.

The state, as being the origin and source of all rights, is endowed with a certain right not circumscribed by any limits.

The teaching of the Catholic Church is hostile to the well-being and interests of society.

The civil government, even when in the hands of an infidel sovereign, has a right to an indirect negative power over religious affairs.

In the case of conflicting laws enacted by the two powers, the civil law prevails.

The secular power has authority to rescind, declare, and render null, solemn conventions, commonly called *Concordats,* entered into with the Apostolic See, regarding the use of rights appertaining to ecclesiastical immunity, without the consent of the Apostolic See, and even in spite of its protest.

The civil authority may interfere in matters relating to religion, morality, and spiritual government: hence, it can pass judgment on the instructions issued for the guidance of consciences, conformably with their mission, by the pastors of the Church, further, it has the right to make enactments regarding the administration of the divine sacraments, and the dispositions necessary for receiving them.

The entire government of public schools in which the youth of a Christian state is educated, except (to a certain extent) in the case of episcopal seminaries, may and ought to appertain to the civil power, and belong to it so far that no other authority whatsoever shall be recognized as having any right to interfere in the discipline of the schools, the arrangement of the studies, the conferring of degrees, in the choice or approval of the teachers.

Moreover, even in ecclesiastical seminaries, the method of studies to be adopted is subject to the civil authority.

The best theory of civil society requires that popular schools, open to children of every class of the people, and generally, all public institutes intended for instruction in letters and philosophical sciences, and for carrying on the education of youth, should be freed from all ecclesiastical authority, control, and interference, and should be fully subjected to the civil and political power at the pleasure of the rulers, and according to the standard of the prevalent opinions of the age.

Catholics may approve of a system of education of youth, unconnected with Catholic faith and the power of the Church, and which regards the knowledge of merely natural things, and only, or at least primarily, the ends of earthly social life.

The Civil power may prevent the prelates of the Church and the faithful from communicating freely and mutually with the Roman Pontiff.

Lay authority possesses of itself the right of presenting bishops, and may require of them to undertake the administration of the dioceses before they receive canonical institution and the Letters Apostolic from the Holy See.

And further, the lay government has the right of deposing bishops from their pastoral functions, and is not bound to obey the Roman Pontiff in those things which relate to the institution of bishoprics and the appointment of bishops.

Government can, by its own right, alter the age prescribed by the Church for the religious profession both of women and men; and may require of all religious orders to admit no person to take solemn vows without its permission.

The laws enacted for the protection of religious orders and regarding their rights and duties, ought to be abolished; even more, civil government may lend its assistance to all who desire to renounce the obligation which they had undertaken, of a religious life, and to break their vows. Governments may also suppress the said religious orders, as likewise collegiate churches and simple benefices, and subject their property and revenues to the administration and pleasure of the civil power.

Kings and princes are not only exempt from the jurisdiction of the Church, but are superior to the Church in deciding questions of jurisdiction.

The Church ought to be separated from the state and the state from the Church.

Moral laws do not stand in need of the divine sanction,

and it is not at all necessary that human laws should be made conformable to the laws of nature, and receive their power of binding from God.

The science of philosophical things and morals, and also civil laws, may and ought to keep aloof from divine and ecclesiastical authority.

No other forces are to be recognized except those which reside in matter, and all the rectitude and excellence of morality ought to keep aloof from divine and ecclesiastical authority.

No other forces are to be recognized except those which reside in matter, and all the rectitude and excellence of morality ought to be placed in the accumulation and increase of riches by every positive means, and the gratification of pleasure.

Right consists in the material fact. All human duties are an empty word, and all human facts have the force of right.

Authority is nothing else but numbers and the sum total of material forces.

The injustice of an act when successful, inflicts no injury upon the sanctity of right.

The principle of non-intervention, as it is called, ought to be proclaimed and observed.

It is lawful to refuse obedience to legitimate princes, and even to rebel against them.

The violation of any solemn oath, as well as any wicked and flagitious action repugnant to the eternal law, is not only not blamable, but is altogether lawful and worthy of the highest praise, when done through love of country.

The doctrine that Christ has raised marriage to the dignity of a sacrament cannot be at all tolerated.

The sacrament of marriage is only a something accessory to the contract and separate from it, and the sacrament itself consists in the nuptial blessing alone.

By the law of nature, the marriage tie is not indissoluble, and in many cases divorce properly so called may be decreed by the civil authority.

The Church has not the power of establishing diriment impediments of marriage, but such a power belongs to the civil authority, by which existing impediments are to be removed.

In the dark ages the Church began to establish diriment impediments, not by her own right, but by using a power borrowed from the state.

The canons of the Council of Trent, which anathematize those who dare to deny the Church the right of establishing diriment impediments, either are not dogmatic, or must be understood as referring to such borrowed power.

The form of solemnizing marriage prescribed by the Council of Trent, under pain of nullity, does not bind in cases where the civil law lays down another form, and declares that when this new form is used the marriage shall be valid.

Boniface VIII was the first who declared that the vow of chastity taken at ordination renders marriage void.

In force of a merely civil contract, there may exist between Christians a real marriage, and it is false to say either that the marriage contract between Christians is always a sacrament, or that there is no contract if the sacrament, or that there is no contract if the sacrament be excluded.

Matrimonial causes and espousal belong by their nature to civil tribunals.

The children of the Christian and Catholic Church are divided amongst themselves about the compatibility of temporal with the spiritual power.

The abolition of the temporal power of which the Apostolic See is possessed, would contribute in the greatest degree to the liberty and prosperity of the Church.

In the present day it is no longer expedient that the Catholic religion should be held as the only religion of the State, to the exclusion of all other forms of worship.

Moreover it is false that the civil liberty of every form of worship, and the full power, given to all, of overtly and publicly manifesting any opinions whatsoever and thoughts, conduce more easily to corrupt the morals and minds of the people, and to propagate the pest of indifferentism.

The Roman Pontiff can, and ought, to reconcile himself, and come to terms with progress, liberalism, and modern civilization.[24]

The Magisterial Role of the Papacy

Hardly had the storm created by the publication of the *Syllabus* begun to subside when the papacy again dramatically voiced its displeasure with the pretensions of the absolute state by summoning an ecumenical council at the Vatican.

One of the reasons for convening the council was the failure of Trent, three centuries before, to refute one of the basic errors of Protestantism: its denial of the hierarchical structure of the Church and her authority to teach unerringly. The fact that no ecumenical council had been called for over three hundred years was unprecedented in the history of Catholicism. In the minds of many well intentioned Catholics, the weapons with which the Church had resisted Protestantism were now become a hindrance and a weakness. What had once forestalled its decline was now a definite impediment to its progress. Invitations to members of the Orthodox and Protestant churches to attend the council were turned down. The Greeks rejected the invitation because it failed "to pay due respect to Apostolic equality and brotherhood." The continental Protestants answered the papal appeal to return to the one fold of Christ by protesting "against every kind of hierarchical and priestly tutelage, against every form of violence to the spirit and oppression of the conscience."

There was a widespread fear in Europe that the council would define the doctrinal points contained in the "Syllabus of Errors," especially the doctrine of papal infallibility. The German theologian Doellinger and the English historian Lord Acton shared a belief that if a definition of infallibility were declared—that is, that the pope could not err in doctrinal matters—Catholicism would suffer a reversal. In many European capitals such a decree was seen as a definite threat to the very security of the state. Bismarck in Germany and Gladstone in England made a political issue of the proposed definition. Yet in July, 1870, the assembled Fathers, though not unanimously, accepted the decree on papal infallibility, which became a dogma of the Catholic Church. After stating his belief in the Apostolic primacy in St. Peter and showing the doctrine to have been perpetual as in the ecumenical councils, especially the Fourth Council of Constantinople and the Council of Florence, the pope clearly delineates the claim that he is supreme in ruling and governing the entire Church.

The decree reads as follows:

> But since in this present age, which especially requires the salutary efficacy of the apostolic office, not a few are found who minimize its authority, we think it extremely necessary to assert solemnly the prerogative which the only-begotten Son of God deigned to join to the highest pastoral office.
>
> And so, faithfully keeping to the tradition received from the beginning of the Christian faith, for the glory of God our saviour, for the exaltation of the Catholic religion, and for the salvation of Christian peoples, We, with the approval of the sacred council, teach and define that it is a divinely revealed dogma: that the Roman Pontiff, when he speaks *ex cathedra,* that is, when, acting in the office of shepherd and teacher of all Christians, he defines, by virtue of his supreme apostolic authority, doctrine concerning faith or morals to be held by the universal Church, possesses, through the divine assistance promised to him in blessed Peter, that infallibility with which the divine Redeemer willed his Church to be endowed in defining doctrine concerning faith or morals; and that such definitions of the Roman Pontiff are therefore irreformable because of their nature, but not because of the agreement of the Church.[25]

It is symbolic that this declaration of the supreme authority of the bishop of Rome took place at the same time that the temporal power of the papacy came to a close. In September of that year Piedmontese troops occupied the city of Rome, and the pope became "the prisoner of the Vatican." It was not until the Lateran Treaty of 1929 that the question of the pope's temporal domains was settled with the creation of the Vatican State.

The fears that the dogma of infallibility would alienate large segments of the faithful were not, however, realized. The popes who followed Pius IX, especially Leo XIII, the worker's pope, and John XXIII, did much to dissipate this fear by abstaining from any ex-cathedra dogmatizing.

With the use of frequent encyclicals, or papal letters, on doctrinal and social questions, the papacy assumed a role of moral leadership hardly known during the centuries when the bishop of Rome was a temporal ruler. Since the Vatican Council, Catholicism has depended more and more on papal encyclicals for the shaping of its dogmatic and moral life. For many Catholics, the teachings set forth in this way are considered as infallible statements. They are held as the teachings of the sovereign authority of the Church.

One of the first important manifestations of this centralized teaching authority was to counter the divisive elements in modern theology by urging a return to scholasticism. Leo XIII found in the philosophical system of Aquinas the only answer to the skeptical relativism evident in modern theology. In 1879 he published the encyclical *Aeterni Patris,* which established the system of Aquinas as the basis of future theological speculation. He wrote:

> Domestic and civil society even, which, as all see, is exposed to great danger from this plague of perverse opinions, would certainly enjoy a far more peaceful and secure existence if a more wholesome doctrine were taught in the universities and high schools—one more in conformity with the teaching of the Church, such as is contained in the works of Thomas Aquinas.
>
> For, the teachings of Thomas on the true meaning of liberty, which at this time is running into license, on the divine origin of all authority, on the laws and their force, on the paternal and just rule of princes, on obedience to the higher powers, on mutual charity one toward another—on all of these and kindred subjects—have very great and invincible force to overturn those principles of the new order which are well known to be dangerous to the peaceful order of things and to public safety. In short, all studies ought to find hope of advancement and promise of assistance in this restoration of philosophic discipline which We have proposed. The arts were wont to draw from philosophy, as from a wise mistress, sound judgment and right method, and from it, also, their spirit, as from the common form of life. When philosophy stood stainless in honor and wise in judgment, then, as facts and constant

experience showed, the liberal arts flourished as never before or since; but, neglected and almost blotted out, they lay prone, since philosophy began to lean to error and join hands with folly. Nor will the physical sciences themselves, which are now in such great repute, and by the renown of so many inventions draw such universal admiration to themselves, suffer detriment, but find very great assistance in the restoration of the ancient philosophy. For, the investigation of facts and the contemplation of nature is not alone sufficient for their profitable exercise and advance; but, when facts have been established, it is necessary to rise and apply ourselves to the study of the nature of corporeal things, to inquire into the laws which govern them and the principles whence their order and varied unity and mutual attraction in diversity arise. To such investigations, it is wonderful what force and light and aid the Scholastic philosophy, if judiciously taught, would bring.

And here it is well to note that our philosophy can only by the grossest injustice be accused of being opposed to the advance and development of natural science. For, when the scholastics, following the opinion of the Holy Fathers, always held in anthropology that the human intelligence is only led to the knowledge of things without body and matter by things sensible, they well understood that nothing was of greater use to the philosopher than diligently to search into the mysteries of nature and to be earnest and constant in the study of physical things. And this, they confirmed by their own example; for Saint Thomas, Blessed Albertus Magnus, and other leaders of the Scholastics were never so wholly rapt in the study of philosophy as not to give large attention to the knowledge of natural things; and, indeed, the number of their sayings and writings on these subjects, which recent professors approve of and admit to harmonize with truth, is by no means small. Moreover, in this very age many illustrious professors of the physical sciences openly testify that between certain and accepted conclusions of modern physics and the philosophic principles of the schools there is no conflict worthy of the name.

Which, therefore, We hold that every word of wisdom, every useful thing by whomsoever discovered or planned, ought to be received with a willing and grateful mind. We exhort you, venerable brethren, in all earnestness to restore the golden wisdom of Saint Thomas, and to spread it far and wide for the defense and beauty of the Catholic faith, for the good of society, and for the advantage of all the sciences. The wisdom of Saint Thomas, we say; for if anything that ill agrees with the discoveries of a later age, or, in a word, improbable in whatever way—it does not enter Our mind to propose that for imitation to Our age. Let carefully selected teachers endeavor to implant the doctrine of Thomas Aquinas in the minds of students, and set forth clearly his solidity and excellence over others. Let the universities already founded or to be founded by you illustrate and defend this doctrine, and use it for the refutation of prevailing errors.

The dominant position of Thomism, especially in the training of the clergy, was reaffirmed by Pope Pius XII in 1950 when he appealed to the hierarchy to accept it as the only system that safeguards the genuine validity of human knowledge, the unshakable metaphysical principles of sufficient reason, causality, and finality, and finally the mind's ability to attain certain and unchangeable truths. He wrote:

If one considers all this well, he will easily see why the Church demands that future priests be instructed in philosophy "according to the method, doctrine, and principles of the Angelic Doctor," since, as we well know from the experience of centuries, the method of Aquinas is singularly preeminent both for teaching students and for bringing truth to light; his doctrine is in harmony with divine revelation, and is most effective both for safe guarding the foundation of faith, and for reaping, safely and usefully, the fruits of sound progress.

How deplorable it is then that this philosophy, received and honored by the Church, is scorned by some, who shamelessly call it outmoded in form and rationalistic, as they say, in its method of thought. They say that this philosophy upholds the erroneous notion that there can be a metaphysic that is absolutely true; whereas in fact, they say, reality, especially transcendent reality, cannot better be expressed than by disparate teachings, which mutually complete each other, although they are in a way mutually opposed. Our traditional philosophy, then, with this clear exposition and solution of questions, its accurate definition of terms, its clearcut distinctions, can be, they concede, useful as a preparation for scholastic theology, a preparation quite in accord with medieval mentality; but this philosophy hardly offers a method of philosophizing suited to the needs of our modern culture. They allege, finally, that our perennial philosophy is only a philosophy of immutable essences, while the contemporary mind must look to the existence of things and to life, which is ever in flux. While scorning our philosophy, they extol other philosophies of all kinds, ancient and modern, oriental and occidental, by which they seem to imply that any kind of philosophy or theory, with a few additions and corrections, if need be, can be reconciled with Catholic dogma. No Catholic can doubt how false this is, especially where there is question of those fictitious theories they call immanentis, or idealism or materialism, whether historic or dialectic, or even existentialism, whether atheistic or simply the type that denies the validity of the reason in the field of metaphysics.

Since a great deal of modern social thought has been concerned with the new role of the state in an industrialized society, the Catholic Church was also forced to come to grips with what it considered the growing menace of state control. In an encyclical entitled *Immortale Dei,* Leo outlined what is generally considered the official position of the Church on the role of the state in modern society. Of course, the encyclical was addressed to countries that were at least nominally Catholic and hence speaks with the uncompromising authority inherent in the strengthened magisterial powers of the Vatican decree on infallibility.

In effect, it stated that every Christian should be a Catholic and that every Christian country should be Catholic in its people and its government. The government is, in fact, obliged to treat Catholicism as one of a number of religions on an equal footing, but in a privileged position as the official religion of the state. The following excerpts sum up the papal position:

> Man's natural instinct moves him to live in a civil society. Hence it is divinely ordained that he should live his life—be it family, social, or civil—with his fellow men. Civil society

has its source in nature, and has, consequently, God for its author.

The Church is a society established to be Jesus Christ, chartered by right divine, perfect in itself, with the mission to guide men to heaven, and its aim and end the eternal salvation of souls. She has for her immediate and natural purpose the saving of souls and securing man's happiness in heaven.

The Almighty, therefore, has appointed the charge of the human race between two powers, the ecclesiastical and the civil, the one being set over divine and the other over human things.

Every civilized society must have a ruling authority; and this authority, no less than society itself, has its source in nature, and consequently God for its author. Hence it follows that all public power must proceed from God.

True and legitimate authority is void of sanction unless it proceeds from God, the supreme Ruler and Lord of all. The Almighty alone can commit power to man over his fellow men. . . .

The State is bound to make public profession of religion; it is a public crime for it to act as though there were no God. It is a sin in the State not to have care for religion, as a something beyond its scope, or as of no practical benefit; or out of many forms of religion to adopt that one which chimes in with the fancy; for we are bound absolutely to worship God in that way which he has shown to be His will. All who rule should hold in honor the holy name of God; and one of their chief duties must be to favor religion, to protect it, to shield it under the sanction of the laws, and to enact no measures that may compromise it. This is the bound duty of rulers to people over whom they rule.

It is not right for the State to treat all and any religions as on an equal footing. It is the duty of the State to give an established position to the religion which God enjoins, and which certain and most clear marks show to be the one only true religion. It cannot be difficult to find out what is the true religion, if only it be sought with an earnest and unbiased mind. It is evident that the only true religion is the one established by Jesus Christ, Himself, which He committed to

His Church to protect and propagate. This Church of Christ is the Catholic Church, Apostolic and Roman.

For all that, though, the Church deems it unlawful to place various forms of divine worship on the same footing as the true religion, she does not, on that account, condemn those rulers who, for the sake of securing some great good, or of hindering some great evil, tolerate in practice that these various forms of religion have a place in the State. And, in fact, the Church is wont to take earnest heed that no one shall be forced to embrace the Catholic religion against his will, for, as Saint Augustine wisely reminds us, "Man cannot believe otherwise than of his own free will."

The encyclical, in spite of its well developed theory of political authority, seems to many inadequate today because it fails to consider the concept of the people in their total relationship to government and the shift from the problem of Church and state to a broader area, the Church and human society. It also fails to take cognizance of the religious pluralism so much a part of the contemporary scene.

John XXIII, while reiterating the themes of Leo XIII, broadens his concern for all humanity in his encyclical *Pacem in Terris:*

Recent progress of science and technology has profoundly affected human beings and influenced men to work together and live as one family. There has been a great increase in the circulation of ideas, of persons and of goods from one country to another, so that relations have become closer between individuals, families, and intermediate associations belonging to different political communities, and between the public authorities of those communities. At the same time as the interdependence of national economies has grown deeper, one becoming progressively more closely related to the other, they may become, as it were, integral parts of the world economy. Likewise the social progress, order, security and peace of each country are necessarily connected with the social progress, order, security and peace of all the other countries.

At the present day no political community is able to pursue its own interests and develop itself in isolation, because the degree of its prosperity and development is a reflection and a component part of the degree of prosperity and development of all the other political communities.

The unity of the human family has always existed, because its members were human beings all equal by virtue of their natural dignity. Hence there will always exist the objective to promote, in sufficient measure, the universal common good, that is, the common good of the entire human family.

In times past, one would be justified in feeling that the public authorities of the different political communities might be in a position to provide for the universal good, either through the normal diplomatic channels or through top-level meetings, by making use of juridical instruments suggested by the natural law and regulated by the law of nations and international law.

As a result of the far-reaching changes which have taken place in the relations between the human family, the universal common good gives rise to problems which are complex, very grave and extremely urgent, especially as regards security and world peace.

On the other hand, the public authorities of the individual political communities—placed as they are on a footing of equality with one another—no matter how much they multiply their meetings or sharpen their wits in efforts to draw up new juridical instruments, they are no longer capable of facing the task of finding an adequate solution to the problem mentioned above. And this is not due to a lack of good will or of a spirit of enterprise, but because of a structural defect which hinders them.

It can be said, therefore, that at this historical moment the present system of organization and the way its principle of authority operates on a world basis no longer correspond to the objective requirements of the universal common good.

There exists an intrinsic connection between the common good on one hand and the structure and function of public authority on the other. The moral order, which needs public authority in order to promote the common good in human society requires also that the authority be effective in attaining that end. This demands that the organs through which the authority is formed, becomes operative and pursues its ends, must be composed and act in such a manner as to be capable of bringing to realization the new meaning which the common good is taking on in the historical evolution of the human family.

Today the universal common good poses problems of world-wide dimensions, which cannot be adequately tackled or solved except by the efforts of public authorities endowed with a wideness of powers, structure and means of the same proportions: that is, of public authorities which are in a position to operate in an effective manner on a worldwide basis. The moral order itself, therefore, demands that such a form of public authority be established.

The Industrial Revolution, which transformed large segments of the Catholic population of Europe and America from an agrarian to a more urbanized mode of life, soon overshadowed the theological problems posed by liberalism and modernism. The complex social and economic changes that occurred during the second half of the nineteenth century gave rise to moral and ethical problems that could not be solved by the simple restating of ancient precepts. The rapid growth of the population of cities created a shortage of clergy and of churches and schools. With the advance of modern medicine and a subsequent reduction of infant mortality the question of birth control and contraception was raised. The increase of literacy among the laity and the rapid spread of news media, especially the popular press, exposed the faithful to the ideas of liberalism and socialism that had hitherto been confined to the intellectuals.

Once again it was the aging Leo XIII who outlined what has become the basic Catholic position on the relationship between capital and labor, the individual and society. The encyclical *Rerum Novarum,* published in 1891, after calling attention to the evil conditions resulting from the Industrial Revolution, rejects the solution of socialism and takes a strong stand in declaring the Christian family as the most essential unit of society. Many of the ideas contained in this famous encyclical had already been formulated by members of the Catholic hierarchy in lands where the Industrial Revolution had alienated masses of the workers from the Church. Cardinal Manning in England, where large numbers of Irish laborers had migrated, and Cardinal Gibbons in the United States, by then the largest of the industrialized nations, had both worked for the improvement of the laboring classes. It was, however, the German bishop of Mainz, Von Ketteler, who first raised the cry for the removal of injustice and indignity in the treatment of labor. In his demand for a more equitable distribution of wealth and rights of labor to organize, he must be listed as one of the first champions of social justice based on the principles of the Gospel.

The encyclical still forms the platform on which the present social teachings of the Catholic Church are based. In 1961 John XXIII reiterated its basic theme in his encyclical *Mater et Magistra*. Many of its ideas have been incorporated in the constitutions of the western European democracies of today. Its salient points are found in the following excerpts:

It is not surprising that the spirit of revolutionary change, which has long been predominant in the nations of the world, should have passed beyond politics and made its influence felt in the cognate field of practical economy. The elements of a conflict are unmistakable: the growth of industry, and the surprising discoveries of science; the changed relations of masters and workmen; the enormous fortunes of individuals and the poverty of the masses; the increased self-reliance and the closer mutual combination of the working population; and finally, a general moral deterioration. The momentous seriousness of the present state of things just now fills every mind with painful apprehension; wise men discuss it; practical men propose schemes; popular meetings, legislatures, and sovereign princes, all are occupied with it—and there is nothing which has deeper hold on public attention.

It is not easy to define the relative rights and the mutual duties of the wealthy and of the poor, of capital and of labor. And the danger lies in this, that crafty agitators constantly make use of these disputes to pervert men's judgments and to stir up the people to sedition. To remedy these evils Socialists, working on the poor man's envy of the rich, endeavor to destroy private property, and maintain that individual possessions should become the common property of all, to be administered by the state or by municipal bodies. They hold that, by thus transferring property from private persons to the community, the present evil state of things will be set to rights, because each citizen will then have his equal share of whatever there is to enjoy. But their proposals are so clearly futile for all practical purposes, that if they were carried out the working man himself would be among the first to suffer. Moreover they are emphatically unjust, because they would rob the lawful possessor, bring the State into the sphere that is not its own, and causes complete confusion in the community.

It is surely undeniable that, when a man engages in remunerative labor, the very reason and motive of his work is to obtain property, and to hold it as his own private possession. If one man hires out to another his strength or his industry, he does this for the purpose of receiving in return what is necessary for food and living; he thereby expressly proposes to acquire a full and real right, not only to remuneration, but also to the disposal of that remuneration as he pleases. Thus, if he lives sparingly, saves money, and invests his savings, for greater security, in land, the land in such a case is only his wages in another form; and consequently, a working man's little estate thus purchased should be as completely at his own disposal as the wages he receives for his labor. But it is precisely in this power of disposal that ownership consists, whether the property be land or movable goods. The Socialists, therefore, in endeavoring to transfer the possessions of individuals to the community, strike at the interests of every wage earner, for they deprive him of the liberty of disposing of his wages, and of bettering his condition in life. . . .

The idea, then, that the civil government should, at its own discretion, penetrate and pervade the family and the household, is a great and pernicious mistake. True, if a family finds itself in great difficulty, utterly friendless, and without prospect of help, it is right that extreme necessity be met with public aid; for each family is a part of the commonwealth. In like manner, if within the walls of the household there occurs a grave disturbance of mutual rights, the public power must interfere to force each party to give the other what is due; for this is not to rob citizens of their rights, but justly and properly to safeguard and strengthen them. But the rulers of the state must go no further; nature bids them to stop here. Paternal authority can neither be abolished by the state nor absorbed; for it has the same source as human life itself; "the child belongs to the father," and is, as it were, the continuation of the father's personality; and, to speak with strictness, the child takes its place in civil society not in its own right, but in its quality as a member of the family in which it is begotten. And it is for the very reason that "the child belongs to the father," that, as Saint Thomas of Aquinas says, "before it attains the use of free-will, it is in the power and care of its parents." The socialists, therefore, in setting aside the parent and introducing the providence of the State, act against natural justice, and threaten the very existence of family life.

The New Devotions

In spite of the revolt of the intellectuals and the apostasy of the working classes, Catholicism throughout the nineteenth and early twentieth centuries showed a remarkable resiliency. It was marked by a revival of monasticism, an increased devotion to the humanity of Christ in His Sacred Heart, and a growing veneration of the Virgin Mary.

After a decline in membership during the French Revolution and the Napoleonic Wars, the oldest of the orders, the Benedictines, underwent a definite revival in the nineteenth century. Prior to 1815, attempts had been made to restore the order in Hungary and Bavaria.

In France, Prosper Louis Pasqual Guéranger provided the vital impetus for a restoration of the order. Guéranger provided the reorganize the monastery of St. Peter in Solesmes in 1833, and in 1837 he was appointed *abbé* of that monastery and prefect of a new Gallican congregation by Gregory XVI. The new communities multiplied but were suppressed in 1880 and finally banned by the French government in 1901. Some of the expelled Benedictines sought refuge in England, others in Belgium. A number of Benedictine congregations were established in America.

It was due to the efforts of Guéranger that an interest in the ancient liturgy of the Church was revived, and the so-called Gregorian chant of the Middle Ages was resurrected.

The leader of the Benedictine revival in Germany was Maurus Wolter who, with the assistance of Princess Katharina von Hohenzollern, purchased an ancient foundation of Augustinian canons at Bueron. Although lost to the Benedictines in 1875 because of the May Laws of the Kulturkampf, Bueron was ultimately restored in 1885 and became the mother house of various monasteries throughout Germany and other European nations. In 1884 Wolter was appointed archabbot by Leo XIII after the constitution of the Bueron congregation had received papal approval. By 1914 the Bueron congregation had expanded to Italy, Portugal, England, Bohemia, Brazil, and Jerusalem. An Austrian congregation was renewed in 1916, and in Spain several of the sixty-six Benedictine monasteries which had been dissolved in a wave of anticlerical sentiment in 1835 were restored. Downside Abbey in England also became the center of a flourishing intellectual and liturgical Benedictine revival. With the appointment of an abbot general in the 1890's, Leo XIII recognized the Trappists as a congregation independent of the Cistercians, and in 1902 Cîteaux received papal recognition as a mother house. The revival of the Franciscans in the nineteenth century was the result of an amalgamation of four branches of the original order. The Observants, Reformed, Recollects, and Alcantarines were united in 1897 under a general and given a central office in Rome. Although the Dominicans had suffered from the French Revolution and anticlericalism, they remained quite numerous, and when oppression ceased they began an industrious rebuilding program. Jean Lacordaire was responsible for their restoration in France.

The Society of Jesus, suppressed by Clement XIV in 1773 and not restored until 1814, continued to encounter resistance within the Church itself and was expelled from numerous countries during the nineteenth century. Despite these deterrents, the society flourished, being active once again in missionary work and education, especially in the United States.

The restored monastic orders, the Jesuits and the numerous

religious societies and congregations founded during the nineteenth century, continue to form the bulwark of Catholic defense in the present century. Their work in parishes and institutions of higher learning sets the pace for the secular clergy, most of whom receive their theological training from them. This is particularly true in the United States, where the Catholic religion was deeply influenced by the restored Catholicism of continental Europe. A chief factor in this development was the emergence in this country, during the late nineteenth century, of the parochial-school system, which placed the education of the laity in the hands of religious sisterhoods.

A striking feature of rejuvenated Catholicism was seen in an increased devotion to the Eucharist. In 1910 a papal decree urged that children should receive the Eucharist when they had reached the age of reason. As a result, many Catholics were introduced into the intricacies of the sacramental system at an age when a deep appreciation of the mysteries was hardly possible. For many, Catholicism was looked upon as a code of ethics rather than a participation in the life of Christ. The first encounter of most believers with the Church was in the darkness of the confessional, where Christ's representative, the priest, presented himself as a judge passing sentence on an interminable list of sins, duly memorized by the frightened penitent. Since there was little opportunity for adult education of the laity, most of them were forced to go through life with the rudimentary capsulary knowledge of religion they had received as children.

Confraternities of the Most Holy Sacrament multiplied and achieved a place of prominence in popular worship. An interesting aspect of this sacramental devotion was the emergence of Eucharistic congresses, begun in Lille, France, in 1881. These international conventions continued in the twentieth century and encouraged local Eucharistic Leagues, whose primary purpose was the glorification of the Blessed Sacrament.

Religious revival was also marked with a new increase in devotion to the Virgin Mary. Indicative of this was the declaration of the dogma of the Immaculate Conception by Pius IX in 1854:

For the honor of the holy and undivided Trinity, for the honor and renown of the Virgin Mother of God, for the exaltation of the Catholic faith, and the increase of the Christian religion, by the authority of our Lord Jesus Christ, by the authority of the blessed Apostles Peter and Paul, and by our own authority, We declare, pronounce and define: the doctrine that maintains that the most Blessed Virgin Mary in the first instant of her conception, by a unique grace and privilege of the omnipotent God and in consideration of the merits of Jesus Christ the Saviour of the human race, was preserved free from all stain of original sin, is a doctrine revealed by God and therefore must be firmly and constantly held by all the faithful. If therefore any shall obstinately maintain a contrary opinion to that which We have defined (God forbid that they do so), let them fully realize that they stand condemned by their own judgment, that they have made shipwreck of their faith, that they have departed from union with the Church. Furthermore, if they dare express in words or writing or any other way what they believe at heart, by that very action they are subject to punishments laid down by law.

Even before this declaration, many religious orders had been founded to foster devotion to the Virgin Mary. In 1816 the Oblates of Mary Immaculate were founded in France; when banned there, they spread to South Africa, Australia, and the western hemisphere. In the same year a similar organization, the Society of Mary, was founded by Jean Claude Colin; it received papal recognition in 1836 with a commission to work in the Pacific missions. The society spread to England and the United States in the twentieth century. A second Society of Mary was founded in 1817 by Guillaume Joseph Chaminade in Bordeaux. Originally named the Daughters of Mary, the society was popularly called the Marianists. Their primary work was the education of youth and care of orphanages. After their expulsion from France in 1903, a large number of members migrated to America and Japan.

Popular devotion to the Virgin was intensified by a number of reputed appearances of the Mother of God, in all cases to small children, in France and Spain. These appearances produced on one hand an intense religious fervor on the part of the laity and on the other a wave of anticlericalism and skepticism. Twice the Virgin was reported to have appeared in Paris in the 1830's, and on the plateau of La Salette two young Savoyard shepherds in 1846 reported that a "beautiful lady" appeared to them and expressed her concern over general religious apathy. In spite of serious doubt expressed by the archbishop of Lyons and many of the clergy, the appearances and miracles which occurred at the spot were declared genuine in 1851 by the bishop of Grenoble and reaffirmed by his successor. The place of the appearance became known as "the holy mountain of La Salette," and pilgrims flocked to it.

Perhaps the most famous and best-publicized appearance of the Virgin occurred in Lourdes, France, in 1858. Bernadette Soubirous, a fourteen-year-old peasant girl, claimed that a lady had appeared to her and identified herself as the Immaculate Conception. Reports of the appearance and subsequent miracles created widespread excitement and brought huge crowds to the grotto. Official response, both civil and ecclesiastical, was initially skeptical, but in 1862, after careful and thorough investigation, the diocesan authorities declared the miracles, most of them cures, to be valid. The crowds which flocked to Lourdes and credence given to the miracles were evidence of a growing vitality of the faith in the midst of a previous desertion of the Church by so many Catholics.

Another well-known appearance of the Virgin occurred in Fátima, Portugal, in 1917. Three young children, Jacinta and Francis Marto and Lucy dos Santos, reported that a beautiful lady appeared to them and instructed them to pray the Rosary and return every month until she revealed her identity and message. The phenomena and miracles that are said to have occurred here continue to attract large numbers of Catholics from all over the world.

The culmination of this growing devotion to the Virgin came in 1950 in the form of a dogmatic declaration by Pius XII that Mary was assumed bodily into heaven:

We therefore, after humbly and repeatedly praying to God, and calling upon the light of the Spirit of Truth, for the glory of almighty God, who has shown great and particular love for the Virgin Mary, for the honor of His Son, the king of immortal ages and the conqueror of sin and death, for the increase of the glory of his great mother, for the joy and exultation of the whole Church, by the authority of our Lord Jesus Christ, of the blessed Apostles Peter and Paul, and by our own authority, do pronounce, declare and define as a divinely revealed dogma: the Immaculate Mother of God, Mary ever Virgin, after her life on earth, was assumed, body and soul, to the glory of heaven.

One of the most popular Catholic devotions of the nineteenth and early twentieth centuries was the veneration to the Sacred Heart of Jesus. Although the devotion was initiated during medieval times, a number of revelations believed made to the French nun Marguerite Marie Alacoque (d.1690) during the seventeenth century brought the devotion to its present-day vogue. This popularity can be attributed in part to promises made to Marguerite Marie, including a guarantee of preserverence in the face of death. She wrote:

The Sacred Heart of my adorable Master has given me to understand that His desire to be known and loved and honored by men is so excessive that He has promised to all who consecrate and devote themselves to it in order to give it His pleasure, that He will never allow them to perish; that He will be their secure protection against all the snares of their enemies especially at the hour of their death, that He will receive them lovingly in His divine heart, thus placing their salvation in safety.

Political overtones were also evident in the movement, as it was recalled that Louis XVI had dedicated the French nation to the Sacred Heart at the time of his execution.

Religious communities and dioceses were also dedicated to the Sacred Heart, and on the eve of the First Vatican Council the entire Belgian nation was so consecrated by a member of the Belgian hierarchy. A French archbishop had circulated a petition desiring Pius IX to dedicate the entire universe to the Sacred

Heart, and such a petition was signed ultimately by all bishops, all heads of orders, and over a million of the laity. The petition was fulfilled in 1875, the bicentennial of the visions, by Pius IX. Leo XIII declared that the supreme accomplishment of his pontificate had been the consecration of all humanity to the Sacred Heart.

In 1956 Pius XII reiterated the benefits of this now deeply rooted devotion in the encyclical *Haurietis Aquas*. He urged the faithful to conjoin this practice with a devotion to the Immaculate Heart of Mary as well:

When so many evils meet Our gaze—such as cause sharp conflict among individuals, families, nations, and the whole world, particularly today more than at any other time—where are We to seek a remedy, venerable brethren? Can a form of devotion surpassing that to the most Sacred Heart of Jesus be found, which corresponds better to the essential character of the Catholic faith, which is more capable of assisting the present-day needs of the Church and the human race? What religious practice is more excellent, more attractive, more salutary than this, since the devotion in question is entirely directed towards the love of God itself? Finally, what more effectively than the love of Christ—which devotion to the Sacred Heart of Jesus daily increases and fosters more and more—can move the faithful to bring into the activities of life the Law of the Gospel, the setting aside of which, as the words of the Holy Spirit plainly warn, "the work of justice shall be peace," makes peace worthy of the name completely impossible among men? . . .

In order that favors in greater abundance may flow to all Christians, nay, on the whole human race, from the devotion to the most Sacred Heart of Jesus, let the faithful see to it that to this devotion that to the Immaculate Heart of the Mother of God is closely joined. For, by God's will, in carrying out the work of human redemption the Blessed Virgin Mary was inseparably linked with Christ in such a manner that our salvation sprang from the love and the sufferings of Jesus Christ to which the love and sorrows of His Mother were intimately united. It is, then, entirely fitting that the Christian people—who received the divine life from Christ through Mary—after they have paid their debt of honor to the Sacred Heart of Jesus should offer to the most loving Heart of their heavenly Mother the corresponding acts of piety, affection, gratitude and expiation. Entirely in keeping with this most sweet and wise disposition of Divine Providence is the memorable act of consecration by which We Ourselves solemnly dedicated Holy Church and the whole world to the spotless Heart of the Blessed Virgin Mary.

A further indication of the Catholic revival in modern times has been a renewed interest in the missions. During the seventeenth century the Church, through the governments of Spain and Portugal, had established flourishing missions in India, Siam, and the Philippines. In China it exerted a great influence in the court of Peking. In 1640 the German Jesuit Johann Schall von Bell reported from Peking that the number of Christians in the Middle Empire was more than sixty thousand. Yet conflict between the older orders, Franciscans, Dominicans, and Jesuits, on the question of ritual and nationalistic rivalry between the Portuguese Jesuits and the Spanish Dominicans and Franciscans often repelled the Orientals from Christianity. Much the same situation occurred in Japan, where most of the Christian communities were exterminated during the persecutions of 1632.

With the eclipse of Spain and Portugal as world powers, the missions in the Far East suffered a decided decline. The severest blow, however, to the eastern missions came with the suppression of the Jesuits. The beginnings of the modern missionary effort can be traced to the efforts of Pope Gregory XVI. Indicative of this new interest was the establishment of vicariates in Madagascar, the Cape of Good Hope, and Algiers during the 1830's. A vicariate was organized in Japan in 1846, and by 1886 eight ecclesiastical provinces with more than twenty bishops were reestablished in India. In China, a series of treaties between 1844 and 1862, enforced by the French government, enabled European missionaries, especially Franciscans, Dominicans, and Jesuits, to lay the groundwork for future proselytizing. By 1890 there were more than a million converts and a native clergy numbering four hundred. There were, however, no native bishops. And although the Boxer Rebellion was responsible for the deaths of thirty thousand Christians, it furthered the work of conversion. By the time of the Communist take-over following World War II, there were more than three million Chinese Catholics. Japan was not reopened to Catholic missionary work on a large scale until 1859. Many of the Catholic descendants of the sixteenth-century converts were once again reunited to Rome, and the missionary appeal was extended to the upper classes. At the present time there are more than two hundred thousand Catholics in Japan.

The Belgian Congo presents an interesting chapter in the spectacular success of government-directed missionary activity. As a result of the Berlin Conference of 1884 on colonial questions, the Belgian government under Leopold II undertook the sponsorship of a vast missionary program in the Congo, and within three generations almost one-fourth of the total population of the country had converted to Catholicism.

In the over-all picture, however, the progress of the Catholic Church in the mission field has been a disappointment. It is for this reason that many present-day theologians feel that the mission question represents the fundamental problem facing Catholicism in the twentieth-century adaptation to different cultures. On its solution rests the very existence of Christianity itself. The reaction of emerging peoples of Asia and Africa against colonialism must be overcome and the Europeanization of missionary methods must be radically altered.

Paternalism—the tendency to look upon the native convert as a child who one day in the distant future might be given a place of responsibility in the Church—has prevailed everywhere. There has been a constant unwillingness on the part of the Church to adapt itself to the various cultures she encounters, and this is coupled with a feeling of cultural superiority.

This failure to adapt the message of Christ to the non-Western mind was recognized as early as the seventeenth century by the Jesuit missionaries Ricci and Nobili. And yet the Church continues to join the words and concepts of *Romanism* and *Catholicism* so that the designation *Roman* has an importance as essential as the word *Catholic*.

A number of reasons have been advanced for this failure, among them the insistence on an unmarried clergy and a Latinized liturgy. But primarily the failure stems from the inability of the Western mind and culture to understand the Eastern philosophy of life. The basic differences between the Asian and European are perhaps best seen in their view of man's meaning in the universe. In almost direct contrast to the Western view of man, the non-European does not look upon man as either the end perfection or the center of nature, but rather as an integral part of it. Thus the Easterner finds man in a close relationship with all of nature, uniting all living and nonliving matter by the same spark of being. In the same respect, the non-European mind does not seek a technical explanation of the world's existence or creation, but is willing to accept the world's being and assumes the eternal continuity of the universe.

The problem has been recently stated by an African bishop:

The crisis in the growth of the life of the Church in Mission lands—Africa particularly—is further accentuated and complicated by the economic and political growth in these parts and also by the contrast which people in relatively obscure areas are presently experiencing with other cultures, especially with that of the West. The result of all this is that the Church is obliged to go through a critical period in her life in the missions. It is a matter of adaptation. But we may hope that this period of adaptation may be short on account of the rapidity with which the people involved are developing socially, politically, and economically. In their eagerness to become respected members of the world community of nations, people who were until recently inactive in world affairs are now forging ahead to realize their greatness and to do this within the shortest space of time. All of this surging activity—economic, political, social, cultural—creates a critical moment for the missionary Church which seeks to achieve a certain stability so that Christianity can take root and shape its surroundings. The question to be asked of missionaries in those areas where a ferment of environmental changes is taking place is "Are we advancing towards a *Civitas Dei* or a *Civitas diaboli?*"

The answer to this question will depend largely on whether or not the Church in this critical period will succeed in causing the message of the Gospel to take firm root in the life of those already converted to the Faith, so that Christianity will become one with their social and political life in whatever milieu they live.

Two great difficulties or dangers for the Church have to be met. The first is the difficulty which people in mission lands face of making the change from old social structures to new. While assuming their new place in the family of nations care must be taken that they do not lose all the good there is in their own culture. The second difficulty involves the danger of falling into materialism, blinded by the attraction of Western technical progress and civilization. Christianity has indeed solutions to these two difficulties, and the missionary work of the past years has already brought to the problem the needed solutions by preaching the gospel. But all this could be lost in a short time, if we did not show our Christians convincingly how to live as Christians in the world according to the social teachings and practices of Christianity—how to live in Christ in preparation for the eternal life, making use of the Liturgy of the Church. In the present situation of the Church in the missions there are probably no more necessary or more urgent matters than these two: social action and liturgical action, and the integration of the two into a mature Christian life.[26]

One is reminded of the advice given to missionaries in England by Gregory the Great in the seventh century:

You know the liturgical customs of the Roman Church in which you grew up. But I ask you to choose carefully, be it in the Roman ritual or in that of the Gauls, or of any other Church whatsoever, every element that seems more apt for a better service of the Almighty God. Select what is particularly adapted to the young Church of the Angles. Collect, then, from each of the Churches the liturgical customs that seem pious, religious and right, and gather them into a set corresponding to the mentality of the Angles and form them into liturgical fashion.

Catholicism at the Crossroads

The pontificate of John XXIII and the opening of the Second Vatican Council in October, 1962, must be considered as a most important chapter in the history of Catholicism. Many feel that the latter will rank with the Council of Chalcedon and the Gregorian reform in terms of changing the image of the Church. For the first time in more than five centuries, the Church has honestly examined its role in contemporary society and found itself wanting. The juridical and the liturgical traditions as well as the philosophizing of theology, so much a heritage of the Middle Ages, are being openly questioned. Thus far the council has responded to the pope's plan for giving more vigor to Christian life, adapting the Church to the needs of the times, and fostering the unity of all who believe in Christ along four lines. It has revolutionized the public prayer of the Church by giving the liturgy the prominent position it enjoyed before the debilitating accretions of the Middle Ages. Within the structure of the Church, two relationships are to be defined more precisely: that of the pope and bishop in government and that of the clergy and laity in collaboration. In her approach to the baptized not in communion with Rome, certain ecumenical guidelines are to be formed that will insure its present "openness." Finally, in bridging the gulf to modern society, the Christian concept of religious liberty is to be properly defined and proclaimed.

The constitution on the sacred liturgy which was promulgated in 1963 cuts like a sword through traditional Catholic concepts and voices a return to the ideals of the primitive Church:

> The wonderful works of God among the people of the Old Testament were but a prelude to the work of Christ the Lord in redeeming mankind and giving perfect glory to God. He achieved his task principally by the paschal mystery of his blessed passion, resurrection from the dead, and glorious ascension, whereby "dying, he destroyed our death and, rising, he restored our life." For it was from the side of Christ as he slept the sleep of death upon the cross that there came forth "the wondrous sacrament of the whole Church."

Just as Christ was sent by the Father, so also he sent the apostles, filled with the Holy Spirit. This He did that, by preaching the gospel to every creature, they might proclaim that the Son of God, by his death and resurrection, had freed us from the power of Satan and from death, and brought us into the kingdom of his Father. His purpose also was that they might accomplish the work of salvation which they had proclaimed, by means of sacrifice and sacraments, around which the entire liturgical life revolves. Thus by baptism men are plunged into the paschal mystery of Christ: they die with him, are buried with him, and rise with him; they receive the spirit of adoption as sons "in which we cry: Abba, Father" (Rom. 8,15), and thus become true adorers whom the Father seeks. In like manner, as often as they eat the supper of the Lord they proclaim the death of the Lord until he comes. For that reason, on the very day of Pentecost, when the Church appeared before the world, "those who received the word" of Peter "were baptized." And "they continued steadfastly in the teaching of the apostles and in the communion of the breaking of bread and in prayers . . . praising God and being in favor with all the people" (Acts 2,41-47). From that time onwards the Church has never failed to come together to celebrate the paschal mystery: reading those things "which were in all the scriptures concerning him" (Luke 24,27), celebrating the eucharist in which "the victory and triumph of his death are again made present," and at the same time giving thanks "to God for his unspeakable gift" (2 Cor. 9,15) in Christ Jesus, "in praise of his glory" (Eph. 1,12), through the power of the Holy Spirit.

To accomplish so great a work, Christ is always present in his Church, especially in her liturgical celebrations. He is present in the sacrifice of the Mass, not only in the person of his minister, "the same now offering, through the ministry of priests, who formerly offered himself on the cross," but especially under the eucharistic species. By his power he is present in the sacraments, so that when a man baptizes it is really Christ himself who baptizes. He is present in his word, since it is he himself who speaks when the holy scriptures are read in the Church. He is present, lastly, when the Church prays and sings, for he promised: "where two or three are gathered together in my name, there I am in the midst of them" (Matt. 18,20).

Christ indeed always associates the Church with himself in this great work wherein God is perfectly glorified and men are sanctified. The Church is his beloved Bride who calls to her Lord, and through him offers worship to the Eternal Father.

The central act of Catholic worship is once again to be understood as a public action of the entire Christian community as God's holy people. The Mass consists of the Liturgy of the Word and the Eucharist. The former is built around the Epistle and the Gospel and focuses attention once again on the long-neglected belief that Christ is present in His Word since it is He Himself who speaks when the Scriptures are read at divine service. The Eucharist is an act of thanksgiving in which the action of Christ the Priest and His Body the Church recall the great things God has done for His people and announce the fruits of His death and His resurrection.

To what extent the liturgical revival will succeed is a matter of great speculation. The great question in the minds of many is that since the present liturgy is so bound in its symbolism with its historical background, ancient, medieval, and baroque, should it not be given up all together? Would it not be better to admit that man in this industrial and scientific age, with its new sociological structure, is no longer capable of a liturgical act? Instead of a renewal, should not an effort be made to consider how best to celebrate the sacred mysteries so that modern man can grasp their meaning through his own approach to truth?

There has been a modification of the role of the bishops which also indicates a return to the practices of the Church before the Gregorian reform. The proposal that the episcopal college, including the pope, holds the supreme ministerial power to govern and teach in the Church is reminiscent of the Council of Constance and the claims of the Gallican bishops. It is significant that the pope informed the Fathers of the council that the common responsibility of the college of bishops is in harmony with the supreme position of the papacy as laid down in the First Vatican

Council. The pope, he claimed, is the hinge and the co-ordinating center of the Church universal. He exercises his supreme office as teacher and legislator in matters which touch upon the good of the entire Church, especially her unity of faith and communion. The world-wide extension of the Catholic Church demands a strong leadership at the center, a central authority "which will be tempered and balanced by an alert and timely delegation of authority and facilities to local pastors." The function of the pope's supreme jurisdiction is, therefore, not to weaken but to strengthen the authority of the episcopate, whether this authority be considered in the individual bishop or in bodies of bishops. Implied in this declaration is the creation of a senate of bishops which would gradually replace the conservative and predominantly Italian Curia in directing the government of the Church.

Perhaps the strongest indication that Catholicism is turning its face to the future has been its condemnation of anti-Semitism and its declaration on religious liberty. The statement of the council on religious liberty asserts that freedom in matters of religion is the right of every individual and thus implies freedom of conscience and freedom of exercise of religion. It marks a turning away from the superannuated opinion traceable to the time of Constantine, which regarded God and the mystery of human salvation as involved in concepts to be manipulated by Church and state.

The proposal on religious liberty takes as its starting point the double task of teaching all nations and announcing to all men the salvation brought by Christ and at the same time of "respecting in all questions in which no agreement has yet been reached, not only the sacred and absolute rights of God, but also the rights and duties of the persons or subjects who are to adhere to the truth." By this formulation it indicates that in human society the rights of the free person rank next to those of God and that the community and the Church also have to respect both. When there is a real or apparent clash of duties, the valid relation between objective order and subjective rights is not subordination but co-ordination. The Church's mission to lead all men to believe in Christ has to be harmonized with respect for man's freedom of conscience, which may be subjectively sincere, even if erroneous. Consequently, Christ's disciples are to be "conscious not only of the mission of proclaiming and defending the truth, but at the same time always and everywhere of the obligation of treating with love, prudence, and patience those who have not yet come to a full knowledge of the Gospel." Christians themselves must observe and respect "the progressive and humane manner with which God leads men with his truth and love."

As well as truth there must also be taken into account the rights and the degree of grace accorded by God to the human beings who are called upon freely to embrace faith. Religious freedom, in the sense of freedom from external compulsion in the practice of religion, is demanded by the nature of the act of faith itself. For man redeemed by Christ cannot accept divine revelation if on the one hand the Father does not draw him and if on the other hand he does not give God a natural and free obedience. Therefore no one can be compelled to accept faith, and so long as anyone is invincibly convinced, he deserves respect and his religious freedom is recognized and defended by the Church. This freedom must be acknowledged by all, for man can only reach his last end if he follows his responsibly formed conscience. In this way, even with an erroneous conscience, a man fulfills God's will, for God Himself so respects personal freedom that this is not destroyed by error.

The council is here defending nothing less than the integrity of human moral acts, of which freedom is a constitutive element. No one can release man from this development in freedom, especially from his decision for or against God. No human authority can take His place. Absolute submission to God, of course, presupposes that a man seeks to know the will of God, that he uses all available means of information, and that regard is had for the rights of others. But if a man has done everything in his power to inform himself about the truth, yet misses it all the same, no human being and no human power has the right to usurp the place of this erroneous conscience, that is to say, to exercise coercion. In this connection the schema declares: "The Catholic Church regards religious intolerance as in the highest degree abhorrent and as a violation of the human person. For by it man is robbed of the freedom to follow the dictates of his conscience, which a man who errs in good faith himself perceives to be the highest and most sacred directing principle."

All this concerns freedom of personal conviction, that is, individual liberty. But the draft goes further than this. The Church, it affirms, does not endorse religious freedom merely as "freedom of opinion," as "freedom to perform the rights of one's own religion or as a personal right not to be prevented from fulfilling religious duties privately and publicly, individually or collectively." The Catholic Church avers that such religious freedom belongs both to individual human persons and to human groups who feel obliged in conscience to join forces "to lead and promote religious life." The right to confess and proclaim faith does not belong to the individual only, therefore, but also to associations. Society must consequently insure that scope for the freedom of denominational bodies which they need to exercise their functions according to the conscience of believers, and it may only restrict this right to the extent that the common good is jeopardized. Public authority cannot impose on citizens the profession of a particular religion as a condition of their being able to take full part in national and civil life. Penalties, discrimination, and confiscation of property on religious grounds, or direct religious persecution, are most rigorously condemned. Freedom from state coercion in religious matters forms, according to the schema, one of the conditions for building an order worthy of man.

The Constitution on Divine Revelation, promulgated at the Second Vatican Council, is a definite departure from the teachings of Trent with their emphasis upon faith as an act of the intellect. Faith is now described as a vital and total response to God. The Word of God, like the word of man, is presented as a matter of self-revelation. Tradition, hitherto limited to the teachings of the Fathers and the magisterial pronouncements of the past now includes not only doctrine but cult and practice. The scriptural idea of religion being a dialogue with God, long a Protestant tradition, is firmly admitted. The document liberates the Church from its traditional insistence on an unchanging moral code and an over conceptualized theology. The Church can no longer interpret the Scripture as it would like to do, but rather it must respect the writings for what they actually are.

It is evident that the spirit of renewal so much a part of modern-day Catholicism is due to those historical processes that have constantly shaped it. The Church's inability to forestall two global wars and the spread of Communism in traditionally Catholic countries have fostered this change of outlook. The Church has gradually shaken off the polemical mentality of the Counter Reformation and loosed itself from the nostalgia of Romanticism. The existentialism of the postwar era has especially placed Catholicism in an entirely new spiritual climate which directs man toward a more personal encounter with the world, a commitment to humanity, and a deeper comprehension of the human condition. Within the Church this existentialism has revised the notion of Catholicism as a living commission and witness to the message of Christ.

This is reflected in a growing tendency to see religion as a personal encounter with God—an encounter which produces a sense of Christian responsibility for the world of man and the human tasks of life. It is significant that this movement has led back to the original sources, both Biblical and patristic, of early Christianity. There has been a return to a sense of history that sees Catholicism as a dynamic part of salvation rather than the guardian of immutable truths and unchanging abstractions. Revelation is once again being understood not so much as the communication of divine truths, but as the self-communication of God to man. God does not reveal truths, but reveals Himself. This He does by acting and speaking in the history of Israel and in His Son Jesus Christ. Revelation comes to mankind in the person of Christ not merely in His teaching but in His life, His actions, and His very existence which is the Mystical Body, the Church.

Thus the image of the Catholic Church as the bark of Peter sailing fully rigged and unchanging over the sea of the centuries is giving way to a more scriptural concept which sees it as the grain of wheat which germinates, sprouts, produces new seed, but remains true to itself in the changing forms it takes on in the course of history. This understanding of Catholicism may dispel the centuries-old belief that since the time of Constantine it has not withstood the temptation to power by bolstering its position with secular privileges. It may also dissipate the assumption that in so doing it has both destroyed the credibility of its claims to a world-wide mission and compromised the impact of that missionary endeavor.

It is now apparent that any concept of the Church which envisions it as a static reality is not only inadequate but false to its biblical sources. The Church is an continuing event, a process in which people are called together by the Spirit. The Church is not one, holy and Catholic so much as it has a mission to become one, holy and Catholic, a mission that is being accomplished in history and through people. Catholicism must imply a universality, an openness to all possibilities. Yet as history so clearly demonstrates the Church has too often opened itself to certain promising directions with the exclusion of others. Within Catholicism there has always been a constant conflict between integralism or closed catholicism and true catholicity which is open to all possibilities and to the fullest expansion and expression of its basic mission. The conflict has not been between conservative and progressive, but between closed and open mentalities. The prophetic insights of Pope John XXIII and his admission that the Church must constantly be reformed have made many Catholics painfully aware of how thoroughly their Church has been hobbled by Roman legalistic and institutional thinking. It has opened their eyes to the post-Tridentine ghetto triumphalism that looks down upon other Christians and non-Christians as "lost sheep" and "prodigal sons." As the decrees of the Second Vatican Council proclaim, Catholicism today demands dialogue with the world, an openness to all cultures and religions.

CHAPTER 6

The Catholic Church of Today

IN SPITE OF the many changes that are taking place in the Catholic Church of today, much of the medieval structure whose development has been described in the preceding chapters still remains. The Roman Catholic considers his church as a divinely instituted organization founded by Christ, the Second Person of the Trinity, true God and true man in which and through which he can work out his eternal salvation. The sacramental system perfected during the Middle Ages is most essential in this program of salvation.

Unless he is a convert, a Catholic is inducted into the Church at the beginning of life through the sacrament of Baptism; at the end he is prepared for eternity through Extreme Unction. While young he receives the sacrament of Penance, that is, the confessing of one's sins to an authorized priest, repenting of them and resolving to sin no more, in order to receive absolution. Shortly afterward he receives Holy Eucharist, the Body and Blood of Christ, and Confirmation, confirming him into the Church. Later he may be married in the sacrament of Matrimony or raised into the priesthood through Holy Orders. Thus the Church provides for the most important acts of a person's life—birth, marriage, and death—through these seven outward signs instituted by Christ to give grace.

The central act of worship in Catholicism is the sacrifice of the Mass which must be attended all Sundays and holy days of obligation, except for a grave reason. There is also a yearly obligation of receiving Penance and Holy Eucharist during the Easter time, from the first Sunday of Lent until Trinity Sunday. Every Catholic must educate his children in the faith, supplemented if possible by attendance at a parochial or Sunday School. There is a hard core of dogma that all Catholics must accept. They must also assume the obligations imposed by the Ten Commandments and the commandments of the Church. Over the centuries thorough interpretation and application to daily life of the commandments has been made by theologians and philosophers, extending Catholicism into the minutiae of daily life.

The Pope

The Roman Catholic Church still remains hierarchical in structure. At the apex is the pope, the bishop of Rome whom Catholics believe to be in direct succession to Peter. The succession of power in the Church proceeds from God through the pope to the bishops, the priests, and then the laity. These first three form the hierarchy, by which is meant two things: the plenitude of power possessed by the Church, and the ranks of the people who share the power. The plenitude of power is further divided into powers of order and authority.

By the power of order is meant the right to sanctify by holy ritual. This power is conferred by ordination and is based on a spiritual mark or character. It is irrevocable and sacramental in nature. The power of authority is given in order to govern the faithful for spiritual ends. It is conferred as a result of appointment to an office. This is the pastoral power of executive, legislative, administrative, and judicial functions combined. It is of the nature of moral relationships and is able to be changed when necessary. A teaching power is also recognized as being related to the other two.

The hierarchy of order is comprised of bishops, priests, and deacons; that of authority is made up of the pope and the subordinate officialdom of the Church. The papacy is the seat of all authority and is self-renewing. The bishops provide the core of the priesthood and are also self-renewing. They share the power of authority with the pope when sitting in an ecumenical council and share the power of order with him as a natural right of their being bishops.

"Thou art Peter and upon this Rock I will build my Church and the gates of Hell shall not prevail against it, and to thee I give the keys of the kingdom of Heaven."

These words, now carved on the inside of St. Peter's dome, and Christ's other command, "Whatsoever you bind on earth, it shall be bound also in Heaven; and whatsoever you shall loose on earth, it shall be loosed also in heaven" conferred on St. Peter and his successors, the bishops of Rome, the primacy of power in Christ's Church. The pope is believed by Catholics to be the visible head of the Mystical Body of Christ, the supreme leader of the Roman Catholic Church. From him either directly or indirectly proceeds every act necessary for the government of the Church. Ruling in the fullness of power, the papacy is actually a form of absolute monarchy. The pope is equal to all other bishops in his power of priesthood as bishop of Rome; thus his decisions are binding on the entire church. He is subject to no court of law, only the judgment of God. He is bound only by the moral law and the discipline of the Church.

The pope is superior to all the bishops assembled in an ecumenical council. Although Vatican II held that the bishops share in the government of the Church, the pope still has the power to convene, preside at, and dismiss the councils, and resolutions passed by it are effective only when approved and issued by him.

Infallibility applies to matters of faith and morals, promulgated by the pope speaking ex cathedra, that is, in his position as head of the Church. This applies to every pope, no matter what his personal life. The doctrine being proclaimed infallible must be found directly or indirectly in Holy Scripture. The doctrine of infallibility is also applied to pronouncements of the ecumenical councils and the ordinary teaching of the bishops of the Church in a body.

Canon law has outlined the duties of a pope. As supreme lawgiver he may defend doctrine against heresy, introduce, alter, or suppress Church law, and regulate holy days, feast days, and fasts. He controls the rites and liturgy but may not add or subtract from the Sacraments. When he censors a book or other work, it applies to the entire Church. He is also charged with the maintenance of religious worship in a pure form and the establishment and extension of the Church.

In his administrative capacity, the pope may set up, suppress, or alter dioceses; appoint bishops and auxiliary bishops; recognize, regulate, and abolish religious orders; found and regulate universities; grant indulgences; canonize saints; and issue liturgical books. Furthermore, he is enjoined to organize and enforce the cultus of the Church.

The pope is also a judge. He can act as a court of first instance, organize other courts, establish rules of judicial procedure, and fix punishments. He may absolve a person from punishments, relax vows and oaths, and give matrimonial dispensations. Certain forms of excommunication and release are reserved to him.

The Cardinals

The pope cannot hope to run the entire Church by himself. To help him, he has the College of Cardinals and the Curia. The Curia is the bureaucracy run by the cardinals, the chief priests of the Church.

The college is the senate and cabinet of the Church, and as such elects the popes. Any priest may become a cardinal if the pope wishes. The pope announces his choice before the assembly of cardinals called the Consistory, where he receives formal approval of his choices. The priests and bishops chosen are usually distinguished by their learning, piety, and administrative abilities. The rule is that no man who has a close relative in the college may become a cardinal, a guard against nepotism; but John XXIII created a second Cardinal Cicognani, a brother of the first.

The former Italian hegemony of the college has been broken. Cardinals are appointed from all over the world, and no longer are Italians in a majority. But the cardinals are still regarded as the titular clergy of Rome.

There are three ranks of cardinals, but the titles have nothing to do with their actual status in the hierarchy. The cardinal bishops are six in number, representing the seven suburbican sees of Rome. The dean of the college holds two sees, his own and that of Ostia. When a cardinal bishop dies, the senior cardinal priest moves. Cardinal priests, the titular parish priests of the Roman churches, are bishops from other parts of the world. The cardinal deacons are the members of the Curia who are not bishops. The senior cardinal deacon announces the election of a new pope. All members of the Curia who actively participate in its work live in Rome. Only the papal secretary of state actually lives in the Vatican.

The Consistory of Cardinals is the last vestige of the old assembly of cardinals. It meets once or twice a year for the creation of new cardinals or the canonization of saints. There are three types of consistories. In the secret consistory only cardinals are admitted. The pope reads a list of all bishops created since the last consistory and the list of new cardinals and says, "What do you think?" The cardinals then give their assent. Some cardinals are named *in petto;* only the pope knows who they are. They are not announced because harm may befall them if this honor is known. Only when it is safe will the pope announce them, but their reign dates from the first consistory.

The semipublic consistory takes place later in the week. Certain dignitaries as well as the cardinals are present. The pope reads an address and gives the new cardinals the scarlet biretta; later he receives them in a private audience and gives them the red skullcap.

In the public consistory they are vested with the red hat that is the symbol of their office. The pope, cardinals, bishops, diplomats, court officials, and other dignitaries attend.

At the consistories for canonizations, the cardinals cast their votes pro or con for the would-be saint as a formality only. At the later public consistory, advocates plead for canonization, and finally the cardinals and local bishops are called in for advice.

The conclave is an assembly of all cardinals for the express purpose of electing a pope. Any cardinal may attend and vote, even those who may have been excommunicated. Since it is so important that the papacy have a continuing succession, very definite regulations have been developed to control every detail of the conclave.

To guard against outside interference, only cardinals, their two manservants (three if necessary), and cooks, physicians, carpenters, and others needed for the bodily care of the cardinals are allowed in the sealed building. The fullest secrecy prevails throughout, excommunication being the penalty for breaking the secrecy.

The election begins between fifteen and eighteen days after the death of a pope. The first day there is no voting; Mass is said, speeches are read reminding the cardinals of their duty, and then the unauthorized leave and the building is sealed. The next day balloting begins.

Three methods of election are recognized. One is by inspiration: without previous discussion or agreement, the cardinals acclaim a pope either orally or in writing at the suggestion of one of their number. Secondly, in an extraordinary situation the compromise method may be used: three to seven electors are chosen unanimously to elect a pope. They receive their instructions to fit the situation, and all cardinals bind themselves to accept the choice.

The third and most common means of election is by balloting. A two-thirds plus one majority is needed; the plus one is added because a cardinal may not vote for himself, and the extra vote eliminates the tedious procedure of checking the ballots to make certain. The ballots are cast in order of seniority. As the ballots are cast, the prelates say, "I take to witness Christ our Lord, who is to judge me that I hereby vote for him who before God I feel should be elected." The ballot is placed on a paten, then transferred to a chalice. If a cardinal is too sick to get out of bed, the cardinal-scrutineers take the box to him.

The chalice is then shaken, and the ballots are counted. If they do not correspond to the number present, they are burned immediately, and a new vote is taken. If all is well, the first teller opens the ballot and passes it to the second teller, who passes it to the third, who reads it aloud. If no pope is elected, the ballots are tied together and, after a second ballot, burned in a special stove. If the votes were inconclusive, damp straw is thrown on the fire, causing black smoke; but when a pope has been elected, they are burned without straw, giving white smoke. The color of the smoke is the only sign of progress available to the outside world. There are two ballots in the morning and two in the afternoon of each day.

When a decision is reached, the dean of the college asks the man if he accepts. As soon as the candidate assents, he becomes pope, the coronation being only a formality. He receives the homage of the cardinals and is presented to the people with the cry, "We have a Pope."

The Curia

The Curia is the officialdom of the Church and the center of ecclesiastical government. The Curia cardinals have no power to make or alter laws, but serve as aides and advisers to the popes. They may not undertake any action of importance without first consulting the pope; all their decisions must be allowed by him unless he has granted special authorization. The Curia consists of twelve congregations, three tribunals, four offices, and numerous commissions.

The most important single man in the Vatican next to the pope is the Secretary of State. He is the pope's right-hand man and principal adviser. He meets with the pope daily and resigns his office at the death of a pope. He is also a member of all the important congregations.

The State Secretariat is divided into three parts. The first section is for Extraordinary Ecclesiastical Affairs and carries on

223 · THE CURIA

the regular business of the Church with civil governments. It draws up the texts of concordats and agreements. It is instrumental in the choice of bishops where the approval of the government is needed and handles all problems which concern the basic policy of the Holy See. The section for Ordinary Affairs deals with all current problems that are not brought to the attention of the first section. It moves faster than the first section and prepares a daily résumé of the news and current trends. This section and the Consistorial Congregation work on the appointment of new bishops where no political questions are involved and suggest nuncios and other papal diplomats. Catholic Action and other lay organizations look to it for guidance in political matters. This section also handles alms and disaster relief subsidies. Honors conferred on ecclesiastics and laymen by the pope are processed here. The third section is that of Apostolic Briefs, having the task of suitably rewriting the documents of the pope and the other two sections.

Two other offices under the Secretary of State are the Secretariats for Briefs to Princes and of Latin Letters. These translate into perfect Latin and send all papal letters to kings, members of royal families, and heads of state. They answer pleas for canonization, and their secretary delivers the oration on the eve of the conclave calling for a new pope.

Under the Secretariat of State and the Congregation for Extraordinary Ecclesiastical Affairs is the papal diplomatic service. The Church must have a way to remind civil governments of the role of spiritual values in life, and the right of the Church to control local religious affairs is safeguarded by diplomatic representation. It also deepens a friendly atmosphere between Church and state. This exchange does not imply recognition of the Church or union with it, but is a friendly act and a matter of prestige.

There are two types of delegates, one to governments and one to ecclesiastics. All are titular bishops and for the duration of their office are accorded Vatican citizenship. They cannot interfere in diocesan affairs without authority. There are four titles, and they report to three different congregations.

Apostolic Nuncios are the true ambassadors. They share in all the privileges of secular ambassadors. By special agreement, each is dean of his respective diplomatic corps, regardless of his seniority. Canon law ascribes to them the duties of fostering good relations with the host governments, watching over the dioceses, and making regular reports on the condition of the nation. For these reasons they are given special powers, such as the ability to grant certain dispensations normally reserved to the Holy See. Apostolic Internuncios, of whom there are presently ten, correspond to envoys extraordinary and plenipotentiary. Setting up an Apostolic Internunciate is usually the preliminary step to full diplomatic recognition.

Having no official diplomatic standing, the Apostolic delegate does not deal with the government but represents the pope to the hierarchy and people of the country. He watches over dioceses, presides at synods and plenary councils, and makes periodic reports to the pope on the progress of the faith.

The fourth official is the Legate *a latere* (Latin: from his very side), who is a temporary personal representative of the pope to important church congresses and other functions. The position is one of religious and liturgical prestige rather than diplomatic in nature.

The various congregations are likened to the departments of the United States government. They are the chief organs of administration, first of which is the Congregation for the Doctrine of the Faith, formerly the Holy Office. With the pope as its prefect, it is supreme in safeguarding faith and morals. It teaches, exercises vigilance over beliefs of the faithful, examines and appraises new doctrines, and gives explanations of difficult ones. It handles mixed marriages, condemnation of books—the Index, heresy, apostasy, schism, profanation of the Eucharist, and antireligious publications. It corresponds with bishops and superiors of religious orders. Its jurisdiction embraces the entire world and its population, save the cardinals themselves.

This Office also acts as a tribunal when judging clerics accused of heresy, belonging to non-Catholic sects, or offenses against the moral law. Its opinions, admonitions, and punishments are mostly jurisdictional; rarely does it impose economic sanctions.

The Consistorial Congregation, with the pope as its prefect, has complete and absolute jurisdiction over all bishops and dioceses, except mission territories. It handles nomination of bishops and creation of diocesan and provincial boundaries and defines the scope of the various other congregations. It also receives the quinquennial reports of bishops, answers their queries, and gives them advice.

The Congregation for the Eastern Church functions in an administrative and judicial power for all Uniate Catholics, those who recognize the supremacy of the pope but still use the Eastern Rite liturgy, and also the Latin Rite Catholics in Eastern countries. It works for an eventual reunification with the various Orthodox churches and the third congregation with the pope as prefect.

The Congregation of the Sacraments regulates the rites and ceremonies of the seven sacraments. It is mostly concerned with the annulment or legislation of marriages and dispensations from vows for the religious. It legislates and administers discipline except for that reserved to the Holy Office.

The Congregation of the Council exercises supervision over the religious and laity. It is concerned with spreading the catechism, the financial affairs of the dioceses, and Catholic Action, and it issues instructions for the observance of fast and abstinence, Sunday service, clerical dress, stipends for masses, and endowments. This congregation also receives and approves acts of the various plenary councils and conducts a council school where priests studying canon law may acquire practical experience in handling problems.

Control of clerical orders is the province of the Congregation of the Religious, a strictly administrative body. It is concerned with all questions of government, discipline, studies, financial and property matters, and rights and privileges. It receives the quinquennial reports of the heads of orders and keeps statistics on the religious orders in the world. The congregation is divided into two parts for greater efficiency. The first section is for ordinary affairs, which is further subdivided into offices for communities of men, communities of women, and societies without vows. The second section, for special affairs, handles whatever problems are placed before it by the prefect.

The Congregation for the Propagation of the Faith works with the missions. It handles administration, expansion, and protection of the mission system as well as for unorganized territories. It takes care of its own finances and runs a news service.

The Congregation of Rites takes charge of church liturgy and canonization of saints. The members are masters of pontifical ceremonies and experts in liturgy and related fields, such as veneration of relics.

The Congregation of the Ceremonial deals with the ceremonies and audiences of the pope, visits of important guests, and protocol, precedence, and etiquette involving the papal court. The prefect of this congregation is the dean of the College of Cardinals.

The Congregation of Seminaries and Universities supervises all Latin Rite seminaries, except for those connected with the missions, as well as all Catholic schools and universities and organizations that foster vocations. It regulates their course of studies, staffs, and administration and controls directly regional seminaries.

The Congregation for Extraordinary Ecclesiastical Affairs works very closely with the Secretary of State, who is its prefect. It is a top-level advisory board closely consulted by the pope. The congregation formulates the basic line of policy, but leaves the details to the Secretariat of State or to the appropriate congregation.

Care of the largest church in Christendom is given to the Congregation for St. Peter's Basilica. It supervises the administration, endowment, repair, and research of the Basilica.

Commissions are small bodies of specialists with a definite and limited purpose. They will go out of existence when their work is completed. They require special knowledge and the study of subjects that cannot be thoroughly handled by the congregations.

The Pontifical Commission for Bible Studies promotes the study of the Bible and makes sure these studies are kept free from error. It also confers scholarships to deserving Bible students.

The Pontifical Commission of Canon Law gives an authentic interpretation of the Code of Canon Law. Another commission compiling a code of canon law for the Eastern Church works independently of that of the Latin Church.

There are other commissions that are continually correcting the Vulgate (the Latin Bible), preserving the faith in Rome, co-ordinating the activity of organizations producing films of a Catholic nature, preserving the historic and artistic monuments of the Holy See, administering the pontifical sanctuary of Pompeii, preserving and increasing the artistic possessions of the Church, supervising sacred archaeology, preserving church archives and encouraging their studies, and co-ordinating relief work done by various Catholic organizations. The two newest commissions were set up by Pope John for Latin America and the ecumenical council.

To complete the picture of the administrative organs, we must consider the offices. These are the lowest administrative bodies in the Curia and serve mostly as centers for executing and sending the directives of the congregations.

The Apostolic Chancery is the executor of orders from the pope and congregations. It draws up papal bulls and documents for the establishment of new bishops and dioceses. The Cardinal Chancellor serves as the notary for the Consistory.

The Apostolic Datary handles the granting of nonconsistorial or minor benefices reserved to the Holy See. It examines the qualifications and worthiness of each applicant and prepares Apostolic Letters of Appointment. It also has the power to dispense with some of the requirements for those offices.

The Apostolic Camera in theory takes care of the revenues and property of the Holy See. The titles and functions of this office are largely honorary, however, while the pope lives. As soon as he dies, the Cardinal Camerlengo takes over the business and financial affairs of the Church during the interregnum. He issues notification of the death of the pope, establishes his headquarters in the Vatican, and seals the papal apartments to prevent the removal of papal documents or personal effects.

The judicial affairs of the papacy are handled by three tribunals. The Sacred Apostolic Penitentiary is the highest ecclesiastical court. Its work is covered by a cloak of secrecy so thick that the judges do not even know the clients' names, and it is concerned chiefly in the sacramental, internal area. It operates under the inviolable secrecy of the seal of confession and corresponds with the petitioners through their confessors. Its decisions are free of charge. Because it is dealing with matters of conscience, it takes quick action in supplementing penance and granting quick absolutions, if they cannot be delayed, in reserved cases (serious sins whose absolution is reserved to the pope). It may also dispense marriage and religious vows, grant indulgences, and convert certain obligations to other ones.

The Sacred Rota is composed of fifteen prelates and a dean, concerned with the annulment of marriages. Decisions are rendered by three judges. It is a court of appeal from diocesan courts, but in some instances is a court of first instance. It also acts as a court of appeal in civil and criminal cases from Vatican courts. In about half the annulment proceedings that are heard, the validity of the marriage is upheld. All pleading is done by writing, though in unusual cases the testimony of witnesses may be heard. The decisions of the Rota, though not infallible, do not need papal confirmation.

The Rota annually publishes a list of lawyers with their fees. There is no set charge; a sliding scale of from $42 to $142 is used, and if the bishop of the diocese decides the petitioners are too poor to pay, there is no compensation demanded. The Rota also conducts a school to train lawyers.

The Apostolic Signature is the ultimate court of appeal. It hears appeals from the Rota only, determining whether all the laws and correct forms have been used. It settles any controversies that arise between lower courts, with the exception of the Holy Office and the Congregation of Rites. There is no limit to the number of judges that it may have.

In August of 1967 the Pope outlined in an apostolic constitution "Regimini Ecclesiae Universae" Government of the Universal Church a new program for reforming the Roman Curia. The more important changes will place more authority in the Secretary of State, making him almost a papal deputy. Thus the Secretary of State will assume the status of a virtual prime minister with powers to coordinate the work of nine other curial departments which formerly were twelve and were semi-independent and equal under the Pope. Equally important was the provision that major curial appointments shall be for a five year period and that they shall terminate on the death of the Pope. Other important changes proposed were the establishment of a new body to deal with the Vatican's foreign affairs and a Prefecture of Economy, a sort of finance and budget ministry.

Vatican City

The pope is a temporal as well as spiritual ruler; he is the absolute sovereign of Vatican City, a small independent state of 108.7 acres surrounded by the city of Rome. In 1929 by the Lateran Treaty (a sign of sovereignty is the right to make treaties), papal lines of communication were declared immune to interference, diplomatic immunity was extended to those ambassadors accredited to the Holy See, and the territory of Vatican City was declared inviolable by secular powers.

The Vatican has its own palaces, churches, museums, art gallery, jail, technical and economic services, library, radio station, railway depot, observatory, and police—the Swiss Guards and Papal Gendarmes.

It has its own printing office, which issues three publications: *Osservatore Romano,* a daily paper; *Osservatore Della Domenico,* a Sunday paper; and *Ecclesia,* a magazine. Further proof of sovereignty is its observance of all the recognized forms of statehood. It has its own civil law, courts, flag, coat of arms, crown, postage stamps, and coins. Some thousand people actually inhabit Vatican City, while about twelve hundred hold Vatican citizenship.

Vatican Finances

This huge bureaucracy of the Church and the works that the Church carries on in the world must be supported by money. The structure of Vatican finances is not entirely clear, since naturally much secrecy surrounds this area, but it is certain that the Vatican is one of the world's great financial powers.

Each year the faithful contribute some $1,500,000 in a collection known as Peter's Pence; this amount is assessed to various countries by mutual agreement between the pope and the contributing bishops. Other revenues include gifts, diocesan collections of Rome, and the proceeds from the $83,000,000 paid in 1929 by the Italian government as compensation for the seizure of the Papal States in 1870.

When the sum was received, the Holy See set up the Special Administration to invest it. Under the supervision of the able Signor Norgara, the money was wisely placed, and since no taxes are paid, the sum has increased considerably. No exact figures can be given, but the sum of $500,000,000 has been mentioned. Recently the entire wealth of the Vatican, including art treasures, was estimated at around 5.6 billion dollars.

This money is invested in the United States, Britain, and Switzerland, but primarily in Italy where the Vatican owns controlling shares in the largest banks, most public utilities, certain real estate companies, hotels, and insurance and investment companies. The Special Administration has recently taken over control of all Vatican funds abroad. In addition the Administration of Holy See Property, the Institute for Religious Work (a bank), and the Administration of the Vatican City State all handle large sums of their own.

Canon Law

To regulate the vast society of the Church in order that affairs may proceed smoothly, a set of laws is needed. The Code of Canon Law provides this order, a compilation of twenty centuries of church regulations promulgated in 1918 in five books. These canons supervise church administration and government. They may be altered at any time and are not be confused with dogma, which is infallible and unchanging.

The Code at the present time consists of 2,414 separate canons divided into five parts. The first book contains eighty-six canons of the General Rule governing the application of the Code to the Church. The 639 canons of the second book deal with the various ranks of persons found in the body of the Church. Book three has 826 canons on the spiritual and temporal means used by the Church. The fourth book has 643 canons on the procedure and methods of the judicial process. The 220 canons of the fifth book constitute the penal code of the Church.

For violation of these and divine and natural law, sanctions exist within the Church. The worst of these is excommunication, excluding from active membership in and from the privileges of the Church. It is not possible to receive the sacraments while excommunicated. If the sinner repents and satisfactorily changes his way of life, excommunication may be lifted. Catholics who enter into marriage before a civil magistrate in some dioceses, or a non-Catholic clergyman, are excommunicated, and the marriage is invalid. However, two non-Catholics married before a non-Catholic authority are validly married, and in the event of a divorce a Catholic authority may not marry either one during the lifetime of the partner. Catholics may be excommunicated for failing to send their children to Catholic schools, but in practice this is rarely carried out. This is for two reasons: there are not schools in all parts of the country, and there is not room for all prospective students in the existing schools. Severe sanctions also exist for priests entering into marriage.

The Bishops

The bishops are the successors of the Apostles, set over particular churches which they govern in virtue of their ordinary power under the authority of the Roman Pontiff. Essentially they have the same powers of order that the Apostles had, save that of personal infallibility. The rule of the bishops, however, is limited to a certain territory: their diocese. Moreover, the pope can limit the powers of the bishops, but he cannot suppress episcopal power or radically change its character.

The pope theoretically can freely name the bishops, but in practice there are several methods of appointment. The bishops of a province usually nominate candidates. In England, the cathedral chapter, a group of priests, also is allowed to nominate candidates. These nominations are submitted every two years. Some governments are allowed the right of nomination.

The qualifications of a possible candidate are listed in Canon law. He must be born in legitimate wedlock, be at least thirty years of age and five years a priest. He must have integrity, piety, zeal, and prudence. He must also be a well informed theologian. The elevation of a bishop is processed by the Consistorial Congregation, except for the mission areas, whose bishops are under the Congregation for the Propagation of the Faith.

The powers of a bishop are ordinary, that is, they are attached to the position. But before he may exercise his power he is obliged to take over his diocese by showing his letters of appointment to the cathedral chapter or to the diocesan consultants. The bishop then has the right to govern in spiritual and temporal matters with power that is legislative, judicial, and administrative. He is the final authority in all cases not reserved to the pope. He exercises his doctrinal authority by his preaching and his vigilant care of every method of teaching sacred doctrine. His most important power is that of administering the sacraments of Confirmation and Holy Orders. His chief duty is to govern the diocese, promote observance of the Church's laws, stop abuses, safeguard the faith and morals, and promote Catholic Education and Catholic Action. He watches literature, administers the sacraments, and may alone consecrate certain sacramentals. A bishop must remain in his diocese nine months of the year and offer Mass on eighty-eight days each year. In addition he must send in a report on the condition of his diocese to Rome every five years and must make a visit to the pope every five or ten years. Finally, he must visit every part of his diocese—persons, places, and things—every five years.

Helping the resident bishop in the government of the diocese is the diocesan curia. This means all who work with the head of the diocese by acting for him in the administrative or judicial government. The most important office is that of vicar-general, the bishop's assistant. He is fully dependent on the bishop and resigns his office at the bishop's death. Auxiliary bishops are elevated to titular sees and then assigned to help a bishop of a large diocese. They do not have the right of succession, as do the coadjutor bishops. The chancellor is the keeper of the archives and registers. He prepares much of the information relating to the bishop's report to Rome.

President of the diocesan tribunal is the Officialis. He has charge of the diocesan courts, which are chiefly concerned with matrimonial cases. The diocesan chapter is the senate of a bishop. He usually consults it before taking any important actions, even though he is not bound by its advice.

At least once every ten years a diocesan synod is called, attended by all clergy and administrators of diocesan foundations. It is consulted by the bishop, but his decisions are final. The synod elects six examiners for ten-year terms to scan the clergy for possible promotions. In America four to six consultors are appointed for three-year terms for the same purpose as the European cathedral chapters, along with administrative duties.

The chief source of diocesan funds is the annual parish collections, with each parish contributing an assessed amount. There are also donations and property grants. Every three years the bishop is required to submit a financial statement to Rome. He controls the parish finances through a board of trustees composed of two men from each parish who for the most part are powerless. He may set debt limits for parishes and announce special collections such as for Peter's Pence, diocesan charities, and the missions. Each diocese is further subdivided into deaneries, made up of groups of parishes, the parish being the basic unit of the Church.

A new decree promulgated in August of 1966, *Ecclesiae Sanctae* has recommended a number of changes for the episcopacy. Among these are the establishment of the new diocesan office of episcopal vicar, provisions for setting up in each diocese a senate of priests to consult with the bishop, a national episcopal conference to propose to the Vatican names of priests to be considered for the office of bishop, and a call for full and juridical establishment of national and episcopal conferences. The decree also recommends the voluntary retirement of priests and bishops at the age of seventy-five.

The Parish

A parish comprises a definite territory in which there are a church, pastor, and congregation. If the population is large enough, there may be several assistant priests to help with the work. Each parish has its own special character, due to the divergent factors that go into its composition. These modify the roles of the parish priest.

The pastor with one or more assistants constitutes the core of this Christian community. The pastor has charge of all souls in the parish. He is like a second father to them, the clergyman who is closest to the people. Thus much depends on his character and personality, including whether a parish will be a vital force in a person's life or just another club to join. The chief purpose of the parish is to involve the people in a common worship of God and to promote good works in the quest of salvation. Without the priest, the parish would cease to exist. All parochial activities directly or indirectly depend on him. The roles of all priests are influenced by the type of class that comprises the congregation and the area of the country in which the parish is located.

Many laymen volunteer to help the pastor carry on his administrative tasks, since in any parish the material needs occupy a more prominent place than the spiritual wants. These laymen help organize finances, building programs, census and other records, and home visitations. Often a parish is divided into zones under lay leaders who keep track of the Catholic population. None of this approaches the boards of presbyters that are existent in many Protestant churches.

The trusteeship controversy still haunts the American Catholic Church, though it only lasted until the Civil War. In early America there was a shortage of priests, so congregations got together, built churches, and then sought priests to staff them. The trustees administered the temporal matters, hired pastors, and determined their salaries. In the 1820's they eventually tried to nominate a bishop of Philadelphia. Rome refused this request, and the militia had to be called in to quell a riot that developed at a meeting of the factions at St. Mary's Church there.

While trusteeism no longer exists, the fear it has engendered of giving the laity a share in the work of the Church persists. The Catholics in America were usually of the laboring class, illiterate or poorly educated, as unable as they were unwilling to assume their proper leadership. Out of sheer necessity priests spoke as authorities in areas rather far removed from church business. In part, due to little lay initiative, they still do.

Helping to carry on the work of God and the Church are numerous parish clubs, in many cases local chapters of national groups. Among the most prominent are the Legion of Mary, the Confraternity of Christian Doctrine, Men's and Women's Auxiliaries, and the Christian Family Movement. There are also the Knights of Columbus and the usual groups of Boy and Girl Scouts. Parishes sponsor lectures and discussion groups, Young Catholic groups, dances, and card parties—anything that will draw the members of a parish closer together in a religious purpose to carry on the Christian Apostolate.

To know God is to love Him. For this reason and to preserve the distinctive Catholic religion, there are parochial schools. Over five million pupils are enrolled in grade or high schools. Every parish tries to have its own school staffed by lay people or nuns. In addition, Sunday Schools are run for all children in public schools, and adult education classes are conducted in many parishes.

Always there is the problem of finance—where to find the money to keep the parish running. Diocesan priests are guaranteed a salary, but the upkeep of the buildings and maintenance of a school require a large amount. Every Catholic is obligated to give a sum for the support of the parish. This is not a fixed sum, but is dependent on the idea of personal stewardship. Much of this comes from the Sunday collections, but many parishes conduct special pledge drives to raise more money. Some parishioners pay their annual obligations in one lump sum. Dioceses also have fund-raising drives to bring in capital for diocesan improvements.

The chief problem of the pastor is his lack of communication with his parishioners. Most priests are too busy to call on their flock at home, and a few minutes a week in the parking lot after Mass is usually not enough. This leaves the initiative for contact up to the people, who often do not make it. There is also the complaint that the priest is too much an administrator and not enough a spiritual father. He is some sort of "super-president" for all the parish organizations instead of a welcome adviser. The fact that many inner-city parishes have been given over to the very poor tends to curtail the religious life there, and many of the suburban parishes and neighborhoods in transition are reluctant to accept colored Catholics into the fold.

For many the parish unit in America is best described as a jumble of 18,000 parochial pieces which has fallen together into a makeshift system. It is an ecclesiastical unit in search of a modernized role that will make it relevant and effective in a changing Catholicism. As a leading American ecclesiastic has remarked: "Today's parish is hopelessly outdated. Patchwork reform is useless. The parish must be struck by the revolution sweeping the Church; it must be completely, radically restructured." The observation might well apply to the overall picture of Catholicism in the twentieth century.

Conclusion

IN SPITE of the many changes introduced into the Catholic Church since the pontificate of John XXIII there is growing unrest among the liberals who feel that the pope has moved too slowly, that he gives with one hand and takes away with the other. The failure of the pope to change the current teaching of the church on birth control was a bitter disappointment to many as was his reiteration of the church's demand for clerical celebacy. Many feel that although the Second Vatican Council accomplished what it set out to do, reform the Church internally, it failed to comprehend the real problems confronting Catholicism today. The reform of the liturgy, for example, merely reveals the gap between public worship and modern man. It remains irrelevant to the young people of our technological society. Much the same can be said of the other reforms introduced during and since the Council. The case of new Dutch Catechism, *De Nieuwe Katechismus* which was to be translated into various foreign languages and given world wide circulation is an example in point. Breaking with the traditional simplistic rote question and answer approach of the past, the catechism takes an undogmatic view of the problems of modern man. No longer presented with apodictic formulation are the questions of original sin, the virgin birth of Mary and the idea of transsubstantion. Original sin is described as a collective guilt in which each human being participates. The catechism provoked the pope to warn against those "who attribute to the council every type of novelty even declaring and those who declare truths defined by the church as matters of opinion." Efforts have been made to ban the publication of the catechism in the United States and England. One critic of the present vacillation policy of the papacy in the matter of renewal strongly suggests that unless changes take place the church will dig its own grave. It is recommended that she divest herself of all claims to worldly power, that its hierarchy drop its Renaissance splendor and that the pope shed his regal vestmenta, quit the Vatican palace and life in Rome. If Catholicism is to be adapted to the modern world, to man's human and social aspirations, its institutional structures must be reformed. The ancient political and ecclesiastical church must be remodeled in such a way that it sees and organizes itself as a community and has the life of a community.

Whether Catholicism will, as many predict, almost disappear and become a church of the diaspora, living in small communities in a post-Christian era or whether it will emerge again as a strong social and political force as it was in the Middle Ages is a question that only the future will answer. Two trends seem to be developing as Catholicism renews itself. One desires that the Church be structured as closely as possible to biblical ideas, another feels that the Gospel should be expressed in concrete terms rather than biblical patterns of speech. Rather than emphasizing liturgy and worship this school sees God as nourishing His people when they are involved in serving others. In both cases it is clear that Catholicism can no longer be a matter of belief in formulas but rather the reality which the forms signify. The great question of the future is whether this reality to be believed can be expressed in what is more in harmony with contemporary civilization and culture. Its success in so doing in the past can be a hope, its many failures in more recent centuries, a warning.

Footnotes

1. Migne, *Patrologiae Cursus Completus, Series Graeca* (Paris, 1857), 13, 83 seq.
2. Denziger, *Enchiridien Symbolorum* (Freiburg, 1952), 41-42.
3. Migne, *Patrologiae Cursus Completus, Series Latina* (Paris, 1844), 40, 1187 seq.
4. *St. John Chrysostom: Baptismal Instructions, Ancient Christian Writers* (London, 1963), vol. 31, pp. 52-53.
5. Denziger, *op. cit.*, 302.
6. Migne, *op. cit.*, 77, 101-104.
7. *Corpus Christianorum, Series Latina* (Turnhout, 1957), XCIV, 91-94.
8. E. Bernheim, *Quellen zur Geschichte des Investiturestreit* (Leipzig, 1913), pp. 47-48.
9. Migne, *Series Latina*, 182, 332-336.
10. Denziger, *op. cit.*, 430.
11. Denziger, *op. cit.*, 695.
12. *Summa Theologica*, III, Quaes. lxxv, art. 1.
13. F. Vetter, *Die Predigten Taulers* in *Deutsche Texte des Mittelalters*, XI, xxxvii (Berlin, 1910).
14. *Corpus Iuris Canonici*, editio Lipsiensis, II, 1245.
15. *Conciliorum Oecumenicorum Decreta* (Freiburg, 1962), p. 385.
16. *Sacrosancta Concilia,* ed. Labbe-Cossart (Paris, 1691), XII, 238 seq.
17. Adapted from the Imitatio Christi cap. iii.
18. Denziger, *op. cit.*, 793-801.
19. *Ibid.*, pp. 940, 946.
20. H. Jone, *Moral Theology* (Westminster, 1946), pp. 196-198.
21. Denziger, *op. cit.*, 360-361.
22. Adapted from the Paris edition of 1648.
23. *Conferences of the Rev. Père Lacordaire*, trans. H. Langdon (New York, 1870), pp. 471-475.
24. Denziger, *op. cit.*, 1701-1780.
25. All following citations from papal pronouncements are taken from the *Acta Apostolicae Sedis, Commentarium officiale*, Romae, 1909 seq., and the *Acta Sanctae Sedis*, Romae, 1854 seq.
26. Address delivered by Joseph Blomjaus, bishop of Mwanza, Tanganyika, at International Study Week on Mission and Liturgy, Nijmegen, 1959.

Bibliography

No ATTEMPT is here made to list all of the works consulted by the author. However the following selections may be found useful to the reader interested in a more detailed study of historical Catholicism.

General Accounts: P. Batiffel, *Le catholicisme des origines à s. Léon,* 4 vols. (Paris, ³1930).

L. Duchesne, *Histoire ancienne de l'église,* 3 vols. (Paris, ⁵1929).

A. Fliche and V. Martin, *Histoire de l'église* (Paris, 1935 seq.).

A. Ehrhard, *Die katholische Kirche im Wandel der Zeiten und Völker* (Bonn, 1937).

L. J. Rogier et alii, *The Christian Centuries,* vol. I, The First Six Hundred Years (London, 1964).

H. Jedin and J. Dolan, *Handbook of Church History,* vol. I. From the Apostolic Community to Constantine (New York, 1965).

A. von Harnack, *Lehrbuch der Dogmengeschichte,* 3 vols. (Tübingen, ⁵1931).

R. Seeberg, *Textbook of the History of Doctrines* (Grand Rapids, 1956).

M. Werner, *Die Entstehung des christlichen Dogmas* (Tübingen, ²1954).

F. L. Cross ed., *The Oxford Dictionary of the Christian Church* (London, 1957).

J. Alberigo ed., *Conciliorum occumenicorum decreta* (Freiburg, 1962).

Chapter I

R. Grant, *A Historical Introduction to the New Testament* (New York, 1963).

J. Parkes, *The Foundations of Judaism and Christianity* (London, 1961).

J. Danielau, *The Theology of Jewish Christianity* (London, 1964).

M. Burrows, *The Dead Sea Scrolls* (New York, 1955).

V. Tscherikover, *Hellenistic Civilization and the Jews* (Philadelphia, 1959).

N. Nilsson, *Greek Folk Religion* (New York, 1961).

J. Festugiere, *Personal Religion among the Greeks* (Berkeley, 1961).

T. Glover, *Conflict of Religion in the Early Roman Empire* (Boston, 1960).

F. Cumont, *The Mysteries of Mithra* (New York, 1957).

A. O. Nock, *St. Paul* (London, 1960).

H. Gregoire, *Les persecutions dans l'empire romain* (Brussels, ²1963).

R. Wilson, *The Gnestic Problem* (London, 1958).

W. H. Baynes, *Constantine the Great and the Christian Church* (London, 1929).

H. A. Wolfson, *The Philosophy of the Church Fathers* (Cambridge, Mass., 1956).

Chapter II

C. Dawson, *The Making of Europe* (New York, 1945).

W. Ullmann, *Medieval Papalism* (London, 1949).

J. Calmette, *Le monde feodale* (Paris, 1934).

F. Ganshof, *Feudalism* (New York, ²1961).

G. Schnurer, *Kirche und Kultur im Mittelalter,* 3 vols. (Paderborn, 1924/29).

S. Runciman, *The Eastern Schism* (Oxford, 1951).

J. Jungmann, *The Mass of the Roman Rite* (New York, 1951).

G. Tellenbach, *Church State and Christian Society* (Oxford, 1959).

Chapter III

E. Benz, *Ecclesia Spiritualis* (Stuttgart, 1934).

L. Gougaud, *Devotions et pratiques du moyên-age* (Paris, 1923).

F. Vernet, *Les ordres mendiants* (Paris, 1933).

E. Davison, *Forerunners of St. Francis and Other Studies* (London, 1928).

R. Bennet, *The Early Dominicans* (London, 1937).

T. Gay, *Histoire des Vaudois* (Paris, 1912).

E. Gilson, *History of Christian Philosophy in the Middle Ages* (New York, 1955).

R. Petry ed., *Late Medieval Mysticism* (London, 1957).

B. Poschmann, *Penance and the Anointing of the Sick* (New York, 1964).

Chapter IV

A. C. Flick, *The Decline of the Medieval Church*, 2 vols. (New York, 1931).

J. Huizinga, *The Waning of the Middle Ages* (London, 1924).

W. Lunt, *Papal Revenues in the Middle Ages* (New York, 1934).

M. Wilks, *The Problem of Sovereignty in the Later Middle Ages* (Cambridge, 1963).

A. Gewirth, *Marsilius of Padua*, 2 vols. (New York, 1951).

L. Loomis, *The Council of Constance* (New York, 1961).

O. Chadwick, *The Reformation* (Grand Rapids, 1965).

H. Jedin, *A History of the Council of Trent,* vols. I and II (St. Louis, 1957).

G. Schnurer, *Katholische Kirche und Kultur in der Barockzeit* (Paderborn, 1937).

J. Oricbal, *Le origines du jansenisme,* 3 vols. (Paris, 1947/48).

Chapters V *and* VI   K. Latourette, *The Nineteenth Century in Europe: Background and the Roman Catholic Phase* (New York, 1958).

A. Aulard, *Christianity and the French Revolution* (London, 1927).

J. Bellamy, *La Theologie Catholique au XIXᵉ Siecle* (Paris, 1904).

M. Petre, *Modernism: Its Failure and Its Fruits* (London, 1918).

T. Granderath, *Geschichte des Vatikanischen Konzils,* 3 vols. (Freiburg, 1903/06).

J. Nichols, *History of Christianity 1650–1950: Secularization of the West* (New York, 1956).

W. Gurian and M. Fitzsimmons eds., *The Catholic Church in World Affairs* (Notre Dame, 1954).

G. Berkower, *The Second Vatican Council and the New Catholicism* (Grand Rapids, 1965).

Current statistical information on Catholic officialdom may be found in the following annuals: *Annuario Pontifice* published since 1912 in Vatican City and the *Official Catholic Directory* published in New York. The latter contains ecclesiastical statistics on the United States, Great Britain, the Commonwealth Nations as well as the Philippine Islands and Mexico.

Index

282.09
D65

Date Due